Seven Steps to Mastering Business Analysis

The Essentials

Second Edition

Jamie Champagne

CBAP®, PMP®, PMI-PBA®

Copyright © 2020 by J. Ross Publishing

ISBN-13: 978-1-60427-160-7

Printed and bound in the U.S.A. Printed on acid-free paper.

10 9 8 7 6 5 4 3 2 1

Library of Congress Cataloging-in-Publication Data
Names: Champagne, Jamie, 1982– author. |
Title: Seven steps to mastering business analysis : the essentials / by
  Jamie Champagne.
Description: 2nd Edition. | Plantation : J. Ross Publishing, 2019. |
  Revised edition of Seven steps to mastering business analysis, c2009. |
  Includes bibliographical references and index.
Identifiers: LCCN 2019033993 (print) | LCCN 2019033994 (ebook) | ISBN
  9781604271607 (paperback) | ISBN 9781604278156 (epub)
Subjects: LCSH: Business analysts. | Business planning. | Organizational
  effectiveness.
Classification: LCC HD69.B87 C37 2019 (print) | LCC HD69.B87 (ebook) |
  DDC 658.4/01—dc22
LC record available at https://lccn.loc.gov/2019033993
LC ebook record available at https://lccn.loc.gov/2019033994

Phone: (954) 727-9333
Fax: (561) 892-0700
Web: www.jrosspub.com

Titles in the
Business Analysis Professional Development Series

This series is for those interested in developing a career in business analysis. Each book within the series will help practitioners develop the knowledge, skills, competencies, and capabilities needed to master the typical business analysis career path. These instructional texts are designed for use in professional training, continuing education courses, and self-learning.

Successful Business Analysis Consulting:
Strategies and Tips for Going It Alone
by Karl Wiegers

Mastering Business Analysis Standard Practices:
Seven Steps to the Next Level of Competency
by Kelley Bruns and Billie Johnson

Mastering Business Analysis Standard Practices Workbook
by Kelley Bruns and Billie Johnson

Seven Steps to Mastering Business Analysis, 2nd Edition
by Jamie Champagne

Mastering Business Analysis Versatility:
Seven Steps to Develop Advanced Competencies and Capabilities
by Gina Schmidt

Agile Business Analysis: Enabling Continuous Improvement
of Requirements, Project Scope, and Agile Project Results
by Kevin Aguanno and Ori Schibi

CONTENTS

5   Your Fifth Step—Know Your Technical Environment 137

6   Your Sixth Step—Know Your Requirements Analysis Techniques. 167

THE PURPOSE OF THIS BOOK

The purpose of this book is to introduce both the practice and profession of business analysis with the practical applications, skill sets, and techniques needed to drive value in organizations both today and tomorrow. Business analysis has grown from its beginnings solely focused on supporting information technology (IT) development to enterprise levels of strategic importance. The goal of business analysis centers on providing value; yet in today's organizations the opportunities are almost limitless as to where these key analysis skills can drive value from individuals and teams. So whether you are called a business analyst (BA) in your official title or are looking for ways to be more successful in your projects, product development, and strategic planning, this book shows you where those opportunities are and what approaches you can take to ensure value delivery.

While the role of BA has become more popular in today's rapidly changing technology world, many other roles continue to utilize key analysis skills—such as project managers (PMs), systems engineers, solution architects, and systems analysts who utilize these skill sets and techniques often. However, the demands of the modern organization of flexibility, adaptability, and innovation mean that many other areas of business are requiring these valuable skills—such as product development, marketing, financial and risk analysis, strategic planning, and even community engagements and nonprofit efforts. This book not only focuses on the role, but emphasizes these key skill sets that are used throughout organizations.

The amount of materials—blogs, templates, videos, etc.—that are available today to anyone searching for information regarding business analysis and the profession is almost overwhelming—especially for someone who wants to start a business analysis career. This book gives you a definition of business analysis and its importance to any organization so that you will have a place to start and essential techniques and skill sets to focus on. This book does go further in explaining the evolution of the role of BAs and how your skills will grow. It also describes some of the evolving techniques needed for tomorrow's changing business environment, as well as the career path options you may take. Regardless of the perspectives that resonate the most with you, the essential items covered here are meant to be applicable throughout your business analysis career and provide you with a solid foundation to always come back to throughout your endeavors.

INTENDED AUDIENCE

This book is intended for anyone who plans to, is already performing, or has found themselves thrust into the wonderful world of business analysis. While many people who hold the title of BA will be able to leverage this book as the foundation of key concepts to support their analysis work, the content and structure applies such that anyone who is doing analysis work and seeking to deliver greater value from current and future efforts in their organization can leverage these essential concepts.

Also, those managers who find themselves leading a team of analysts who seek to deliver results will better understand what can be expected from analysis work, along with the ideal career growth path for those maturing analysts. This book will help them define the BA role and to realize the distinction between junior levels, mid-levels, and senior levels of business analysis performance. It will also lend itself to helping define the expected responsibilities of anyone who will hold a title of *analyst* in an organization.

A theme that will be highlighted throughout this book is both the profession of business analysis and the practice. The titled role of *BA* may come and go and shift and alter with the same fluid dynamics of the constantly changing world around us, yet the essential skill sets presented here will remain valuable for years to come. The most successful BAs today are going beyond simply asking why and following through to ensure and validate the delivery of value. This book provides key concepts that remain the fundamental skills that all analysts should grasp while walking you through how to grow and expand your reach in business analysis.

HOW IS THE BOOK ORGANIZED?

This book is divided into seven chapters—each representing a step toward mastering the essentials of business analysis work. Each chapter, or step, covers a significant skill area for the successful business analysis professional. The chapters do not need to be read in order, though, and can be quickly referenced based on the activity being performed.

- Chapter 1: Your First Step—Understand Business Analysis: the Role and the Work Involved
- Chapter 2: Your Second Step—Know Your Audience
- Chapter 3: Your Third Step—Know Your Project
- Chapter 4: Your Fourth Step—Know Your Business Environment
- Chapter 5: Your Fifth Step—Know Your Technical Environment
- Chapter 6: Your Sixth Step—Know Your Requirements Analysis Techniques
- Chapter 7: Your Seventh Step—Increase Your Value

The seven chapters serve as the essential building blocks upon which novice analysts may begin to master their business analysis work. This book has been created so that aspiring BAs can start from the beginning and work their way through each chapter sequentially. This gives junior BAs the entire picture of business analysis today and identifies the key areas where they need to begin working to grow their skills. Practicing BAs or those who have been doing analysis work for some time might find it more beneficial to simply jump right into the chapter of interest for their current situation. The chapters are independent such that if you are having a hard time articulating your role to management, you might read through Chapter 1 and utilize some of the concepts in your discussions. If you are working with a large stakeholder group that you have never worked with before, then the discussion in Chapter 2 on stakeholder groups and how to approach them might be most beneficial. Chapter 3 will be most helpful to those transitioning to organizations where project management and PMOs are more mature in organizing project work. Chapter 4 is very helpful for those BAs who have resided traditionally in IT roles, while those BAs who come from the business perspective may benefit from spending some time in Chapter 5 in order to understand *why* they need to know about technology in today's analysis world. The techniques in Chapter 6 are beneficial to all analysts and can help remind those seasoned veterans of the foundational concepts that make the techniques work—the concepts that we too often forget when in the middle of working with excited stakeholders. Chapter 7 is a must-read for all analysts. Since we often spend so much of our time helping organizations add value, we sometimes fail to measure (and therefore improve) our own performance. Our quality of work will never get better if we always use the same approach and/or refuse to seriously measure how we do things.

Chapter 1, *Understand Business Analysis: the Role and the Work Involved*, introduces you to business analysis and the definition of the BA role. It explains the relationship to technology roles while also highlighting how the role has evolved in organizations. As an introduction to those seeking to learn more about the role and possibly pursue the profession, this chapter presents questions for you to consider when deciding whether or not the role is right for you. You will read about the potential career progressions that a BA may take and delve into the key terms that BAs use to drive value on a daily basis.

Chapter 2, *Know Your Audience*, then brings in all of those people that the BA will find themselves working with on their change efforts. What's important here is that the chapter focuses on the similarities and relationships that a BA will have with the PM and also the considerations when there is only one person to fulfill both roles—as is too often the case, unfortunately. This chapter also highlights the definition of subject matter experts (SMEs) and when they may or may not truly be an expert, along with what a BA can do to best work with an SME in any situation. Once you know whom you will be working with, you then need to consider *how* you are going to work with them. Teams today are often physically separated and typically have cultural and language differences that must be taken into account in order to deliver successful change efforts.

Chapter 3, *Know Your Project*, dives right in with understanding business cases that drive the decisions to start projects. Since many BAs conduct project-based work, understanding both why and how those projects are initiated is important in order to be successful. Significant here to the BA's success is how they align their work with different architectures (enterprise, information, technology) of the organization to achieve maximum value from any change effort. This chapter then goes through all of the considerations for a project's initiation so that whether or not there is a PM assigned to manage the project, you will start the effort headed in the right direction for success.

Chapter 4, *Know Your Business Environment*, details the business analysis world by taking a look at how to understand the business environment, beginning with some useful elicitation techniques. The elicitation techniques highlight traditional approaches such as reviewing documentation, observation, and interviews while also introducing you to more modern approaches that include context diagrams, collaboration games, and personas. This chapter also discusses the thought process that a BA should have when it comes to understanding business processes. All of these techniques are key tools and approaches that a BA needs to have in their toolbox to help implement successful change initiatives.

Chapter 5, *Know Your Technical Environment*, focuses on the importance of technology even if your BA role is no longer found in the IT department. Almost every activity performed in an organization utilizes or relies on technology in one shape or form. A BA can be more effective in identifying needs and offering possible solutions when they understand key technology areas from hardware and software to data, usability, and testing. The emphasis here is not to become a programmer, but rather to emphasize how the more you know about any given area, the more helpful a team member you can be in adding value. This chapter also explains the different methodologies in use today that are no longer constrained to the technical teams, but apply to project-based work across organizations. Knowing these and their differences is crucial to a BA when planning and defining your approach to analysis work.

Chapter 6, *Know Your Requirements Analysis Techniques*, details the analysis techniques that are needed to deliver quality requirements. Categorization of requirements, both on traditional and agile or adaptive methodologies, is provided to remind the BA that the work of requirements is to enable the delivery of value. The rest of the chapter contains information that BAs will want to keep handy since it walks them through a variety of the most common and powerful analysis techniques and presentation formats.

Chapter 7, *Increase Your Value*, then balances the hard technical analysis skills with the softer personal skills and qualities that a BA should possess in order to be an effective analyst. Time and relationship management techniques coupled with strong communication skills are explained to highlight how valuable these traits are toward successfully helping organizations deliver valuable change. However, to be an effective analyst, your own personal growth needs to be considered. This chapter addresses your own analysis planning and improvement plans so that you will continue to grow and thrive in your business analysis role.

HOW TO USE THIS BOOK

Each chapter is a valuable step on your path to mastering business analysis. Mastering each concept presented helps you build the foundation that is required to be successful when working with organizations to deliver value.

If you are just starting out, you should begin with the first chapter and work your way through the sections until the terms become quite comfortable. You should not move on to the next chapter until you can easily explain the concepts presented in Chapter 1 to a colleague. Then you should proceed through each subsequent chapter in the same manner. This will give you the foundation required to build and grow your business analysis skills such that you are mastering the business analysis work daily in your organization's change efforts. If you are a senior BA who has years of practice under your belt, this book should be used to refresh your skill set in order to move your career forward.

ACKNOWLEDGMENTS

This book would not have come about without the support of an amazing community, trusted colleagues, and a wonderful family. The fantastic business analysis community, whom I have met through conferences and events around the world and in my own Hawaiian backyard, is the reason I am able to write about this topic and have been lucky enough to make a career out of it. I am fortunate enough that there are far more amazing people in this growing community than there is space to thank them all; but know that every single one of you are extremely appreciated and I am truly grateful.

I must give special thanks to Dr. Paul G. Schempp for mentoring and guiding me on this journey—encouraging and motivating me to constantly do bigger and better things.

And, of course, grateful appreciation goes to my husband for supporting me in this endeavor and to little baby bubbles who was kind enough to listen to my constant dictation and review sessions.

ABOUT THE INTERNATIONAL INSTITUTE OF BUSINESS ANALYSIS™

 International Institute of Business Analysis™

The International Institute of Business Analysis™ (IIBA®) is a professional association dedicated to supporting lifetime learning opportunities for business and professional success. Through a global network, the IIBA connects with over 29,000 Members, more than 300 Corporate Members, and 120 Chapters. As the recognized voice of the business analysis community, IIBA supports the recognition of the profession and discipline and works to maintain the global standard for the practice and certifications. The IIBA multi-level competency-based core BA certification program recognizes Business Analysis Professionals knowledge and skills and supports their lifelong business analysis career progression. Each level includes its own eligibility requirements and competency-based assessment (i.e., exam) and is aligned to *A Guide to the Business Analysis Body of Knowledge®* (*BABOK® Guide*).

For more information, visit iiba.org.

IIBA®, the IIBA® logo, *BABOK®*, and *Business Analysis Body of Knowledge®* are registered trademarks owned by the International Institute of Business Analysis in one or more countries. CCBA® and CBAP® are registered certification marks owned by International Institute of Business Analysis. Certified Business Analysis Professional™, Certification of Capability in Business Analysis™, Entry Certificate in Business Analysis™, ECBA™, Endorsed Education Provider™, EEP™ and the EEP logo are trademarks owned by the International Institute of Business Analysis.

ABOUT THE AUTHOR

Jamie Champagne goes beyond her *passionate BA* title and truly embodies business analysis to add value to those around her every day. An accomplished speaker and trainer, she enjoys sharing with others ways to improve their analysis skill sets and defining metrics to demonstrate measurable results. Her company, Champagne Collaborations, collaborates with and brings powerful insights to growing organizations and entrepreneurs, helping them and their teams reach the next level of success. Jamie's background in information technology, business analysis, project management, process improvement, and knowledge management has given her the opportunity to work across industries with organizations around the world.

She was the first Certified Business Analysis Professional (CBAP®) in the state of Hawaii and helped found the IIBA chapter there, where, in their first year, they won chapter of the year. Jamie is also a certified Professional Business Analyst (PMI-PBA)® and certified Project Management Professional (PMP)®.

Jamie is passionate about volunteering knowledge and time to the business analysis and project management communities. When she's not busy collaborating with her business partners, you can find her collaborating with her friends and family in the Hawaiian waters on a surfboard.

Web
Added
Value™

This book has free material available for download from the
Web Added Value™ resource center at *www.jrosspub.com*

At J. Ross Publishing we are committed to providing today's professional with practical, hands-on tools that enhance the learning experience and give readers an opportunity to apply what they have learned. That is why we offer free ancillary materials available for download on this book and all participating Web Added Value™ publications. These online resources may include interactive versions of the material that appears in the book or supplemental templates, worksheets, models, plans, case studies, proposals, spreadsheets and assessment tools, among other things. Whenever you see the WAV™ symbol in any of our publications, it means bonus materials accompany the book and are available from the Web Added Value Download Resource Center at www.jrosspub.com.

Downloads for *Seven Steps to Mastering Business Analysis, The Essentials, 2nd Edition*, include:

- A business analysis skill set check list (list of competencies discussed for self-assessment)
- A chart on how to work with various business analysis stakeholders
- A business analysis survey for those thinking of a career as a BA
- A matrix of techniques listed in the book mapped to tasks

CHAPTER 1

YOUR FIRST STEP—UNDERSTAND BUSINESS ANALYSIS: THE ROLE AND THE WORK INVOLVED

This book is intended to help business analysts (BAs)—including aspiring BAs, those who are fairly new to the profession, and professionals who are expected to perform the activities of a BA in addition to their primary role—master the essentials. It is designed to also help those who are responsible for hiring or managing BAs to gain a thorough understanding of the role and the work involved, along with identifying the traits of people with the greatest potential of becoming highly successful. In addition, this book will help executives gain an understanding and appreciation of the value this role can bring to an organization.

In order to master business analysis, you must first possess a clear and complete understanding of the essential skills of a BA. Business analysis spans across all areas of organizations around the world today. BAs perform activities ranging from basic problem solving to complex systems thinking and strategic planning. The actual definition of the skill sets and techniques of analysis work is becoming more clear and easier to reference, yet the role of those who are performing business analysis continues to change. Our consideration of what makes a BA successful has greatly evolved over the years, yet fundamental questions are still being asked, such as:

- Are BAs more than requirements experts?
- Are BAs only found in information technology (IT) departments?
- What skills and techniques do BAs need to grow in their profession and careers?
- What *soft* skills and characteristics do business analysts need in order to work in our dynamic environments of today and tomorrow?

This book aims to help you answer these questions while pushing you to consider what elements you enjoy and really get satisfaction in performing well. There is passion needed to bring teams together, research emerging technology, facilitate meaningful dialogues, analyze market trends and the competition, and drive value-centered solutions. These abilities will all be covered in this book because they produce better business outcomes—which is what great business analysis delivers to the organization.

WHAT IS BUSINESS ANALYSIS?

"The role of those performing business analysis continues to evolve."

Business analysis is centered on the idea of adding value. The International Institute of Business Analysis™ (IIBA®) defines business analysis as: *the practice of enabling change in an organizational context by defining needs and recommending solutions that deliver value to stakeholders.* Project Management Institute (PMI) also has updated their definition of business analysis to: *the set of activities performed to support the delivery of solutions that align to business objectives and provide continuous value to the organization.* If you are not quite sure what these mean yet, that is okay. The role has evolved into so many areas of business that these definitions have gotten more diverse to cover the growing spectrum of application. Regardless, some key elements should stand out to you that are core to business analysis, including:

- Change efforts—activities and tasks
- Focusing on solutions
- Understanding context
- Aligning to business objectives
- Delivering value

This vagueness surrounding specific activities is due to the many ways that business analysis can support an organization, especially with changing technology, innovations, and evolving markets. And yet, specific key activities are still at the core of the BA role because they continue to ensure the delivery of value:

- Identification of business problems and opportunities
- Elicitation of needs and constraints from stakeholders
- Analysis of stakeholder needs to define requirements for a solution
- Assessment and validation of potential and actual solutions
- Management of the change, solution, or requirements scope
- Evaluation of current solutions and continuous process improvement

These key activities of the business analysis discipline have emerged from work that was previously done by project managers (PMs) (gathering high-level business requirements) and systems analysts (designing functional requirements for software behavior). This is why some organizations still struggle with the placement of BAs in their organizational structure—some are found on IT teams, others are in project management offices (PMOs), and still others have strategic-level roles. Regardless of where they are placed, BAs elicit, analyze, communicate, and validate requirements for changes to business processes, policies, and information systems that deliver value. The business analysis professional understands business problems and opportunities in the context of the requirements and recommends solutions that enable an organization to achieve its goals.

Today's business analysis professionals are no longer finding themselves just on simple projects that might contain software or IT components, but are also working on more business-focused and strategic opportunities and co-creating solutions with customers. IT aspects are not disappearing from business analysis, but are becoming more seamlessly integrated as part of the solution with IT BAs providing direction on how to gain the most value out of technology investment. The essential work of business analysis, though, remains focused on elicitation, analysis, validation, problem solving, and solution delivery throughout all manner of change efforts and project-based work.

These skills, which we will discuss throughout, remain relevant on various types of work in any organization and can easily translate from major IT projects to new market opportunities. All of these projects will frequently require a change in process, utilize some form of technology, and even reorganize the personnel structure, ensuring that business analysis skills will continuously add value.

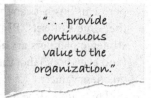

"... provide continuous value to the organization."

Business Analysis's Relationship to IT

Unfortunately, some organizations still feel that business analysis is an *IT position* and is only involved when there are technical components to the solution. Not only are the organizations not leveraging their employee skill sets properly, but this kind of approach can lead to issues where the technical requirements are delivered as requested, but the solution is still not acceptable—the "we-did-exactly-what-we-were-told" symptom. This is why the BA role has continued to evolve. Technical analysts will push to ensure that their technical solutions align with business goals, while business and product owners drive to ensure that the customer experience they are designing is realized. The future of business analysis skills lies in organizations that are leveraging the capabilities of emerging technology while providing experiences that delight customers and support successful long-term relationships.

This shift to focusing on delivering business value not only expands the role beyond IT-related projects, but also allows the role and skill sets of business analysis to then transcend across industries. Business analysis helps the IT solutions deliver value in a technical organization the same way IT solutions can help bring value for a healthcare or financial organization. Simply implementing technology does not bring organizational value; it must be aligned and leveraged. Business analysis originated in IT departments due to their focus on knowing the technology while analyzing how to drive solutions. That same approach is also useful in every area of an organization and that is why when we talk about the structure of business analysis in an organization, there continues to be more variety than standards. People who work in finance understand the processes and models and how financial activities help support the organization in the same manner as these technical BAs. Finance analysts can utilize this industry knowledge while applying analysis skills to help with any project or company initiative in order to drive revenue or increase their customer base. People who have good analytical skills, who understand their environment and context (including competition and market shifts and flux), and who work well with others make good BAs regardless of the functional area of the organization in which they work.

The Role of the BA

The business analysis profession emerged with the explosion of technology. The need to translate business needs into technological requirements quickly grew to ensure organizational success. This need still remains and has evolved so that organizations now require greater business analysis skills for strategic planning, designing user-centric solutions, and optimizing their existing systems to leverage innovation. The same foundational communication and facilitation skills and analytical aptitude that was required of the first generation of BAs still remains essential for the next generation of strategic and specialized BAs.

The role of the BA has matured to the point of being a defined profession, leading to organizations such as the IIBA to specify the role and the skill set. However, with the definition of a BA being "anyone who performs business analysis tasks" (IIBA 2015), this continues to leave room for many other roles to utilize the same skill sets. PMs, systems analysts, software engineers, solution architects, product owners, and strategic planners are all titled roles that utilize business analysis skill sets frequently. One might expect (and even hope) that there are numerous roles around an organization that are performing tasks that drive business value.

This might drive us back to the frustration of the challenge of defining the role, but it also opens up opportunities for those wishing to pursue a business analysis career. IT professionals can continue their business analysis roles on project-based work, sticking to a more breadth-wise knowledge of the organization and IT functions so as to bring these two areas together. This also exposes the opportunity for a BA to pursue a more concentrated knowledge in the IT field and pursue subject matter expertise knowledge of various components of technology—i.e., networks and security, infrastructure, and even software and development—while still growing his or her business analysis skill sets. Data analysts, solution architects, and other subject matter expert (SME) roles become incredibly valuable to organizations as they are intimate enough with the technology to guide solution decisions while still keeping a keen awareness of organizational goals and drivers so that the solutions are valuable to the organization. This same skill set is just as applicable, if not more so, outside of the IT organizational structure. Financial analysis, marketing analysis, and industry expertise are areas where BAs may not only pursue their passions, but also are finding many titled BA positions. Again, these analytical people who get the stakeholders together to design solutions in the best interest of the organization are some of its most valuable staff.

This explosion in the need for proficient analytical skills increases the opportunities for BAs. To aid in this development, BAs now have teams and centers of excellence (COE) for business analysis. These centers facilitate the creation of senior BAs and managers of BAs as positions that help to define a growth model for BAs to consider when it comes to their own career planning.

BA Traits

Most people who are drawn to the business analysis profession have certain traits in common. Analysts in general enjoy learning new things and have a natural curiosity. There is fundamental enjoyment in problem solving. In addition, BAs have a rare combination of the ability to see the big picture (conceptual thinking) while being very detail oriented. This combination of traits results in a successful BA. The *people* skills necessary to be a successful BA are many and varied, yet are the most important. BAs need to enjoy and be comfortable working with people. Stakeholders are often opinionated, narrowly focused, and easily excitable; they may lose sight of the fact that the BA's facilitation skills are his or her strongest asset when it comes to the solution goal. Strong communication skills (both verbal and nonverbal), listening, and patience are a must. BAs must ask good questions and probe deeper for detailed information while keeping the goal in mind. Leadership abilities, such as running successful meetings, encouraging team members, and supporting corporate goals, are common with successful BAs. Again, the main focus is on working well with people, realizing that each person is different, and understanding the need for diversity to help bring creative problem-solving solutions to the customer.

"Your facilitation skills are your strongest asset."

When BAs apply their specific expertise of analysis, it will then drive their additional skill sets and capabilities in order to deliver value. IT BAs and other technical analysts find value in understanding today's technology. Having a basic understanding of software development approaches, organizational IT standards, data design, storage strategies, and software usability principles leads to better decision making when the solutions include IT. If you are a specialized analyst, such as a data analyst or IT security analyst, knowing the current trends, capabilities, experts, and competitors lends tremendous value in your role on teams in order to leverage the technology. The same goes for those who focus on an aspect of business such as financial analysis or other common business functions. Knowing the common tools, methodologies, and the ways they affect business decisions and outcomes are key areas of concentration in which to build your skills. Having strong knowledge of the area you are working in allows you to utilize the terminology and language of these functional teams and helps you facilitate targeted discussions. These concentrated BAs often offer subject matter insight from their responsible areas on cross-collaborative teams to help decisions and therefore solutions, quickly come to fruition.

More broad-based BAs seek to understand their industry, markets, and customer segments, along with how their organizations create, deliver, maintain, and evolve value. These BAs seek to understand methodologies that go beyond IT, project management, and business so that they know multiple ways to approach problem solving. Systems thinking and understanding how processes are interrelated and incorporated throughout an organization are key skills of these enterprise-level analysts. They must bring together people from various areas of the organization and facilitate decisions by getting SMEs to provide their valuable insight for the solution.

Regardless of your concentration or focus of business analysis work, as a BA professional, you must stay abreast of current trends and capabilities and be able to communicate effectively with any type of team. One of the most sought out skills in BAs is to be not only a quick learner, but also a constant learner. Since the role of a BA requires so many different skills, most individuals in this role are constantly working on improving and increasing their skill sets, learning new methodologies, exploring how various parts of the organization operate, and looking for ways to expand their horizons. Effective BAs are always challenging themselves to learn new techniques and improve their use of analysis tools.

History of Business Analysis

Traditionally, everyone involved with software development came from a technical or IT background. They understood the software development process and often had programming experience. They used textual requirements along with American National Standards Institute (ANSI) flowcharts, data flow diagrams, database diagrams, and prototypes to document the software design. Frustration with software development was caused by the length of time required to develop a system that did not always meet business needs. Business people demanded easy-to-use, sophisticated software and wanted it better and faster.

Many business people got tired of waiting for large, slow-moving IT departments to roll out yet another cumbersome application. They began learning to do things for themselves or hire consultants, who were often BAs. These consultants would report directly to business management and help with software design and development. As businesses experienced the benefits of having a person dedicated to finding solutions to business problems, the number of BAs increased. Individuals from the business units became BAs with varied backgrounds such as marketing, accounting, payroll processing, and claims administration.

BAs inside of business units were sophisticated users who were anxious to take advantage of new technology and were willing to look outside the enterprise for help. Their focus on reporting directly to a specific line of business in the organization led to some functional departments purchasing software packages without consulting their own IT departments. Other BAs hired outside developers to create new software. These stand-alone systems caused even more problems for IT, which was suddenly asked to support software that it had not written or approved. Small independent databases popped up everywhere, with inconsistent and often unprotected data. IT organizations realized that creating a BA role internally was critical for continuing to support the business and stay in control of software applications. In addition, as some software development projects were outsourced, the need for quality, detailed requirements, and validation of deliverables became painfully obvious.

Several other factors have increased the need for and value of dedicated business analysis professionals. The explosion of customer-facing web pages demanded an increase in the understanding of usability and human factors in design. The International Organization for Standardization (ISO) set quality standards that must be adhered to when conducting international business. Carnegie Mellon University created software development and organizational quality standards with CMMI® (Capability Maturity Model Integration). Six Sigma has provided a disciplined, data-driven quality approach to process improvement aimed at the near elimination of defects from every product, process, and transaction. Business process management products are dedicated to improving efficiency and consistency at an enterprise-wide level. Service-oriented architecture (SOA) encourages improvements in software design and reuse of system components (called services).

All of these movements have been driven by frustration with the quality, timeliness, and applicability of business support from technology groups. Many studies of software development failures show that incomplete, incorrect, and missing requirements are the main reason for failures. And today, this focus on providing solutions that meet and even delight customers has made it clear that the technology, product, and solution development processes need a category of professionals who are dedicated to eliciting, analyzing, and utilizing requirements from an organization's value perspective and who will make sure that the business needs are met in the development and the solution.

Where Do BAs Come From?

BAs continue to come from both IT backgrounds and business areas. In the best situations, the business analysis professional has a combination of IT and business skills and experience.

From IT

BAs with an IT background tend to be analytical individuals who enjoy problem solving. They are attracted to technical development because of its emphasis on solution design, logical thinking, and discipline. Systems analysis and design involves the same type of critical thinking skills as business analysis. These individuals are often strong designers and developers because of their inherent logical thinking patterns and attention to detail. They are often promoted to more analytical roles because, in addition to their strong problem-solving skills, they have strong communication skills. Many people in IT have experienced the transition from being assigned a junior, task-focused position to a more concentrated system position, and eventually evolving to recommending solutions from positions such as solution architects or technical designers. As the technical skills grow, often the interpersonal and communication skills grow as your audience expands from a responsive nature to a proactive and driving role in IT.

Real World Example: BA Role from an IT Position

I got to oversee a major enterprise IT program at an organization with my duties focused on the technical setup and architecture so that staff could *realize* the benefits of the program. Even though the system had been well set up, users were not taking advantage of it and were continuing to rely on antiquated shared drives and e-mail. So I met with end users to ask them why they were not using the program. They knew exactly how to use the features, but were not sure of the value of the program for them. How could it help them do their jobs more successfully? Thus I had to be familiar enough with the technology to explain what the program was capable of doing, but also had to learn the specific business processes the end users were trying to accomplish. I had to show them how to use the program with the goal of streamlining their processes, while also bringing back their business requirements to the developers so that the program could be tailored for end users to gain maximum value.

Often, new analysts with IT experience limit recommendations for potential solutions to software. They may not consider process or organizational changes as effective methods for problem solving or understand the time required to implement a change in business procedures when new software is deployed. These analysts need to look for business solutions without assuming that technology is the answer to every question. They need to learn to think like a business person, understand the goals of the enterprise, and then adjust their view of technology to one that supports the business goals rather than drives them.

From Business

Individuals from business units have also moved into business analysis. In many cases, BAs who have work experience have been acting as SMEs on projects, making them familiar with project structure and requirements. These BAs bring a wealth of subject matter knowledge with them and are promoted within the business line because of their intelligence and ability to see more than just their job. They often recommend procedural or workflow changes to improve efficiency in their areas. In addition, they show strong analytical and problem-solving skills within the business area, along with strong communication skills with management and their coworkers.

Real World Example: BA Role within the Business Area

While working on a marketing project, our team had a cross-functional mix of people from the IT, compliance, communications, and marketing departments. The marketing team had the vision and idea of what they wanted to create for their new product. Team members from IT, finance, and compliance

continued

were participating in order to bring their independent expertise to help shape the solution. There was a marketing person (product manager) who was vital to this team. The product manager reported to marketing but often worked with the customer and business market teams to ensure a customer-centric approach. She would constantly ask great questions to clarify requirements as to whom our intended audience was, how we were planning to differentiate this product, and how we would reach and engage our customer even after release of the product. She would come to the team meetings with research as to what our competitors had in the same market space, what was happening in similar markets across the United States, and how the industry was engaging with our intended customer audience. Her leadership and clarity of expectations helped bring the team together and allowed the functional SMEs of the group to focus on their areas (e.g., IT was able to research appropriate technologies that would support all the requirements). Again, her title was not that of a BA, but she contributed to the team the analytical questions and mindset of a BA so that the solution would ultimately deliver value—or in this case, profits.

This is a great example of someone who brought the analytical problem-solving and communication skills of a BA from the *business* perspective. When BAs follow this path, they can then choose to focus on specific business lines of operations or become SMEs that are typically required on projects. They can also begin to expand their roles by taking these same skill sets and asking the questions of the organization as a whole. These are often the analysts that eventually become enterprise BAs because they begin to look at how products across the entire organization work together to drive organizational value. They grow successful because they still continue to learn about IT development, financial analysis, human resources talent management, and other areas of business while being able to converse openly and strategically with business teams throughout the organization.

Where Do BAs Report?

The value that business analysis brings is being acknowledged and sought after in more and more areas of business today, although "analysts" may hold a variety of titles. This recognition of the skill set of the role leads to the expansion of where BAs are found in organizations. BAs are commonly found in IT departments and PMOs. Some organizations have even created their own BA COE or BA teams. Regardless, BAs can be found with all sorts of analyst titles throughout many individual business units. Figures 1.1, 1.2, and 1.3 show some example organizational charts of where BAs may report.

BAs who are assigned inside business units have a different perspective and a different emphasis than those from the IT area. BAs working in a business unit will be much more aware of the business conditions, competitive issues, and financial challenges; they are aware of how other groups see their business unit and how these other groups work with their business. This perspective allows the BA to analyze and solve business problems at a detailed level. BAs working in the business area are often involved in writing business cases, documenting current workflows, and re-engineering processes. They also understand how critical IT support is to business workers. When a BA is sitting in an office next to a customer service representative and hears that person's frustration over daily system crashes, the BA is acutely aware of how much disruption this system problem is causing. By being close to the business, the analyst is better able to articulate the importance of launching a change effort to correct the problem. Also, understanding the competitive nature of a business unit, especially in the sales or marketing area, helps the analyst recognize why new product ideas must get to market as soon as possible. There is usually a window of opportunity that, if missed, will decrease the long-term sales of the product.

When a BA reports to a business unit, the challenge on project-based and cross-functional work becomes the ability to focus on solutions rather than simply the goals of the business unit. BAs must now not only perform their business unit duties by reporting to their business managers, but they must also work on the cross-functional teams and give their insights and recommendations as a piece of the overall puzzle by also reporting to the PM or team lead. Those who focus on *what is best for the organization* rather than their specific department often reveals your true BAs. These are those individuals who constantly look

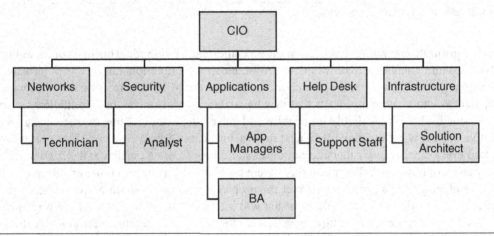

Figure 1.1 IT organizational structure

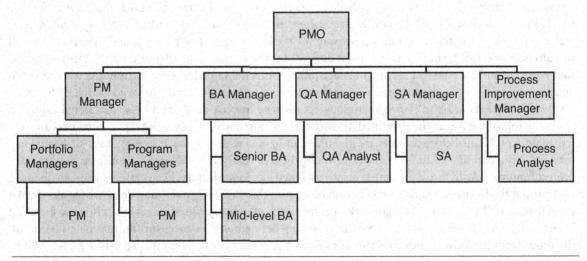

Figure 1.2 PMO organizational structure

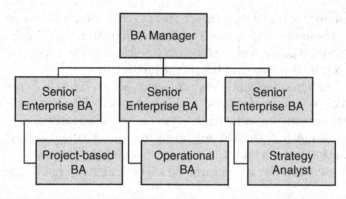

Figure 1.3   BA COE organizational structure

for overall organizational value, regardless of the give-and-take of individual business units, as opposed to those business unit analysts who only look to drive their specific functional line of work forward.

BAs who are working in IT will be much more aware of the technical environment, the availability of new capabilities, other current projects that may be related, and, of course, how technology is developed and maintained. This allows the BA to analyze and solve business problems from a strong technology perspective. If a BA is sitting in an office next to someone at an IT help desk and hears that person voice frustration every day because callers do not understand how to use a particular application, the analyst is acutely aware of how much disruption this system problem is causing and is better able to articulate the importance of launching a project to correct the problem. Also, understanding the architectural nature of software helps to design better solutions that will interface smoothly with surrounding applications. When BAs have a deep understanding of what is possible and what IT resources are available, they are able to set more realistic expectations and help customers envision more powerful solutions.

When BAs report to IT management, they often have access to resources and technologies of which the business unit may not even be aware. A challenge with this organizational structure is that IT may feel the need to drive the business as opposed to the business driving the need, and ultimately, requirements. Or worse yet, IT may feel that it should simply wait for the business to state its needs and then react—an all too dire scenario for the business. It may be difficult for the BA to be an advocate for the business when they report to and are paid by IT. This challenge for IT BAs is the same for business unit BAs who report to and are paid by their respective business area. Both are trying to put organizational goals first by focusing on overall solutions while still bringing the subject matter expertise needed on cross-functional teams.

As the role of the BA has been refined, the work of the position has grown. BAs in the business area often analyze problems before projects are identified, utilizing techniques such as root cause analysis. They may identify potential solutions and perform cost/benefit analysis, developing a business case to gain project funding. BAs in the IT area are typically assigned after a project has been approved and are focused on learning the business requirements and making sure the technology solutions meet those needs. An experienced, well-rounded BA could work in either arena effectively. Often this is when BAs are included in the PMO. Here the BAs get the opportunity to help define business cases for future projects based on the input from business units while also considering organizational needs. As projects are approved to move forward, the appropriate BA skill sets can be added to the project team to help drive execution of the requirements while still keeping the overall organizational goals in mind. Further, having your BAs involved at the enterprise level also creates the opportunity to look back at project outcomes and evaluate if the most value for the organization is being achieved or whether more can be done.

A business analysis COE is a business unit expressly created to support individuals who are performing business analysis work. The idea for this group comes from the PMO concept, but remains centered on value generation. While often supporting project-based work, the scope can frequently expand to evaluating new markets, research and development, and optimizing existing solutions and practices (think process improvement techniques). The advantage of having a department that is expressly focused on business analysis work is that the best practices and guidelines are more easily standardized and available for the entire enterprise. Business analysis professionals share lessons learned from their work to improve future work. BAs have support and guidance from other BAs.

A business analysis COE supports business analysis professionals by providing a list of approved analysis techniques with diagramming and naming standards—not for the sake of compliance and structure, but rather to give a basis where reuse and evolution of foundational concepts can be employed. A mature COE may provide analysts with software tools to support the development of requirements, requirements management, and requirements tracing. For those performing business analysis, these tools enable them to not have to start from scratch, but can leverage the established processes and value creation methods already in place at the organization. The center becomes the place to start for new BAs to work within the organization while leveraging and encouraging continuous improvement of seasoned BA expertise.

Managers who are considering reporting lines in their organization should weigh the advantages and challenges of each option. These decisions depend on the enterprise philosophy toward business analysis work and the organizational culture. Consider who is driving the development of new solutions: marketing? sales? IT? Where do your projects and change efforts start? How well are the projects completed and reflected upon? Consider how well the value of business analysis work is understood by the organization. BAs can demonstrate their value quickly regardless of where they report as long as they are given the time and resources necessary to elicit and develop quality requirements.

WHAT MAKES A GREAT BA?

There are several important characteristics and skills that are necessary for success in business analysis work. The BA must:

- Be flexible, be naturally curious, and enjoy learning new business domains
- Be an outstanding communicator and enjoy working *with* people
- Understand general business concepts and be able to advocate for the business
- Have an understanding of technology and specific technical functions
- Enjoy detailed research, recording, and analyzing
- Be skilled at organizing and managing large amounts of information in various formats
- Understand project management, software development, product development, and organizational change processes and methodologies

- Be able to see the bigger picture
- Look to connect pieces of work to understand how systems function
- Be able to work through complex business problems and determine the root cause of a problem
- Come prepared with a toolkit of techniques to elicit, analyze, and present excellent requirements

The business analysis profession requires a wide breadth of skills and extensive business experience. You may be considered a competent BA after you have a few years of experience, but learning and increasing your abilities should continue throughout your career. Compare this with the skills and ability of a musician. Many people play the piano successfully, both professionally and as amateurs. Beginners can learn to play many songs and accompany groups. Intermediate and advanced players compete and win awards. Career players may be invited to join symphonies and orchestras around the world. Some virtuosos have solo careers that include concert tours and recording contracts. Yet, they are all pianists. Ask anyone who plays whether they have mastered the piano—100% of honest pianists will say: "No, I have not mastered the instrument." When asked if they could improve, most will answer: "Yes, I could improve with more lessons and more practice." Their answer will never change throughout their lives. BAs should take the same approach. There is always more that can be learned. Mastering business analysis involves working on different types of projects and change efforts, dealing with different stakeholders, using different techniques, creating different deliverables, and analyzing different business areas. Skills can always be improved and honed. BAs can continue to grow within the profession throughout their careers.

Note that the number of years of experience alone is not a good indicator of business analysis expertise. If you have been doing the same tasks in the same business area for many years, your other analysis skills may be lacking. For example, a BA who supports maintenance changes to a particular application system may know exactly how to write functional requirements and design changes to that system. The projects all follow a similar process and the stakeholders are always the same people. This BA may be very proficient in those projects and have a very satisfied sponsor. But if this same BA is moved to a different department or assigned to work on a different application, he or she might not be able to be effective because a different project might require different techniques and skills—including perhaps a different perspective.

Many successful BAs are individuals who have worked as consultants in different organizational settings, on many different types of projects, and have used many different analysis techniques. Others have worked for several companies, gaining experience in different industries and working with different types of stakeholders. This may be considered a *fast track* for the business analysis professional. If you are interested in developing into a master business analysis professional, ask to be assigned to different business units and types of projects with various ranges of applications, development methodologies, and tools. The more varied your experience, the more flexible and adaptable you become. Agility, flexibility, and adaptability are key skills for BAs—both today and for tomorrow.

"Agility, flexibility, and adaptability are key skills for BAs—both today and for tomorrow."

So, how does a person learn business analysis and become a senior BA? To take the piano analogy a little further, you must first learn the basics and then *practice, practice, practice.* Pianists learn the basics like reading music, memorizing the notes created by each key, understanding the use of the pedals, and fundamentals of technique (e.g., when to use the thumb versus the index finger). They then use what they have learned on simple pieces to start to put all of the knowledge and skills together to create *music.* At this point, they can then use their own creativity and insights to apply different techniques to new environments and actually evolve their talents and outcomes. They do not start out playing Chopin—they often start out with *Row, Row, Row Your Boat!*

Similarly, a BA must start by learning the basics:

- What is a need?
- What is a requirement?
- What techniques are used to define, elicit, analyze, and present requirements?
- What are stakeholders and what is my responsibility toward them?
- How are business problems solved?
- What methodologies, approaches, and technologies are available?
- How do I obtain and then utilize feedback?

The BA puts all of this knowledge together regarding a project or initiative (hopefully a small, simple one at first) in order to perform *business analysis*. The basics of business analysis are: an understanding of the role of the BA, understanding requirements, scoping solutions, and learning to think analytically and critically while learning the techniques to perform each of these tasks well (see Figure 1.4).

There will be missed notes along the way. There will be hesitations and stalls as the BA works his or her way through the organizational maze. Have you ever listened to someone who is just learning to play the piano? It can be painful on the ears! They are encouraged to practice alone. But the best way for BAs to practice is on real projects, right in front of everyone. And this is part of being a BA—immediate feedback

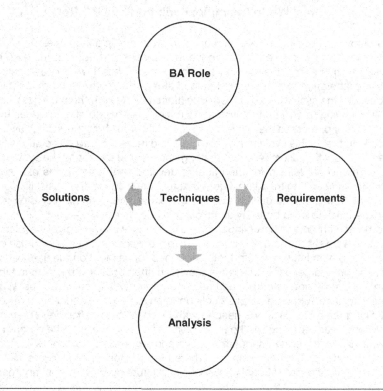

Figure 1.4 BA basics

that drives improvement of not only the project or initiative, but also yourself and your career. See Chapter 7 for more on measuring and improving your skills.

As with any complex work, there are always prodigies. Mozart started playing piano at the age of four and by the age of six, he was accomplished and giving performances. There are some individuals for whom analysis, problem solving, and solution design are as natural as walking. There are also individuals for whom asking questions and probing for detailed information are part of every interaction. These individuals are natural-born analysts and will quickly develop into very successful BAs as they learn formal techniques and guidelines within which to harness their talents.

Understanding the development of a business analysis professional and his or her maturity level is very important for managers/PMs who are assigning resources. If possible, new BAs should be allowed to work with experienced BAs who can coach and mentor them through their first few assignments and change efforts. Quality training in analysis techniques and communication and collaboration skills should be provided. Ideally, those pursuing BA careers should have an intern period at their organizations, almost like doctors, where they are guided and supervised by an experienced BA, before they are left on their own. Support, help, and guidance for new BAs will best help them develop their skills. Experienced analysts often require little supervision. Learn to recognize prodigies who may not produce a requirements deliverable exactly according to standards but will probably have an excellent vision of a possible solution.

Real World Example: Evolution of a BA Role

The best part I enjoy about being a BA is getting to work in multiple industries and lines of business. I was on an IT team where I was given one of those fun "specialist" titles that more or less feels like the popular "analyst" title that every other person at an organization has. I was hired to help with the training on an enterprise collaboration tool. The more I trained others, the more I learned about the system. I was also the help desk for the system, so the more questions I answered, the more I got to know the users and what they were trying to do with the system. With time, I began to offer up ideas to the users about ways to automate other processes they were doing manually or to show them ideas as to how the system might be able to help them. This evolved my role into being more focused on solutions. Management enjoyed the expanded work that users were conducting and wanted to expand the system. To do this, clear requirements needed to be defined for the offshore development team. I was excited for the detailed analysis and quickly jumped into the team. I got great feedback on my analysis skills concerning the way the development team was able to quickly and easily work with our organization's project team. Overall, it was a great experience to build both my technical and analytical skills.

While still working with enterprise collaboration systems, I was moved to the planning department where my functions were still the same—deliver value to the users through the best use of the system. My experience with the system left me comfortable enough to focus more on the users and to learn the different approaches from a larger user base rather than worrying about how the system functions. Here, my communication skills really got a workout and helped further my BA competencies. When I then shifted entire industries—again to support enterprise collaboration systems—I could bring my experience to the IT teams on defining the relationship we needed with business to be effective. The more I worked outside the department I was reporting to, the more I learned the business of the organization, how things worked, and what perspective the users (employees and external customers) were focused on. It was then easy to shift to an enterprise analysis role where I was no longer *system specific*, but could widen my scope to really look for organizational challenges and figure out how to best approach solutions.

Many others have had similar growth patterns that stem from paying attention to what they enjoy doing when performing analytical work, drawing out information from users, learning about new and emerging technology, and understanding how businesses deliver value. These are skill sets that allow you to evolve your analysis career in both breadth and depth as well as industries and environments.

BA Suitability Questionnaire

This may seem obvious, but if you are more interested in being a BA than simply having the title of "analyst" at an organization, paying attention is an important factor to really drive your career. Focusing on business goals and value helps you deliver strong measurable results, but they come with work and effort and a commitment to constantly learning and utilizing different techniques while remaining flexible. The road to becoming a successful senior BA is one that is filled with constant learning from challenges and from working with all kinds of stakeholders, industries, technologies, and even entire organizational re-designs.

If you have found yourself wearing the title of BA without understanding what the role involves or have simply been "promoted" into the role by managers who do not understand the skills and characteristics required, then this is your opportunity to decide to learn and grow the role as it is being described here. If you are not interested in the problem solving and the ever-changing solution opportunities you could create, you might consider a change in title that reflects the tasks that you enjoy.

For those who are curious about the BA role (and yes, this is a natural tendency of BAs), the upcoming questions are intended to help you to determine if the BA role is appropriate for you and how well-suited you are to the profession. Use these questions to honestly assess yourself. That is something BAs do quite frequently—they create assessments, do the work, evaluate the results against the assessment, and then define improvement plans and ways to leverage their success. These questions can be answered by anyone who is interested in or working in the business analysis profession. If you are feeling frustrated in your role, you may find out that you are not well-suited for it. If you are well-suited to the role but are having difficulty being successful, it is likely that the role is not being supported adequately by your organization. This questionnaire could also be used by career development managers to assess an individual's interest in moving into the business analysis profession. As you read each statement, decide whether you agree or disagree.

Suitability Questionnaire

1. I enjoy organizing information. My personal finances are filed and easy to reference.
2. I enjoy, and am good at, preparing documents that are clear and easy to review.
3. I am good at drawing diagrams (e.g., maps, floor plans).
4. I am able to simplify a complex topic.
5. I have a list of tasks that I need to complete daily.
6. I enjoy learning new technologies and techniques. I am very curious.
7. I love problem solving. I enjoy puzzles and logic games.
8. I really enjoy getting into details.
9. I can step back and see the big picture.
10. I am able to motivate myself to get work done.
11. I appreciate constructive criticism and feedback so that I can improve myself.

12. I love working with people.
13. I am comfortable dealing with conflict.
14. I am good at negotiating solutions between two other people.
15. I enjoy project-based work. Change excites me!
16. I get personal fulfillment from the act of working on more than the delivery of a particular product.
17. I am comfortable making presentations in front of groups.
18. I am good at conducting meetings—keeping everyone on topic and on schedule.
19. Before I start every task, I think through how I am going to do it.
20. When I receive an e-mail message, I take a few moments to think about to whom and how I am going to respond rather than just reacting.
21. When someone does not understand something that I am explaining, I can explain it in another way.
22. I create positive relationships with people.
23. I love starting new projects, but also take pride in showing the completion of a project.
24. I am good at getting others to share their stories—preferring to listen to their details rather than telling them my stories.
25. I am constantly reading books and blogs and following people, often of varied interests

How do you feel? The more statements with which you agree, the more likely you are already analytical in nature and are already driving down the path to a business analysis profession. The purpose of this assessment is to honestly answer the question: "Do I want to be a BA and will I excel in this role?" If you do not enjoy the type of work that BAs perform or these are not your strongest skills, it may be better for you to find out now. Keep in mind also that there are various levels of BAs and you will probably start at the lowest one. Beginning BAs will refine and improve their skills as they gain more experience.

Do not worry—managing and supervising others, carrying out enterprise-wide analysis, and helping to make multi-million dollar decisions are not the first things a junior business analysis professional encounters. The best part of the career path is that you normally start out very task-focused—a part of project teams where you have specific deliverables. As you complete your activities the importance is on paying attention to what you enjoyed, determining where you think there is room for improvement, and then taking action to improve those gaps. This will allow you to naturally grow your career since the more comfortable you get with your own skills, the greater the challenges you can take on regarding your work.

This is just an example assessment that you can use of some generalized themes that often come up when BAs get together and talk about the future of business analysis. There are many formal assessment tools that may be useful to consider if you want to get a better understanding of how you work and how you best communicate with others. Communication skills and work preferences are so important to business analysis work that as an analyst you must understand your own style and preferences. An analyst works with many different stakeholders and is rarely able to convince a stakeholder to change his or her style. The analyst must adapt and conform to the most effective style for each stakeholder interaction. This requires significant self-awareness, along with the ability to read and assess other people—just another aspect of the life-long learning that BAs must do.

> "The analyst must adapt and conform to the most effective style for each stakeholder interaction."

And remember, if you do any sort of self-assessment, how you perceive yourself is often very different from how others perceive you. And that perception by others varies with different projects and types of work. You might be very driven and focused when completing your own tasks, but then very analytical and reserved when working with stakeholders in order to understand their challenges. Taking multiple assessments—from DISC® to Myers-Briggs Type Indicator (MBTI®) to even organizational or team-created assessments—are ways to continuously look at yourself from new perspectives and see what opportunities might be possible.

BA Career Progression

Having experience with the various business units in an organization can provide you with a breadth of knowledge in the industry of your organization. For example, if you have years of business experience in a financial company and decide to change jobs, you are likely to move to another financial company because your knowledge of the industry is valuable regardless of whether or not the new position is in the same business area. BAs with this kind of industry experience and knowledge will also be excellent candidates for business consulting roles because they are often able to see how processes function across the organization. These individuals will be valuable as executive managers in their area of expertise because of their understanding of the business issues and their analytical capacity to imagine and implement solutions. If a BA is interested in moving into management, their experience will easily transfer to more strategic positions in the enterprise. Their skills will grow as they deepen their industry knowledge.

BAs who have IT, marketing, or other functional area positions may find themselves moving in slightly different career paths. Your functional expertise continues to grow in depth the more projects that you are involved in, the more opportunities you have to improve daily operations, and the more chances you have to bring in new ideas and technologies that are applicable in your business domain. Growth in your line of business can easily lead to management positions since you know the value of the roles that your team provides. Your communication skills also expand since you have to articulate the value of the SME knowledge that you bring to cross-functional change work. And those communication skills transfer appropriately to consulting careers where you need to bring solutions based on your expertise—solutions that can benefit the organization. This focus on a business line also gives you a great opportunity to learn new industries, as the concepts you bring are still applicable to most organizations regardless of industry. And even better, you get to learn about new industries, further enhancing your skills and experience.

To successfully understand the business requirements without having worked in the business unit requires a person who can learn quickly and can imagine a situation *without* actually having been in it. These individuals must understand business requirements at a high level and translate them into solutions with valuable insight from their experience. When your focus shifts to providing business value to the organization regardless of functional area ownership, there is often a natural transition to project-based teams. Those analysts who want to ensure every effort delivers value and work to prove the value of those efforts naturally progress to enterprise BAs—either in PMOs or enterprise business analysis teams. And if you are determined to drive that solution to completion, a project-based BA is a great fit because of your goal-oriented approach. It allows you to identify and leverage the requirements in order to validate that your solutions are adding value.

There are different types of business analysis work, and the people who perform it do not have exactly the same skills. A large organization may have many individuals doing different types of business analysis work. Recognizing that the organization will benefit from a variety of analyst roles often leads to a set of job descriptions, titles, and career paths supporting business analysis professionals. Formally creating professional standards for business analysis work is one of the goals of organizations like the IIBA and PMI. Experienced BAs are committed to elevating the profession, setting professional standards, and bringing recognition to the role. The more well-defined the positions and job descriptions, the easier it will be for professionals to find the appropriate positions for their skill sets and their interests.

One of the best things you can do to progress your career into business analysis whether you are a new BA or you have been working in an organization for a while is to find a mentor—formal or informal—and utilize that person at every opportunity. Do not be afraid to ask for help and direction, or even better, to bounce ideas off of them regarding ways to utilize techniques and approach different stakeholder groups. Seek out people who are BAs in multiple areas of business, industries, and even titles (again, capable BAs love to research and learn as much as they can about a subject). Mentors can be one of the best assets in a BA's toolkit. They will expand your techniques, outlook, and perspectives on business aspects that may be hard to accomplish naturally.

> "Find a mentor—and utilize that person at every opportunity."

KEY BUSINESS ANALYSIS TERMS/CONCEPTS

In general, companies use terminology very inconsistently. One of the roles of professional standards organizations is to standardize definitions and the use of terms throughout their respective professions. Language is very important to the role of the BA. BAs must learn to be precise and consistent in their use of language. Words, concepts, and ideas are all used to convey requirements. Listen carefully to the way stakeholders use words so that you can communicate back to them in a language that is familiar. When a "customer" is referred to as a "client," the BA should do the same. It does not matter if that is not the best or most appropriate word. It does not matter if that is not a word with which the BA is comfortable or familiar. When that specific term is used by the business, it must be used by the BA to facilitate and demonstrate understanding of the business and their natural language.

BAs must recognize that terms have different meanings to different stakeholders and they must be able to translate these words and meanings to the concepts they represent. There are a few key business analysis terms and concepts that will be used throughout this book. They are introduced here.

What Is a Requirement?

The word *requirement* is the most important word in business analysis work. BAs must understand the uses of this term. In the industry, the word requirement is used inconsistently and can mean various things to different people so having a solid foundation to rely on allows you to pull out the true requirements from any conversation. One of the best definitions to date has come from the IIBA *Business Analysis Body of Knowledge*® (*BABOK*® *Guide* 2015) which states that a requirement is *a usable representation of a need*. Your job is to dig out the true need—not the want—and articulate it in such a way that everyone involved sees the same picture/representation of the end solution.

> "The IIBA defines a requirement as a usable representation of a need."

However, take note of the fact that this definition—as well as others by PMI and the Institute of Electrical and Electronics Engineers—do not say anything about the format or representation of the requirement. Analysts are free to represent it in any way that clearly communicates the need. This is why creativity is especially important as the business environments, technologies, customers, and solutions themselves rapidly evolve. The ability to focus on solutions regardless of methodology is part of your requirements analysis skill set. There is also no definition of who owns or manages the requirement. This is where your communication and facilitation skills come into play—to focus on why the requirement is important and what value it adds to the effort at hand, the solution (once it is deployed), and even future efforts for reuse.

A requirement can be documented and presented as a(n):

- Sentence (The system shall . . .)
- Structured sentence (as in a business rule)
- Structured text template
- Table or spreadsheet
- Diagram (workflow)
- Model (diagram with associated details)
- Prototype or simulation
- Graph
- Storyboard
- Any other format that communicates

Remember that a requirement has to be *usable*, thus, the format chosen should be one that makes it easiest for someone to use the requirement. The format or representation does not qualify it as a requirement; it is the intent and the stakeholder need that make it a requirement. You will find your stakeholders interchanging other words such as *specification* or *functionality* when describing requirements and design components. And that is okay if it works. However, be careful that someone does not use the word *need* when articulating a *want*. Make sure the requirement is actually required.

Since the definition of requirement is so broad, it is helpful to think of requirements in terms of categories or components. These core requirements components are the building blocks upon which complex business areas and systems can be described. You might compare them to the letters of the alphabet: understanding the letters and how they can be combined into words allows you to make sentences and communicate difficult ideas and concepts.

Core Requirements Components

When describing a business, there are four basic requirements components: people, information, processes, and rules. The *people* component may include individuals or departments inside or outside of the organization (called external agents or actors). The people component also represents *systems* or other business areas. *Information* is data. *Processes* are manual or automated activities or procedures that the business performs. *Rules* include business rules, guidelines, constraints, regulations, or policies under which the business operates. Think of rules as encircling the other three components because rules guide the use of the other components (see Figure 1.5).

This is a simple way to start thinking about analyzing any business area. See Figure 1.6 for an example of the breakdown of requirements components for a grocery store.

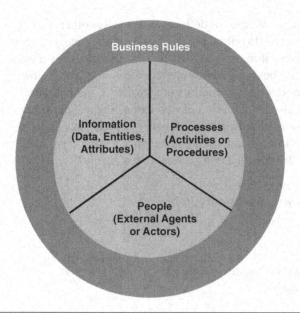

Figure 1.5   Requirements components

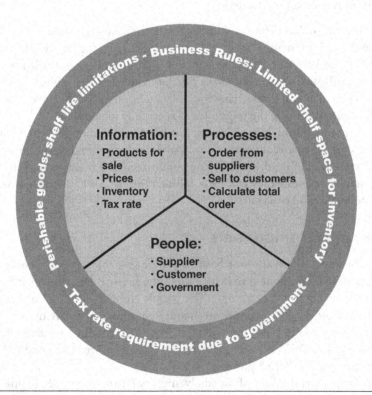

Figure 1.6   Requirements components for a grocery store

By breaking requirements into their core components, BAs begin to see the business more analytically. They can identify specific parts of the business that may need improvement and develop more specific questions to get more detailed requirements.

Why Document Requirements?

Regardless of your experience, the question as to what to document often comes about and is sometimes heatedly debated. Different methodologies encourage or challenge the notion of capturing what is going on, especially when you consider how fast things change in a business environment. Will what you have captured be obsolete by the time someone reads it?

One point about which there is agreement is that requirements are often elicited from stakeholders and shared with project teams to deliver the solution. The BA is generally found in the role of eliciting requirements because not only is the skill set of facilitation key to BAs, but also the unbiased solution view of a BA becomes incredibly valuable toward ensuring that the team is heading in the right direction in order to accomplish their goals.

Regardless of who ends up capturing the requirements, here are some essential reasons why requirements should be captured:

- *People forget things*: Business stakeholders will sometimes forget what they tell solution teams—and solutions teams will sometimes forget the requirements. This leads to a lot of wasted time while team members try to remember what was discussed. The challenge is to capture the outcome of any discussions and not necessarily all the *meeting minutes* that led up to decisions.
- *Verbal communication is fraught with errors*: Remember playing the game telephone as a child? A message that is passed from one person to another changes significantly as more people are involved. Requirements are very specific, detailed items that can easily be changed by using a different word or phrase. You want everyone literally on the same page with what representation they are picturing. Verbal communication can leave plenty of room for interpretation.
- *People sometimes answer the same question differently if asked twice*: Business stakeholders often give different answers to the same question at different times. This may be because after the first discussion a stakeholder has had time to think about the question further, or it may be that a stakeholder has simply changed his or her mind. BAs are experts at asking the same question in different ways before documenting a requirement, just to be sure that the stakeholder has really answered definitively.
- *Writing something down forces a person to think about it more carefully than they do when they say it*: For example, a stakeholder may say that he wants a report to show totals by month, but when he sees a report layout with 12 columns crammed together, he realizes that he actually wants the last three months only.
- *It ensures accuracy and identifies missing requirements and undocumented assumptions*: When a user is requesting something, have someone other than the user write down the request, such as the BA. Then have the user review it for accuracy. This will highlight ambiguity and poorly defined requirements.
- *New people joining a project need to quickly get familiar with the goal, the approach, and the requirements that the team is working on*: Having the requirements easily accessible to any team member at any time keeps both new and assigned team members on the same page.

Why Do Requirements Need to Be Detailed?

Many times, the person who captures the requirements is not the same person who is developing or delivering the requirements. To clearly communicate the needs, the details must often be further refined—especially if you consider remote and virtual teams that are not able to be colocated. Defining a marketing campaign that is *eye-catching* is a great business requirement to ensure the exposure, but it is hard for your offshore team to deliver the same expectation that the marketing director may have. Detailing requirements allows you to validate expected behaviors, experience, and results *with* your customers so that the resulting solution delivers value.

> "... validate expected behaviors, experience, and results *with* your customers."

Now, the greater the detail, the longer it will take to define, capture, analyze, and organize requirements. This is often where the debate comes up regarding the value of capturing requirements and how long it takes to get them. But some good BA planning and collaboration with your project team can help with this decision. If you are on a project in a highly regulated or risk-averse industry, then greater details on your requirements will facilitate better testing and validation with limited rework required. You will then be able to use the captured requirements for audits and reporting requirements—again, without having to create whole new documentation. If you have the ability to work more closely with your customer for iterations of feedback, such as in agile and adaptive approaches, then your requirements may be at a much higher level that is *good enough* to allow the team to produce partial solutions. You should constantly utilize what is produced in order to elicit from your customer exactly what reflects their vision and what needs to be refined. These become your requirements for the next iterations. You have not wasted valuable time documenting specific details that simply changed in the next iteration, but have focused on moving forward the delivery of value.

The capturing of requirements is often best accomplished when discussed in the context of the business, the change, the solution, and the environment. Even small functional changes to systems usually have impacts to end users and the resulting customers. Articulating how processes work and are changing or impacted by the requirements helps the best solutions for a given situation to emerge, while keeping everyone on the same page. Greater discussion on capturing requirements can be found in Chapter 6.

Complex Business Rules Must Be Found

Many business rules are not exposed until low-level detailed requirements are documented. Many business rules and guidelines are not mentioned during requirements elicitation because they seem inconsequential (too detailed) or because the business SMEs take for granted that everyone knows them. These business rules often drive exception processing and cause major problems if omitted. Every business rule that will be automated by software must be explicitly stated in the requirements. With business rules, the requirements should include the desired exception processing, including the exact wording of any warning or error messages. Helping the business SMEs think about how they expect to see business rules enforced often exposes other business rules and more detailed requirements.

Requirements Must Be Usable

Originally, BAs were often the translator role between business and IT. They would be able to articulate the business needs down to a detail that the developers could utilize and build. This was natural since the technology departments often had the same challenge: seeing exciting IT solutions but not knowing how to get the business to buy-in—thus enters the BA.

In today's world, requirements must be understood by all team members who will not only use them, but also will be affected by them. Ideally, the BA will be able to express the requirements in a format and style so that everyone on the team sees the same outcome. This is the reason why expressing requirements in text is sometimes discouraged. Using text requires both audiences to share an understanding of terminology that must be very exact. For finance people to learn IT language or for IT people to learn marketing language (and so on) is not necessarily of value to the participants. However, understanding the expectations and opportunities identified by various team members leads the team to successful solutions. Business analysis professionals should have the skills necessary to present requirements in visual formats that can be clearly understood by all parties. Customize the presentation of the same information based on the audience that will be utilizing it—in this way, the requirement itself is never lost, but can be split logically or summarized as the audience dictates. Again, whenever there is lack of clarity and team members do not understand each other, this creates an opportunity for the BA to utilize his or her skills by defining the requirements with various details so that everyone understands not only their own role, but the bigger picture into which they fit.

An example of diagrams helping to define the requirements can be found in a user experience with technology. In the process of designing an app, marketing may have great ideas, but deliver you vague requirements such as "user-friendly," "easy-to-use," and "eye-catching." If you handed these over *as-is* to the development and communication teams, do you think they would all have the same representation of the final product? The answer is—*probably not*. The BA's job, in this case, is more valuable than simply translating business requirements down to technical requirements. BAs must help articulate the features that drive value and initiate the discussion on options that allow technical teams to create solutions from their experience rather than being told how to program. They help articulate the functionality that will drive the user experience as described. In the discussion, they then create process maps that walk the customer through the entire experience from start to finish—not only explaining expected behavior to technical teams, but also supporting communications, training the help desk staff on how to troubleshoot, and identifying marketing opportunity points. There should also be records establishing when the product is to be upgraded or changed, giving you a starting point to work with. Of course, you always want to consider your environment, the project approach, and what your teams need in order to deliver value. Some teams will need very detailed descriptions to use for testing and validation when it comes to addressing specific regulatory requirements. Other teams are looking for the vision from the product owner and are excited to deliver ideas for feedback. The skill set of experienced BAs lies in helping to ensure that requirements are detailed to the level required of those delivering the solution. You will need to adjust your approaches, techniques, and deliverables based on what is most needed of your team and the current challenge while always thinking of how to leverage your efforts for additional future value.

What Is a Project?

A *project* is a temporary endeavor—with specific start and completion dates—that is undertaken to create a unique product or service that brings about beneficial change or added value. It is critical for business analysis professionals to understand the nature of project work versus the strategic planning that

> "A project is a temporary endeavor that brings about beneficial change or added value."

goes into the decision to do projects or the operational activities to keep a business functioning. Projects, regardless of their level of technology involvement, are funded to accomplish a specific objective. Once the project goals have been accomplished, a project is complete. The challenge is that many organizations will do *initiatives* or other endeavors and not realize they are projects. Sometimes efforts on a smaller level are called projects, even if managed completely by the person responsible for doing and delivering the work. BAs get the opportunity to be assigned as a resource or even to drive the work on all these levels. This takes us back to why business analysis has such a broad definition. You may help problem solve an existing operational issue (operational work), be assigned as a key resource to help deliver a new product or service (project-based work), or may even find yourself helping with business case development and market analysis (strategic analysis).

What Is a Product?

Business analysis work is concerned with products that deliver value. To ensure that appropriate value is constantly being achieved in an organization, many projects are undertaken to create, implement, change, or even retire obsolete or inefficient products. The challenge is to see that products today are not always tangible and money-generating items. "Products" are also processes, market share, brand awareness, employee engagement, and investments; items that BAs will need to incorporate and leverage into the organization's business model to drive value. Projects will have a specific and limited scope. Products have larger visions that evolve and change. It is important for BAs to understand the concepts of project and product—and be able to differentiate between the two so that you know how best to facilitate that continued value.

What Is a Solution?

> "The IIBA defines a solution as a specific way of satisfying one or more needs in context."

A solution is a *specific way of satisfying one or more needs in context* (IIBA 2015). This is the main focus of business analysis in providing solutions, not simply a product. A product can still address the needs, but the solution will include training, communication, customer feedback, and continuous improvement to ensure that the organization gets the value it needs from that product. Having a keen focus on solutions by validating that the value is achieved is what makes BAs so valuable. This is often the argument when it comes to why managers should hire BAs from *in-house*. BAs constantly look at solutions, whereas many consultants simply provide products or only the deliverables listed in a statement of work. There are process changes and other incorporation tasks that have to be done to a product in order for it to work well in an organization. The BA helps follow and facilitate the project to deliver products that are true solutions for the organization.

Real World Example: What Goes into a Solution?

Have you ever had to upgrade your smart device (such as a cell phone) or even upgrade an app? People typically just accept the disclaimer message and move on in order to hurry up and get the newer product—ignoring the recommended link to learn more about the upgrade. You then turn on your cell phone, for example, and find that the features that you previously accessed from the home page are no longer there. You start trying to find them and only get frustrated. These "disappearing features" typically happen when those behind the update decide to make *simple* changes without considering the entire user journey—what may happen and who else may be affected. When you go online to search for where your features went, the first results are news articles of what changed in the update and how to use the new features. Then finally you'll find a page that explains where the old features are (though maybe the project team should have considered if you skipped the *helpful links* reference . . .).

Now consider a user experience where a BA had helped the project team consider not only the changes but also how to communicate with the public concerning those changes. Marketing requirements included use of all communication channels, including social media and videos, to help advertise the new features and how to find the old ones. Call centers and retailers were given advanced information on the changes, scripts, and instruction guides so as to help their customers when asked. User manuals were updated with a history of changes recorded for reference and even feedback opportunities were incorporated into the design so as to decide how it would be best to consider future upgrades that would change the development process itself. The BA gives the cross-functional view, stakeholder analysis, and scenarios to help the project team think through the initial changes and prepare itself for continued value.

Traditionally, IT analysts have focused on software as the solution and often underestimated the significance of the business changes that must be made to accommodate new software. BAs are in the unique position to understand the ramifications of a change to the entire business area. As can be seen, the evolving business analysis professional is working to broaden the perspective by acknowledging that software is often a part of the solution, but it must be combined with procedural and organizational changes to effectively improve the business.

BAs must approach each assignment with an open mind—even when someone has already recommended a solution. Focus on the need. A need can have many solutions; however, a solution itself is only one option. The act of analyzing prevents jumping to conclusions or choosing a solution until you completely understand the problem or opportunity and have considered all the ways in which you may address the need. Each element and even product possibility may produce the solution that your organization ultimately needs.

What Is a Deliverable?

Understanding deliverables is important to any change effort, particularly project-based work. Deliverables are *any unique or verifiable work product or service that a party has agreed to deliver* (IIBA 2015). These often help you answer the question: are we done yet? Since it is a distinct piece of work, you can verify the item. Be comfortable with the *goal* of the deliverables because stakeholders can often misuse or even overuse the term due to a misunderstood definition, so it is important to ensure that everyone is on the same page.

Deliverables are the separate items that contain some value but ensure overall value of the solution is achieved. BAs use traceability with deliverables to help validate that the solution is delivered (see Chapter 6 for more on traceability). When you have verified that all of the deliverables are completed (i.e., delivered) then you can usually verify that the solution is delivered. Examples of deliverables include a workflow diagram *delivered* to a stakeholder for review and approval, a staffing matrix *delivered* to HR for review and feedback, a training plan with identified resources *delivered* to the team to coordinate, a database design *delivered* to a database administrator with the expectation that they will create a new database, and a new data entry screen *delivered* to software users to improve their process efficiency. It can help you on project work to distinguish the type of deliverable and then help assign ownership. For example, business analysis professionals create requirements deliverables for their stakeholders to confirm their understanding of requirements, get approvals, communicate requirements to various team members, communicate needs to vendors, and validate solution components. BAs will have business analysis deliverables that will include requirements documentation, process maps, and other outputs of analysis activities that are discussed in more detail throughout the remaining chapters of this book.

Some organizations have formal structures and formats for producing business analysis deliverables that might include requirements tools, repositories, and templates. Different methodologies also have preferences on the type and format of expected business analysis deliverables, such as user stories on agile projects. BAs must be aware of the mandatory and recommended requirements deliverables for the organizations that they are working with and also for each particular project or change effort. In addition, the BA may decide to create other deliverables in order to present requirements that are not completely represented by traditional techniques. BAs need to pay attention to the needs of their teams and produce the appropriate business analysis deliverables that continue to drive the delivery of value. This focus allows them the flexibility and creativity to adjust their approach based on each change effort. Open communication with your team to explain how you aim to help achieve the goals is required, but can be as simple as talking and planning with your PM or business units.

System Versus Technology

Consistent use of terms is important in all BA communications to help everyone be on the same page. The use of *system* has become all too popular with standard business vocabulary today due to the proliferation of technology; however, not every system that your stakeholders describe is a software application nor do many people realize the systems in which they work and function daily. BAs are often systems people in that they are concerned with the larger picture. To a BA, a system is focused on the outcomes produced by the interaction of various interconnected components (IIBA 2015). This can include technology, the people who utilize it, the processes they follow, the regulations and laws that govern it, and more. With this focus, BAs need to be clear in conversations with stakeholders when they are talking about a specific software application and the core functions the system performs or the technology and how it relates to the day-to-day business value of the organization.

"A system is focused on the outcomes produced by the interaction of various interconnected components."

Be aware that when you use the word system alone, your audience will envision something based on their background and experience. If you are talking with an IT person, they will think software. An electrical engineer will think electrical system. A business person will think about a business system. Use the word "system" carefully and with a specific purpose.

It Depends

One of the most common phrases that business analysis professionals use is *it depends*. Much of business analysis work is complex, abstract, and dependent on current circumstances. When a BA is asked about a recommendation for a particular approach or analysis technique, often they will start the answer with, "It depends." Every situation is unique, and BAs bring their problem-solving, communication, interpersonal, and teamwork skills and knowledge to tailor an approach to each new problem. This is another reason why planning your business analysis work is so important and will be continuously highlighted throughout these chapters. Do not be afraid, though, to say, "It depends." Simply follow it up with some good investigative questions on the situation to help you provide meaningful recommendations.

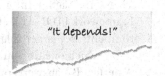

"It depends!"

BUSINESS ANALYSIS CERTIFICATION

As a BA, constant learning and growing are common traits of not only your profession, but often your personal curiosity. Certification in business analysis allows you the opportunity to not only concentrate on the details of the profession, to know them at an intimate level that may not be common in your workplace, but also gives you the professional recognition of someone devoted to their vocation. In your own research and analysis, you will find there are different options in which to pursue advanced learning. Certificate programs acknowledge that an individual has completed a course of study. They are evidence that an individual has satisfactorily completed an approved curriculum and has demonstrated the ability to perform the tasks required. As you get into higher levels of certifications, experience with practicing business analysis is usually required as well.

There are many options for certifications. The IIBA now offers multiple certifications that include various levels of experience. These range from the Entry Certificate in Business Analysis™ (ECBA®) that is focused on entry-level analysts with no work experience (but requires BA training) to seasoned professionals with years of experience such as the Certificate of Capability in Business Analysis™ (CCBA®) and the Certified Business Analysis Professional™ (CBAP®). As of this writing, the IIBA (2018) has over 10,000 certification holders in the world. PMI also has emerged with their business analysis certification, the PMI Professional in Business Analysis (PMI-PBA)®, and while it is a newer certification, it already has over 2,000 worldwide certification holders (Khan 2018). This one is more project-based and aligns well with PMI's *Project Management Body of Knowledge (PMBOK® Guide)*. It also requires experience as a BA along with professional BA training.

Additionally, you can find business analysis certificate and diploma courses through many providers such as vendors, training organizations, and even universities. Some of these are single courses with no experience required and last from a few days to a few weeks. Others include multiple classes with group projects and presentations. They give you professional-level training and knowledge you can take back to your organization and utilize in your BA role.

Additionally, those wishing to take a specific concentration in business analysis topics will also find many certificate programs and even industry certifications available. Data analytics and business architecture are two areas of business analysis that have full industry certification programs. Also, never discount the value of certification in methodologies and techniques. Project management approaches (PMI, PRINCE2®, agile), Information Technology Infrastructure Library (ITIL), The Open Group Architecture Framework (TOGAF), and Six Sigma are all great certifications that will enable you to understand environments, see larger solutions, and work better with your stakeholders on change efforts.

So which one do you need or which one is going to benefit you the most? It depends (I know, right? A perfect BA answer!) on why you want the certification and what you are going to do with it. Proof that you have attended business analysis training and/or have knowledge of the profession shows that you are aware of industry terminology and techniques. It will always be considered positively by employers and will make your transition into new environments easier because of not only the knowledge, but the certification that shows the initiative to keep learning and growing. Standardized certifications from the IIBA and PMI give you industry-level recognition that is now becoming required more often for those who desire senior BA positions; and it gives hiring managers a common criteria with which to compare candidates. Having a broader certification helps you attain greater experience in a variety of environments, which is essential to growing your skills and becoming comfortable in larger, more strategic work.

From an employer's perspective, evidence that a BA possesses not only business analysis knowledge but also the ability to apply that knowledge in a day-to-day, real-world, business analysis environment is invaluable. Consider your current situation and where you want to be in three or five years when making this decision. Also, the process of obtaining certification can be a great way to re-energize your business analysis work by walking you through the fundamentals. We often get too excited in our day-to-day work—we forget the purpose and goals of our techniques, which we have molded to fit our own situations. Certification can be a great way to ground you again and really advance your skills.

Because many organizations use the BA title differently or combine the role with project management or quality assurance, certifications can be a great way to standardize expectations and experience. Hiring managers are looking for help in discerning the tasks that are typically performed by BAs, and since managers often do not have personal experience with performing these tasks, they need help evaluating a candidate's capability. Hiring managers can look to certifications to help them define the expected tasks of the role of a BA for not only promotion within the organization, but then in finding candidates that best suit the needs of the organization.

BUSINESS ANALYSIS FOUNDATIONAL MATERIAL

As you venture into learning more about business analysis, you will find it rewarding to reference the organizations that are devoted to the practice and profession of business analysis in all formats, along with their practitioner-created materials. These valuable resources not only further your understanding of business analysis, but also give you the industry-accepted vocabulary and standard terminology to use when communicating with other professionals inside and outside of business analysis.

The IIBA has their *Business Analysis Body of Knowledge® (BABOK® Guide)* that gives you a guide into the activities and areas where business analysis is providing great value to organizations. It was created and refined in each version by the global community of business analysis professionals who bring their real-world experience to this foundational guide. It explains the key knowledge areas, tasks, techniques, and underlying competencies that BAs should be familiar with as they perform business analysis. If you need help overcoming challenges or are entering a new area of analysis work, referencing the various sections can give you guidance on how best to approach your BA work. Additionally, all IIBA certifications are based on this guide when preparing for examination. You should make yourself quite familiar with all the key concepts, even if you do not apply them daily.

PMI has continued to focus on requirements and business analysis skills and in 2015 produced *Business Analysis for Practitioners: A Practice Guide*. This is an excellent guide to key activities that a BA may perform on project-based work. Core concentration on requirements and change management are discussed throughout the entire project life cycle to help focus on delivering valuable solutions. In 2017, PMI released the *PMI Guide to Business Analysis*. This includes both an ANSI-accredited foundational standard and PMI's *Business Analysis Body of Knowledge* in one publication. This publication gives the core foundational knowledge of business analysis across various project delivery methods and ways to produce change in organizations. Both guides are great companions to PMI's *PMBOK® Guide*, following the structure of how to approach the various elements of project-based work. Emphasis on the evolution of BAs to seek to evolve their techniques to match the situation is highlighted. These materials are great references when you need guidance, but are not necessarily the step-by-step *cookbook* to performing business analysis well. Use these along with your knowledge, soft skills, and especially team skills to help successfully apply these concepts in your day-to-day work. Both of these guides from PMI are also key resources for helping you prepare for PMI's Professional in Business Analysis Certification—the PMI-PBA.

SUMMARY OF KEY POINTS

The first step in mastering business analysis is to acquire a very clear understanding of the work involved and the role of the BA. Business analysis work continues to evolve and will be performed by many people with various titles, but it always involves:

- An understanding of the definition of business analysis and how it can apply to not only technology, but to any analysis work done in an organization for business value
- Awareness of the evolving role of BAs and why they may be found in various locations across an organization from IT to enterprise levels in order to help support true business needs
- Insight into some of the key traits and perspectives that a passionate BA leverages to support organizations
- Consideration on how to enter, grow, and succeed in a business analysis career that may drive even further learning through experience and certification
- Providing definition and references for organizations that are looking to define the business analysis role and structure the various positions, along with how to look for possible candidates
- Awareness of key business analysis terms and vocabulary and why communication of these aspects is so important to successful BAs

BIBLIOGRAPHY

International Institute of Business Analysis (IIBA). (2015). *Business Analysis Body of Knowledge® (BABOK® Guide)*. IIBA: Toronto, Ontario, Canada.

IIBA. (2018, March 31). "Listing of Certification Recipients." http://www.iiba.org/Certification/Certification-Registry.aspx.

Khan, A. (2018, January 31). "PMI Credential Holders Worldwide." *360PMO*. https://www.360pmo.com/pmi-credential-holders-worldwide/.

Project Management Institute (PMI). (2015). *Business Analysis for Practitioners: A Practice Guide*. PMI: Newtown Square, PA.

PMI. (2017). *A Guide to the Project Management Body of Knowledge (PMBOK® Guide)*. PMI: Newtown Square, PA.

PMI. (2017). *The PMI Guide to Business Analysis*. PMI: Newtown Square, PA.

ADDITIONAL READING AND REFERENCES

IIBA. (2017, November 6). "The Digital Transformation Is Here, Relevant and Your Opportunity for Success." *BA Lens*. http://balens.iiba.org/?q=content/digital-transformation-here-relevant-and-your-opportunity-success.

KPMG. (2016). "Business Analysis—Positioning for Success." KPMG LLP, Canada.

The Myers & Briggs Foundation. (2018). "The Myers Briggs Foundation." Gainesville, FL. http://www.myersbriggs.org/.

The Open Group. (2018). "The TOGAF® Standard, Version 9.2." Overview. Retrieved from http://www.opengroup.org/togaf.

Paul, D., J. Cadle, and D. Yeates. ed. (2014) *Business Analysis, Third Edition*. BCS Learning & Development Ltd., United Kingdom.

PRINCE2.com. (2018). "What Is PRINCE2"? https://www.prince2.com/usa/what-is-prince2.

Saboe, D. (2017, June 13). MBA128: "Where Should the BA Reside?" Mastering Business Analysis. http://masteringbusinessanalysis.com/mba128-business-analyst-reside/.

Whittenberger, A. (2017). "How Business Analysis Services Add Business Value." IIBA. https://www.iiba.org/ba-connect/2014/august/how-business-analysis-services-add-business-value.aspx.

Wiley, J. (2018). "Everything DiSC." John Wiley & Sons, Inc. https://www.wiley.com/WileyCDA/Brand/id-43.html?&category=For+Working.

CHAPTER 2

YOUR SECOND STEP—KNOW YOUR AUDIENCE

While we will talk further about the capabilities and techniques that business analysts (BAs) use on the job, the heart and soul of a BA is working with people. Some of your most valuable analysis is done with coworkers. The soft skills of communication, collaboration, elicitation, and facilitation are what allows BAs to leverage all of their knowledge, regardless of the area of interest, in order to drive greater value, gain experience, and grow into more senior roles.

The word *stakeholder* is common terminology used by a BA or anyone doing project work. A stakeholder is the generalization for anyone (group or individual) who has a *relationship to the change, need, or solution* (IIBA 2015). This definition is important for you to understand. Stakeholders are the decision makers who are examining business needs, those working the projects to deliver the change required, and those using, supporting, and evolving the resulting solution. An example stakeholder scope diagram is presented in Figure 2.1. Each layer of audience will have different needs from both the project team

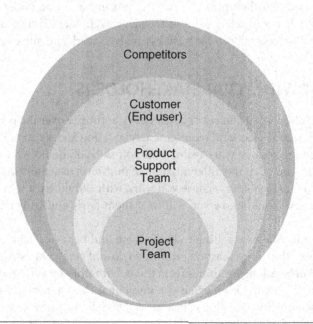

Figure 2.1 Example stakeholder scope diagram

perspective as well as from the final solution perspective. When you have a complete view of all the stakeholders involved, better solutions are designed.

A part of knowing the scope involves knowing the stakeholders. While we refer to stakeholders in these general terms, remember that each individual has a unique perspective and with that comes unique goals and desired outcomes. The listening and elicitation skills of the BA should be used to draw out a stakeholder's perspective and to understand each individual; this is paramount when it comes to working successfully with stakeholders. The people you work with often have titles and are filling roles on your project or team. Something as simple as remembering their names can instantly help you form the relationships needed to work *with* them to accomplish your goals.

It is essential that BAs develop a mutual understanding with stakeholders as they gather information and then follow up to ensure clarification of needs, desires, and ideas since they must be able to present the information that has been collected and analyzed to various other individuals. How you present the requirements to the technical team is much different than how you would present a formal business case to executive leadership. You must tailor your presentation for the audience to whom you are speaking. Presenting BA deliverables clearly and accurately is made more efficient when you know the characteristics of the person(s) with whom you are communicating.

"You must tailor your presentation to the audience to whom you are presenting."

This chapter discusses the different individuals with whom the typical BA will encounter and often work with. It discusses how and why the BA must learn as much about each stakeholder as possible, regardless of how short of a time span is involved. Often the area of stakeholder analysis is something that project managers (PMs) and BAs will work closely together on for their project work, but it is important to understand that you each have a unique perspective on what your relationship is to each stakeholder. Clearly, understanding your team members is critical to the success of both the business analysis work and any change initiative as a whole.

ESTABLISH TRUST WITH YOUR STAKEHOLDERS

As a BA, you have very little formal control or supervisory authority over the people with whom you will be working. Your best chance at successful requirements elicitation and solution identification will be your stakeholders' confidence and trust in you. Again, these soft skills of the BA—trustworthiness, ethics, personal accountability, etc.—are often the differentiators of mid-level to senior BAs as the keys to delivering valuable solutions for your stakeholders. Those you work with should trust that you will treat them with respect and kindness. They should know you will treat them fairly and truly have their best interests in mind.

You establish trust with people by getting to know them and behaving with integrity. As a BA, acting with integrity means doing the things that you promise to do and being honest, direct, and consistent. You gain trust from people not by asking for things from them, but rather by asking what you can do for them. And when asked, answer honestly—even when you know that the listener may not like the answer. This can be as simple as responding to a question whose answer you do not know with, "That's a good question! I do not know at this time—but I will find out."

Stakeholders must trust that you will not use the information they provide to harm them. Information is powerful. People who have access to large amounts of information have a responsibility to treat it with respect. You are going to be gathering and compiling large amounts of information; and you will be learning about what other people's jobs are, how they perform their jobs, what problems they have, and more. How you use that information and how you represent your sources will tell your stakeholders about your integrity and professionalism. Some information must be kept confidential for political or legal reasons. However, your job is about pulling the needed information out in an unbiased way to help the team focus on the solution. Keeping sources confidential by stating facts and working to drive the team forward toward their goals will help build trust and minimize your worry about trying to please everyone or trying to be *nice* over being *effective*.

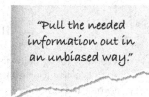

"Pull the needed information out in an unbiased way."

WITH WHOM DOES THE BA WORK?

Every change effort has a myriad of stakeholders who each play a role in ensuring solutions for business success. Although each organization and each project is different, there are several common roles with whom a BA works with on a regular basis, including:

- Business executives
- Product owners
- Project sponsors
- PMs
- Other business analysis professionals
- Subject matter experts (SMEs) and users
- Quality assurance analysts
- Scrum Masters
- Solution architects
- IT (information technology) developers and various IT SMEs
- Testers
- Trainers
- Vendors and external consultants
- Customers

Business Executives

While senior BAs will often find themselves working at a more strategic level with business executives, even junior BAs should keep in mind that their analysis work is helping decision makers to make faster, smarter decisions with the information they deliver. Your business executives have the charge of leading the organization, determining the strategy that will drive business success for years to come—all while providing their stakeholders with value.

Again, understanding your stakeholders starts with understanding the nature of the business in which you work. Understand that your organization may have multiple stakeholder groups they are trying to please with each and every strategic move. BAs use the stakeholder knowledge of those involved—those who are impacting or impacted by the change—in order to drive their analysis work to deliver information that helps decision makers see the options, risks, and impacts surrounding the decisions they are looking to make.

Real World Example: Pleasing Multiple Stakeholders

Working for a major financial corporation, the challenge on every initiative and project was also to remember the four stakeholder groups that the organization answered to. These included the end customer, the employees, the community, and of course, the shareholders. A project to bolster employee satisfaction and reduce turnover included extra cost and effort. If the value returned from the effort accomplished the goal of increased employee satisfaction and less employee turnover, then many of the team members argued that the effort was easily justified; however, part of the project's justification had to include how the effort would also positively impact the organization's customers, the community, and the shareholders. This was where the analysis work came into play to show how knowledge of products and relationships between customers and long-time employees resulted in higher profits and better product selection for the customer. Being attuned to customer needs supported the development of greater business investments that positively impacted the community. And, of course, increased profits led to increased dividends (and therefore, happier shareholders).

Product Owners

Regardless of the project management approach that the team may take with an initiative, BAs work with product owners regarding the development of a product, the requirements to maintain the product, and which factors may lead to the product's retirement—such as technology changes, competition, and even a change in leadership or business strategy. Product owners, as their name implies, are the ultimate responsible parties of the product that an organization manages. Decisions on changes, as well as daily operations, are driven by them and they prioritize those decisions based upon perceived business value.

Now, how does the product owner make these decisions? Often, they need to consider what is beyond their scope of management—such as external influences, competition, and even something as simple as what other products the organization is utilizing in their business model. Here is where the BA role comes into play again. BAs from a more senior to mid-level perspective often work closely with product owners, delivering enterprise analysis as to how the product fits in the organizational business model as well as subject matter expertise on the line of business. Even if you are a more junior analyst, bringing information to the decision maker is what the relationship is all about. What risks and impacts are there with multiple decisions? What is the potential return on investment (ROI)? How do we quantify the business value of even small changes to the organization, not just the product owner?

"Bringing the decision maker information is what the relationship is all about."

Helping the decision maker understand how decisions can affect all stakeholders is one of the most powerful roles the BA can provide in this relationship.

Here is a quick note on product owner versus product manager: the term *product owner* is more commonly used today with the proliferation of agile methodologies on projects. Yet, whether your project uses agile or any other methodology, there are sometimes members identified in the role of product manager. A *product manager* is, as the name implies, responsible for the product. From the creation of the business case through production, upgrades, and changes, to retiring it from the organization's product offerings, the product manager makes the decisions on the product. A product owner may or may not be the product manager. A product owner can be a business SME assigned to a project to help the team quickly make day-to-day decisions to move the project forward. They act on behalf of the business. The product owner reports to the product manager, providing updates, and sometimes consulting when there are major decisions or directions in strategy to consider. Regardless of the title, knowing what the person is focused on and thinking of how you can best provide valuable information to help them with their decision making are your key considerations as a valuable BA.

Project Sponsor

The sponsor is effectively the *boss* of the project. The sponsor has secured funding for the project or change effort and has specific objectives for the funds. The sponsor determines the success of the project or change effort based on how well it meets his or her objectives. Project-based work can even have multiple sponsors sometimes, especially when the project is very large and complex. You might encounter not only a project sponsor, but also a business sponsor or executive sponsor as well. All of these individuals are key stakeholders—not only for the project work, but also for your own performance. They will have an opinion on how much value you contributed to the successful outcome of the project. The most important thing for you to learn about the sponsor (or sponsors) is why they want this project carried out and what their success criteria will be. The answers to these questions are part of the project initiation or project scope phase. At the beginning of a project, you may be working with a PM or you may be working alone. Either way, your main goal is to gain a thorough and complete understanding of why the organization has decided to spend money on this project and why the sponsor feels there is significant value to pursue this effort with their name on it. This will be discussed further in Chapter 3.

The biggest mistake that can be made with a sponsor (or any stakeholder, for that matter) is to waste their limited time listing excuses and problems. The sponsor is usually less concerned with what has happened and more concerned with what is being done to ensure that maximum value is being achieved. Communication with sponsors is focused around accomplishments and requirements to be achieved, along with action plans and risk responses for moving forward, rather than excuses and complaints about the current situation. Often on project-based work, you will provide this information to the PM for them to communicate to the sponsors and all stakeholders as appropriate. And remember that your communication has to be tailored based on your audience. The higher up the corporate ladder, the less detail and more concise summaries you will need to provide. PMs are going to want to know some details to consider risks and dependencies (and hopefully you are helping explain them). However, executives are too busy to read long, detailed reports; they want the BA to cut to the chase and give them the highlights. Do not let your attention to fine details derail you from presenting information concisely to sponsors that is valuable to their decision making. This is where you need to use conceptual thinking on top of your stakeholder analysis. A couple of key questions to address in executive summaries are:

> "Present clarity to sponsors surrounding information valuable to their decision making."

- Are we still achieving value from our efforts?
- Is the project going to accomplish the goals we intended?

Remember to point out the value achieved, regardless of your progress. The PM will report on the milestones that have been reached to date and together this information gives the sponsor a clearer picture to confirm that the project is still on track to accomplish the defined goals as expected by the sponsor. Knowing not only the PM's desire to report accurately on the status of the project, but also the sponsor's need to know what is being done helps you be a more effective BA.

Real World Example: Working with and Presenting to a Project Sponsor

I was assigned to a project where I was working with a PM on the implementation of a large IT system that was to bring about new customer features while significantly improving the internal processes for technical and customer support. This project made sense to the organization and had garnered support because we had an IT sponsor, a business sponsor (for customer impact), and an executive sponsor who reported on the project through his portfolio and budget.

The PM and I started off by ensuring that the business case and project charter were solid so that we understood exactly what we were charged to change; then we detailed the value that we would deliver at the end of the project. As we were starting our initial analysis and beginning to pull in team members, we started having trouble finding the positive level of impact that was described during the initial assignment. Analysis continued longer than planned, but we could not get the detailed analysis to produce the business case that was being asked. Initially, the PM had done a great job of articulating the status to the sponsors regarding the fact that our planning would take more time in order to ensure that we started the project off on the right foot. I had to provide estimates of how long my analysis work would take, along with who and what I needed to complete the analysis. I additionally gave her a summary status of milestone dates that could be achieved based on my analysis (i.e., approved project charter and business case on a certain date).

But as we completed the analysis, we realized that we were not seeing the benefits that were initially forecasted. Rather than move forward, we had to present our findings to the sponsors. We prepared a very clear and concise presentation that articulated what goals we were told were expected to be met on the project, the key metrics we had identified through our analysis, and then most important, we presented the sponsors with a series of options. This included moving forward as planned but constantly measuring the value to determine whether or not we were seeing results. This carried the most risk because our initial planning was not showing the value to be achievable. The second option involved breaking the one project into two parts with separate goals and approaches. This meant basically canceling the project and reconsidering whether or not there were other alternatives as to how to approach either providing the customer features that were desired or the internal infrastructure support that was hoped to be achieved. And then as a third option, we shared the idea of a pilot project where we limited the implementation but still completed the changes in their entirety to measure and report on the value impact to the customer and internal processes. The presentation was only a few minutes, though we came prepared with all of the details and analysis that led us to these recommendations. The data helped us respond to questions, but we did not have the data clutter the clear presentation on what decision needed to be made. The end result was a quick decision by the sponsors that resulted in the selection of the third option—the pilot idea—to demonstrate what value was possible with this project.

When communicating with sponsors, brevity is the key. Be brief and to the point. Stay at a high level, supplying details only when necessary to make a point. Be concise, clear, and respectful of their time. They want to know what the bottom line is. Do good research and planning prior to every meeting with them so that you stand on your facts and do not operate by gut instinct. If you feel intimidated by your sponsor, you may not be able to ask good questions and get the information that you need in order to be successful. Take opportunities to talk with executives whenever you can. Put yourself in the sponsor's position and tailor the communications appropriately. Remember your goal—you are often asking for a quick decision to move forward in a specific direction. Are you making it as easy as possible for them to see the information and give you a timely response?

PM

Effective project management is critical for successfully delivering change efforts, not only in IT, but also across all areas of the organization. Most firms have also learned that a great PM does not necessarily have to be a great technician. The growth in popularity of the Project Management Institute's PMP® certification in both IT and non-IT departments demonstrates this realization. Most large organizations also have a project management office where PMs are supported and project management methodologies are administered. The growth and recognition of the role of the PM is the same growth and recognition we are now seeing with the role of business analyst.

Project management and business analysis are two distinct professions with two intersecting skill sets. A PM is responsible for managing a project and making sure that it meets its objectives. Project management work includes identifying project requirements, establishing measurable objectives, and managing the resources, time, scope, and quality of a project. Projects are typically assigned to PMs or even business owners (who are now playing the role of a PM) to carry out and deliver the expected changes. BAs who are doing project-based work will often find themselves assigned as a resource of the project, reporting to the PM on assigned tasks. The BA work on a project includes eliciting, capturing, and managing requirements; testing; verification; validation; and operational turnover analysis.

How do a PM and a BA work together to make a project a success? Fundamentally, the PM manages project tasks (resources, timelines, tracking, and reporting) and the BA manages the solution (requirements, tracing, testing, validation, and operational support). The BA reports to the PM on their progress on the assigned business analysis tasks. If there are both a PM and BA assigned to a project, a great tactic is to have the PM and BA sit down at the very beginning of the project and plan out their approaches, potential challenges and risks, and discuss not only the overall project but also their working relationship and responsibilities.

> "The PM manages project tasks and the BA manages the solution."

This sets a solid foundation for the project so that as things get moving, they each can begin to focus on their respective responsibilities. Excellent PMs and BAs will work hand in hand to make the most of each other's strengths.

Often on projects, there is overlap with the work a PM is expected to perform and the defined business analysis work. In many organizations, PMs have actually been expected to do all of the project management work in addition to all of the business analysis work. In this case, the PM relies on the SMEs that are part of the team to identify their requirements and ensure they are validated through the solution. The PM will spend time supporting cross-functional collaboration and discussions to ensure overall project needs are addressed, rather than individual needs or desires. Other times, the BA may be asked to manage a project. This is typical of smaller work efforts. Here, the BA still focuses on doing the analysis to identify and deliver the requirements, but must keep a healthy watch on the timeline, the needed resources, and the budget, as appropriate. The BA in these cases will need to ensure that they communicate and report on the project status more often and with larger stakeholders than simple daily work efforts. When lucky enough to have both roles on a project, there are also the challenges of the appearance of overlap of scope of the PM and BA role. The challenge that often arises on projects is that the PM is very project-focused while the BA is very product- or solution-focused. The solution scope can sometimes be beyond the project scope. Again, creating a solid foundation between these two roles and their responsibilities, while defining clear objectives and a vision of the final solution, will help ensure the two roles can be more effective together.

The Business Case for a BA on a Project

As project management skills have matured with the explosive growth and variety of project-based work, many of the tasks on a project often completed by BAs are being performed by the PM. This can come from a lack of resources (i.e., there is not a BA available), a lack of understanding of the roles and their values and differences, or simply because the scope of the project is relatively small enough that a PM with experience doing analysis work can handle the tasks of both roles.

However, having two separate individuals (a BA and a PM) on a project leads to greater results and is worth the cost of the additional resource. Since a PM will manage risks on the project, sponsors need to be made aware that not having a BA is a risk factor to not only successful completion of the project, but also the success of the resulting solution. The simple act of having to manage and coordinate all the project tasks, schedules, and budgets makes project management a full-time position and the analysis of requirements that drive the necessary tasks can be minimal to almost nonexistent on many busy projects without a BA. Ensuring that there is coordination in the design of the solution is a key success area handled by the BA that is often overlooked. Some of the key factors to present to sponsors in your business case are to articulate the value of the BA role on a project, along with how they mitigate risk and accelerate the successful delivery of the solution beyond just the scope of the project. While the project may work out okay with only a PM, the analysis work still needs to be done by someone. Having a BA with this skill set can produce faster, higher quality results than relying on your PM to complete the analysis work.

Even if the role of BA is not accepted or defined in your organization's project methodology, knowing that there is analysis work that needs to be completed to ensure that you're building the right solutions for the right challenges (i.e., solving the right problems) is paramount to any project. This is where business analysis still has a place in project-based work regardless of methodology. But you need to make the business case as to whether or not a dedicated role should be identified and assigned or whether it is as effective to have the analysis work performed by those resources who are already assigned to the project. And again, this might be where you find that a BA has been assigned, but he or she ends up doing the work of the product owner. While not ideal since the roles have separate functions and responsibilities, the project can still be successful regardless of the roles as long as the key activities of analysis, validation, and defining and prioritizing the desired value and outcomes is done by someone competent who can align project and organizational goals for lasting, valuable solutions.

PM and BA Skills Comparison

Common Skills

One of the reasons why many organizations assign one person to act as both the PM and the BA is that people who operate well in these two roles have many skills in common. Both the PM and the BA must have very strong communication and collaboration skills. This is probably the most important skill needed to operate effectively in either role. Individuals in either role must also have an understanding of how projects are accomplished and an awareness of the methodologies and approaches to designing and developing valuable solutions. Facilitation is often a key skill since both roles remain responsible for bringing together groups of people, negotiating, and gaining consensus on how a particular solution will be implemented. The approach to finding ways to implement changes requires individuals to be natural problem solvers who are interested in understanding how things work and who then use strong interpersonal and client management skills to help those they are working with add greater value. Neither of these roles have decision-making authority, yet they are expected to present clear definitions of situations with value-adding recommendations that lay a clear path forward.

Unique Skills

There are also unique skills for PMs and BAs that allow them to perform the tasks for which they are responsible. PMs are exceptional at managing tasks, dependencies, and removing roadblocks that prevent team members from completing their defined duties. BAs excel at diving into the details to understand not only how things work, but also what elements drive the related behavior of processes, systems, and organizations. PMs have an eye toward scope and confirming what is in scope and especially what is out of the scope of work in order to keep teams keenly focused on the tasks at hand and ensure that they achieve their goal(s). BAs, through their analysis skills, look at solutions beyond immediate needs and assess the value the solutions will have for both the current group of stakeholders and into the future, including the effects on the entire organization and communities surrounding the solution.

Similarities and Differences Between the Two Roles

The PM is responsible for ensuring that the desired changed is delivered to the customer on time and within budget. The BA is responsible for ensuring that the desired change produces value through defined designs and requirements. This difference in focus between the two roles is the reason why having both on the team is so critical. Together, they ensure that the change produces the desired value (or greater) as designed—on time and within budget.

The following is a list of some of the qualities and duties found in the role of a PM:

- Responsible for planning the project and ensuring the team follows the plan
- Manages changes, helps clear obstacles, and keeps the project moving
- Manages people, money, risk, and project scope
- Chief communicator of good or bad news to the sponsor and management
- Usually the first person assigned to a project

The following is a list of some of the qualities and duties found in the role of a BA:

- Responsible for ensuring the solution delivers the intended value
- Learns the business needs, context, and environment in detail
- Manages requirements throughout the requirements' life cycles
- Chief analyst of situations, challenges, and recommendations to support decision making
- Usually assigned to a project after it has started

Traditional Versus Adaptive Projects

Much of the conversation so far on PM and BA roles has come from the traditional approach (often termed *waterfall*) to project management. Further discussion of the different roles and titles used on adaptive or agile project management methodology is found later in the chapter; however, awareness of the perspectives and key activities of a PM and a BA on any project-based work, regardless of methodology, will help your change initiatives succeed. No matter how short your timelines are or the differences in titles of the roles being fulfilled on your project, awareness of your project scope and intended outcomes are key success factors. There is always some planning that is done to ensure that you have the right resources and are gathering the needed information. There will always be analysis work done to ensure that the solutions are delivering value during and long after the change is implemented. Formality will be different on your deliverables and communication styles, but cohesive and productive team coordination and collaboration will always be required regardless of the titled role that facilitates it. These key elements and clarity on the value of both the project management and business analysis skill sets will help you focus on learning and growing the skills needed to be a valuable change agent regardless of your title, organization, or the methodology employed.

> "There will always be analysis work done to ensure that solutions deliver value."

Dynamic Duos

When assigning PMs and BAs to a project, executive management should be aware of the importance of this dynamic duo. Their success depends on their respective experience, knowledge, and skill sets. The results will vary depending on the individuals selected.

If a strong PM is assigned to work with a weak (inexperienced, unskilled, or insecure) BA, the requirements-gathering and analysis tasks may be rushed and important requirements may be missed. The PM will be pushing for the project to make progress and the BA may not be strong enough to convince the PM that complete, accurate requirements are critical to project success. This may result in rework late in the project when the missing requirements are identified. This type of rework usually results in schedule and budget overruns.

In the opposite situation, if a weak PM is assigned to work with a strong BA, too much time may be spent in requirements gathering and the project may fall behind schedule. BAs can sometimes push to get every single detail 100% correct before moving forward, and if the PM lets the BA try to accomplish this virtually impossible task, the schedule will be jeopardized. Also, if the PM does not strictly enforce the change-control procedure, the BA may allow the business to add more and more requirements, resulting in *scope creep* and project delays.

Obviously, the worst-case scenario is a project with a weak PM and a weak BA. No matter how involved the SMEs are, or how good the technical team is, a project is likely to fail without strong leadership and clear requirements.

Therefore, the best-case scenario is a project with a strong PM and a strong BA. Assuming the rest of the project team is competent, this project will be well run and the end product will be of the highest quality. There is a balance between thorough requirements gathering and project progress. The project will be on schedule and meet the expectations of the sponsor.

The PM is much more of a director than the BA. The PM directs the project team, making assignments, giving specific directions, removing barriers, and ensuring that team members are working on the appropriate tasks. The PM requires strong management skills, while BAs are more focused on listening and analyzing. They must listen carefully to SMEs and discover requirements—not create or invent them. The BA is actually looking for problems, issues, or even opportunities that may not have been identified during project scoping but could impact the success of the project. The BA alerts the PM to these potential problems and ideas and works with the PM to address them. The BA requires strong investigative skills. The PM is focused on helping the team get work done and remains project focused, while the BA is focused on helping people describe the work they do and communicates all identified needs across different functional teams to elicit and listen for suggested solutions.

During the course of a project, the PM manages the change control process. Any changes to a project will impact the original plan, so the PM identifies this impact, works with the executive sponsor to decide whether a change will be accepted, and then revises the plan to accommodate any changes. BAs often help with the analysis of these changes, the risks involved, and the potential impacts. The analysis work helps provide clear business justification for courses of action that the PM can communicate with decision makers and quickly get an answer to move forward. BAs will manage any changes and impacts to requirements so they can report to the PM regarding any impacts to scope, schedule, and/or budget.

Tips for Those Performing Both Roles

If you happen to find yourself playing this dual role, the challenge is to be aware of the conflicting focus and to try to act in one role at a time. You may find you are having disagreements with yourself, and it may be helpful to have a fellow PM or BA listen to your internal debate to try to help you make decisions. Be aware that you probably have a preference for one role or the other and you may find yourself neglecting the tasks of the role you enjoy the least. If you prefer doing PM work, you may miss requirements. If you prefer doing BA work, you may allow the schedule to slip or forget to direct your team members. This situation is further complicated if you are also assigned to other project responsibilities (e.g., you are also the technical architect) or assigned to work on other projects. Your project schedule, budget, and product quality may be affected. Be sure to plan for the time needed to do both jobs adequately.

If you frequently find yourself in this situation in your organization, use your detailed analysis skills to identify the risks and potential impacts. Then use your communication skills to heighten management's awareness regarding these competing roles. Make management and your team aware of your opposing responsibilities and the challenges associated with them. BAs must remain focused on providing valuable insight to challenges and opportunities so the business can make decisions quickly.

Other Business Analysis Professionals

For large projects, more than one BA may be needed. When multiple BAs are working on the same project, they need to plan the business analysis work together and then divide the work appropriately. When one of the BAs is designated as the senior BA, he or she will usually decide which tasks will be assigned to each BA. BAs must work especially close together during project initiation and requirements elicitation since they may be working on closely related business areas.

There are many different strategies for dividing business analysis work. Some teams delegate one BA as the data analyst, one as the process analyst, and one to gather business rules. This division allows each analyst to focus on a particular type of requirement and then cross-check their work by linking or tracing their requirements' components to the others. Another delegation strategy is by high-level business process. Each BA is assigned to a high-level business process and is responsible for analyzing all of the requirements components needed for that process. Regardless of the delegation approach used, BAs should consolidate their requirements and make sure that all relationships between requirements components have been documented and traced so as to ensure the solution adds the desired value to the organization.

SMEs and Users

An SME is a person who has a particular expertise needed on a project. The expertise may be on the business side (a person who understands business needs), on the technical side (a person who can provide technical design ideas), or outside the organization (an external customer or agent). The acronym SME has become popular because it can be used to describe anyone on a project who has expertise in a given area.

Business domain SMEs understand the business area being analyzed. Ideally, they are experts on the business or a particular area of the business. The business domain SMEs can be workers in the business area, managers, or even people outside of the business who have some interaction with the particular area of the business being studied. These business domain experts are often the people who are considered the BA's customer; these are the people for whom the BA is trying to solve a business problem and create a solution that will make the business more efficient and effective. It is always important to know the *customer* of your solution since many change efforts include internal business processes and are not focused on external purchasing customers.

"It is important to always know the customer of your solution."

During the requirements elicitation phase, it is valuable to talk with experts on the business. The SME provides critical understanding of the business: why things are done, how they are performed, what the results are, and ideas on what the business needs to be successful. Without these SMEs, there is often no business analysis. Some of the SMEs may report to the sponsor, but many will not. On small projects, the SME may be the head of a department using application software that interfaces with other departments. SMEs can be business people from various organizational units who have varying amounts of interest in your project. As the BA, your biggest challenge is to convince these people that they should spend time with you and tell you everything that you need to know about their business. Successfully convincing them that you are on their side and working to help them is the secret to being a successful BA. This is why your communication, collaboration, and facilitation skills are often more valuable than your knowledge of analysis techniques.

You will also frequently hear about the *user* role. This term refers to a person who *uses* the solution, product, or process that is under discussion. Many people prefer the term "SME" to "user" because it sounds more positive and because it is more accurate during analysis and requirements elicitation. Be aware that although many SMEs may also be *users* of the solution, many are not directly engaged. Department managers may be SMEs because they understand the business goals of the department, but they are not *users* in this sense because they do not perform the business process directly—for example, entering data into the application. Alternatively, a user is not necessarily an SME. A data entry person who simply enters data on a computer screen without any knowledge of the reason for the data entry is not an expert.

All SMEs are not created equal. Expect many challenges with personality types, working styles, and motivations. Understanding and winning over these experts will not be easy. It will require you to get to know these individuals, do research before meeting with them, and use every bit of charm that you can possibly command to convince them that they should tell you their deepest, darkest secrets. These are not personal secrets, but honest revelations about how they do their jobs, what their most important issues are, and why broken processes are not working. Your goal is to build a trusting relationship where these business experts can share with you not only the business information, but even their own ideas on how to make things better.

As mentioned earlier, business analysis professionals must be able to ensure that they accurately communicate the same picture (the representation of the goals, objectives, and ultimate solution) to all stakeholders in the appropriate format for that particular stakeholder group. As a result, BAs will use varied language when speaking and writing in order to best communicate with the intended audience. Titles and role names of stakeholders are often used inconsistently. An analyst should clarify terminology and titles when they are used and be consistent. For example, some people use the word "customer" to mean a person external to the organization who purchases products. Some IT people use the word "customer" to mean anyone inside the organization who uses IT services. A simple misinterpretation of this term can cause requirements elicitation to take longer than anticipated. Even if the BA is not driving the conversation, taking the time to clarify what is meant by the role name in front of the team will lead to better discussions and developing faster solutions as you keep everyone on the same page and focused on the goals.

Getting to Know Your SMEs

Ideally, you will be given the names and titles of your SMEs before any project meetings or facilitated sessions are scheduled. This will give you a chance to do some research before you meet with each one. Start with your own BA planning—identify what you already know about the individual (not just the role) and what areas you believe the SME can be of most help with when it comes to the change initiative. Then use your analysis skills to begin to build a picture of the SME before you meet with him or her, such as looking up their position in the organization, who they report to, and who reports to them. Also ask your PM and other team members if anyone has worked with any of the SMEs that you are unfamiliar with in order to obtain more insight into the person and their background. The more you understand the person, their role, and their potential perspectives, the faster you will be able to focus on the value-adding details of the change initiative and move forward.

Think of it as doing research before going on a job interview. You will want to make a good impression on these people the first time that you meet, so anything you know up front will help. And do not be afraid to learn some personal details or areas of interest regarding each person. While it may not appear

"A successful BA builds numerous trusting relationships."

business related, you are building an overall relationship to help with the larger goal. The more trust you can build into the relationship and show that you value them as a person, not just as a change resource, the more information you will be able to collect and utilize to move the effort toward a valued solution. Successful BAs build numerous trusting relationships with people inside and outside of their organizations. These relationships help the BA to be successful not only on the current challenge, but also to then have a solid foundation on which to be successful throughout many future endeavors.

Business analysis is as much analysis on the people affecting or affected by the change as it is on the business itself. Understanding social styles, work ethics, and general likes and aptitude helps you plan your approach to be as effective as possible. This can be as simple as learning that the person comes to work early every day and then asking them if a morning interview might work best. These seemingly small gestures will improve the speed at which you can elicit requirements and, more important, give your SMEs—your customers—a confident sense that you know what you are doing.

So how do you do this research? You are trying to learn as much as you can without anyone suspecting what you are doing. Think of yourself as a private investigator:

- Walk by the SME's cubicle or office to observe their workspace.
  - Does it appear well-organized or cluttered? This may give you an idea about how this person works.
- Are there a lot of people around socializing with the SME or do they seem to prefer to work independently?
  - This will give you an idea about how willing the person will be to talk with you.
- Are there any certificates or awards hanging on the walls of their office?
  - This may indicate experience, training, and pride in work accomplishments.
- Are there posters or pictures that indicate outside interests? Family photos?
  - Finding a common interest outside of work can be a great icebreaker and a way for you to develop a friendship with an SME.

If you know other BAs or PMs who have worked with this person in the past, talk with them. Carefully, discreetly, subtly ask questions about how the SME participated on the last project. Did they show up for meetings on time? Were they prepared with information that was requested at previous meetings? Did they contact the BA with questions or follow-up information or wait for the BA to initiate all contact? How knowledgeable was this individual about their business? How comfortable was he or she with the change?

If you know someone else in the business area who works with the SME, talk with that person. Again, carefully, just mention who you will be working with on your next project and that you are looking forward to getting to know him or her. Watch for facial expressions and body language. Does your contact give any hint of a positive or negative reaction? If so, ask a follow-up question, like, "What has your experience with this person been?"

Obviously, if you have worked with this SME before, you already know the answers to many of these questions. Even so, try to keep an open mind and learn even more about the person. If you did not have a positive experience on the last project, think about what you might do differently this time. The more you know about your customers, the better you will be able to service them. However, there are some common challenges related to SMEs as discussed in the following sections.

Managers Who Do Not Understand Their Employees' Work

Sometimes the manager of the business area is the main stakeholder and the only person available to provide information on a business domain. While quite knowledgeable with the business area's function and how the team members provide value to the business, he or she may not know the specific details of how work processes are carried out or how systems function. This causes difficulty for the BA because interviewing the manager does not result in accurate business models or requirements to the details that are required for validated solutions. Since the information comes from a trusted source, the BA initially may not even be aware that the requirements are incomplete. A solution may be delivered that is inadequate to support basic key business functions.

To be successful working with your stakeholders, you not only need to know the characteristics of those you are working with, but you must also be very clear as to the information you need in order to help validate that you have the correct people involved. Are you able to articulate what information the team needs to solve the challenge at hand? And then are you able to further parse this information as it applies to the business area you are working with? Being clear on what types of information you need and how it helps design the solution will keep the BA role from evolving into an SME who is expected to provide all the answers. When you ask to meet with someone, your request—whether informal over the phone, in person, or more formalized with an e-mail or meeting invite—should clearly articulate what information you are after so that the person can identify whether they are the correct SME to provide the desired information. Your time is valuable as well, so ensure that you are meeting with the right person at the right time. The communication skills that you use to articulate what information is valuable to the solution at that time are also key to working well with your SMEs.

Real World Example: Identifying Appropriate Stakeholders

While working on a website redesign project, the project team identified the various departments that needed to be included in order to ensure that we were delivering a valuable solution. These included marketing, IT, the various product owners, and even legal and compliance departments. As the BA assigned to this project, I was explaining to the team that I would need to spend some time independently with each business area before bringing everyone together to identify needs and specific requirements. The marketing director said that she would be the point of contact for any marketing questions.

I was grateful for her support for the project; however, I had to consider whether or not she was the most appropriate person for the tasks that I needed to complete. We set up a meeting for the two of us to go over the requirements. I came to this meeting with a list of all the types of information that I felt marketing could answer in order to help define the requirements and bring ideas to the team for defining the solution. These included questions surrounding what statistics they had on the current website, including sources of referrals, top selling online products, and most-used features. Additional questions were more focused on the business strategy—asking about near-term and long-term marketing vision and strategic goals of the department. Finally, I also inquired about what branding requirements

continued

were to be included as we discussed designs so that they were built into the solution, not brought up after development was complete. As I went through my initial list with the marketing director, she started identifying some team members of hers who could give me more detailed data, background, and specifics to support my requirements definition. She would address the strategy and vision discussions herself.

Doing my analysis and preparing questions ahead of time helped me articulate the type of information I needed so that I did not have to actually tell people they were the incorrect person. Rather, I focused on the goals and outcomes and asked those identified SMEs if they were able to provide the information—or if not, could they tell me who could offer the necessary information?

Doing your own analysis of what the solution needs and what your options are for getting the information helps you work more effectively with your stakeholders.

When the Expert Is Not Really an Expert

Although they are called SMEs, BAs may not necessarily be working with an expert within the context of meeting their current goals. Sometimes the manager of a business area assigns a person to the project team who does not have significant work experience in the business area. This is common because, from their perspective as the business area manager, they cannot afford to have their best people away from their normal, everyday work in order to attend project meetings. Thus, it is typical to send a less experienced employee to project meetings. So what does a BA do when the *so-called* expert who attends the meeting is not really an expert?

When assessing your requirements team, determine whether you have been assigned an SME who is not an expert. Be careful not to jump to any conclusions. Just because someone is new to the area does not mean that they are lacking in valuable knowledge. You should give the person a chance by interviewing him or her just like you would any other SME. Understand the SME's role, expertise, and their functions within the business area. Remember, someone may be new to the organization but actually have years of industry experience. And this outside perspective can sometimes be even more valuable to the organization. Those fresh ideas can help build the solutions that your organization so badly needs.

Once you use your communication skills to understand more about the person you are working with, go back to the goals of why you are trying to gather information and consider what you expect the SME to provide during the course of the project. Since many people may not like to admit that they do not know something or are potentially not the best person to be interviewing regarding this subject, you have to plan your validation activities even better when you are unsure of the source. This means that you will still approach the SME with your requirements and analysis needs and verify the information with them; however, you may have to plan more work to validate the information, such as additional interviews with other business members, more document analysis, and possibly even multi-department team meetings to flush out the solution requirements versus business-area-dependent requirements. This will confirm the SME's understanding (or lack thereof).

Keep an open mind when it comes to the stakeholders that you are working with and presume the best on all accounts. Again, restating the goal of helping the organization get more value (this is not about your job, the SME's job, or punishing anyone) will help you stay focused on the larger objective. If you really feel that you are not moving forward toward the goal or that the person participating is not helping to achieve the solution—regardless of whether it is out of a lack of knowledge or that he or she simply does not care or want to help—you must then rely on your own (solid) analysis skills. You will want to first have a private discussion with the PM, but bring clear facts on the situation, including the risks, the impacts, and what options and recommendations you have for keeping the project on track. BAs must perform analysis work under any circumstance and provide valuable recommendations that help the business make quick, yet well-informed decisions. Simply state the facts about what information you are trying to achieve and by what date. An uninformed or uncooperative SME is a risk that you need to mitigate because it affects the time it takes to produce your BA deliverables and complete your project tasks.

> "The best thing analysts can do is provide valuable recommendations for quick, yet well-informed decision making."

There might not be an option to change team members, stakeholders, or SMEs. If this is the case, then simply look at it as another challenge and develop options for finding the best solution. The less comfortable you are with your stakeholders, the more validation you will have to do. Inform the PM that your BA tasks may take longer to validate due to the availability of resources. You will need to plan your activities in much more detail and have additional options on ways to validate the information and feel comfortable on the input to the final solution.

When the Expert Is Truly an Expert

This should be the ideal situation for a BA. You have been assigned an SME who knows everything there is to know about the business. So what is the problem? Well, the SME may know the business so well that he or she fails to tell you simple, critical facts—assuming that you already know them. When experts talk about something within their area of expertise, they use terminology that is specific to the area and make assumptions about the listener's general knowledge of it. Think about the last time your doctor explained a test or diagnosis to you. You probably had to ask follow-up questions or maybe you left the doctor's office feeling like you did not really understand the situation. You need to ask a lot of questions and validate your understanding of every requirement. The SME knows the business so well that it seems very simple to him or her. The tendency is to oversimplify complex processes, forget to mention common exceptions, and minimize the size of the business area by explaining it too quickly. The SME may also get impatient with you and your lack of knowledge. On the other hand, some SMEs enjoy sharing their wealth of knowledge, even getting outside the scope of the project. They may provide irrelevant history or so much information that it is difficult to pull out just the pieces that you need.

Your approach to eliciting requirements from a true expert is preparation and repetition. You have access to all of the information that you could ever want, but you need to pace yourself in terms of how fast you can take it all in. It is important for you to understand your most effective approach to learning new things, along with the pace at which to do so. If you are a visual learner, you should ask for diagrams and pictures of how things work. If you learn best with repetition, then you should explain to the SME that you will want to go over the same requirements a couple of times on different days to make sure that you truly understand them.

You may want to schedule a greater number of short interviews so that the expert can quickly give you a lot of information and you can go back to your desk to process it before your next meeting. You also might want to remind the SME that they are the expert and that you are just learning. You may have to ask the same question several times before you really understand the answer. Ask the SME to be patient with you and work to make the best use of his or her time. This may be a situation where you would benefit from talking with a less experienced person first—one who can help you get an initial foundation of understanding before talking details with the expert.

Before you discuss the project with anyone, experts or otherwise, you should make sure that you are clear as to what you already know about the business area or topic and what role this person is expected to play. Regardless of the individual's level of knowledge, your business and stakeholder analysis before any elicitation session is a key planning activity. Always plan your approach and your verification and validation activities. The level of expertise by those you work with will affect how much pre- and post-work you will need to do so that every engagement provides valuable results.

The Expert Who Is Reluctant to Talk

Some SMEs do not feel like experts. They are hesitant to tell you anything because they are afraid that what they tell you may not be correct. This fear may be based on experiences where mistakes were punished by unsupportive management, or they simply want to ensure that the solution works and they are not at fault if it does not perform as intended. The key to working with this type of SME is establishing trust and developing a relationship where the SME feels safe talking to you.

One approach to working with an SME who is reluctant to talk is to present your understanding of the business first and ask for corrections or confirmation. Since you do not know much about the business, your initial presentation will be naïve, incomplete, and probably even incorrect in places. That's fine. As the SME points out the missing pieces and corrects your errors, that individual is building confidence in their own knowledge. The SME will begin to realize that he does know a lot more about the business than you do and that you are really interested in learning what he knows. This should make it easier for him to share information and explain complex topics. Keeping the goal clearly defined and articulating how you are trying to help the business and organization keeps you focused on the *work* and not the *worker*. If this is challenging, you may consider holding interviews with two or three SMEs at a time. The reluctant SME may be more comfortable if other experts are there to help with the answers to your questions.

The Expert Who Is Angry about Previous Project Failures

Many business analysis roles in organizations exist from lessons learned—where projects failed to deliver valuable solutions. A large, established organization may have tens if not hundreds of project failures in its history. In most of these projects, there was at least one SME who was interviewed and involved with the project. You may meet people who were involved in several of these projects. They may be angry and frustrated because they have not seen or been affected by project success. Try to put yourself in an angry SME's shoes. The SME was assigned to a new project and initially was enthusiastic about it, spending time with a BA or other analyst to carefully explain their business processes. The SME patiently answered questions, made suggestions, and reviewed requirements and design documents. The project may have even made its way to the testing phase. And then, for one reason or another, the project was canceled or the solution that was developed did not look at all like the SME expected it to—all that work and time wasted.

Then, a new project is started and the SME does it all over again. It is hard to blame an SME who dreads a new project with a new BA knocking on the door asking for a description of their business. "Describe my business? I've already done that several times! Didn't you people write anything down? Don't you all talk to each other? Why bother? You never listen anyway. If by some small chance the product actually gets developed, it never does what I want it to do! Why should I bother?" Good questions! Many projects, especially outsourced and cross-functional solutions, fail to address the expectations of all users who may be involved, affected, or concerned with the effort.

So how do you start up a dialogue and relationship with this angry SME? First of all, search for any notes, artifacts, documents, or plans from previous projects so that you do not have to start from scratch. If you can find some of the previous work, the SME will at least feel like someone listened to him on the last project. Again, your BA planning is paramount here as to how you will approach the stakeholder. Another important part of your initial conversation with this SME requires you to show empathy and regret for all of those previous failures. Even though they were not your fault, from the SME's perspective, you represent the group of people who failed—and he wants to hear that your group is sorry about the wasted time and the frustration.

This is a critical step in getting past this anger. It does not cost you anything to apologize. All you have to say is: "I know that you have worked on similar projects in the past that have failed. I am very sorry that your time was wasted. We have learned from those failures and are hoping that you will help us again, using our new approach. As the BA, I am your advocate, and my job is to make sure that your business needs are met on this project. I will be working with the solution team to make sure that they understand what you need and that they design and build it to address those needs." Apologizing and taking responsibility for the source of the SME's anger and frustration will disarm him. The SME may be able to let go of their anger simply because you have listened. Once you get past this, your interactions with him will be much easier. As you earn more trust, not only will the SME be more forthcoming with you, but they will also be more engaged with the project and help to make it a success.

The Expert Who Hates His Job

Occasionally, an SME may be someone who is very unhappy in his current role. You will detect this unhappiness from the person's body language, tone of voice, and attitude—or the SME may tell you directly. An SME who hates his job will not propose solutions to problems, will not be enthusiastic about the project, and will not be easily engaged in the process. Offer to meet the SME in his office or in a conference room located near his workspace for your first meeting. Allowing someone to be in a familiar environment will put them more at ease. Start out your conversion on a positive note by telling the individual that you are looking forward to working together. Introduce yourself very briefly and watch for body language. Is the SME interested in who you are or anxious to get on with the meeting? Another approach is to meet the SME somewhere away from the work environment. Going out for coffee or lunch will allow the SME to relax and get to know you with a more positive attitude.

As with many negative emotions, it is often helpful to allow the SME to talk with you about specific work frustrations. Listening empathetically and showing interest may lessen the intensity of the negative feelings and allow the SME to focus on your questions. You do have to be careful not to let any negativity pervade the interview because it can prevent you from eliciting true requirements. It may be helpful for you to acknowledge the problems and then move the conversation on to a more positive or at least neutral footing. For example, you might say: "I can see why you would be frustrated with this situation. Hopefully, our new system can make your job a little less tedious [or whatever the complaint is]." You may also want to explain why the SME was selected for this project. They may have specific expertise that will increase the likelihood of project success. You may be able to say that the SME was *hand-picked* to participate because of his or her knowledge and value. Put a positive spin on the SME's participation in the project based on what you know about the situation.

Finally, make sure that SMEs understand the project. Explain your understanding of why the project has been initiated along with the project objectives. Tell the SMEs what the project will do for them. If you can convince an SME that their job will be more tolerable if the project is a success, you may have an ally. Set expectations about what you will be looking for in your requirements gathering activities. Remind the SMEs that you are there to collaborate *with* them throughout the entirety of the project to ensure that the project results in a viable and valuable product.

SMEs provide the materials (information) upon which to build a solution. It is critical that a BA work closely with all of the SMEs on a project in order to ensure accurate requirements.

Quality Assurance Analyst

A quality assurance (QA) analyst, regardless of their official title, is a gift that many BAs never receive. People who are experienced, knowledgeable QA professionals add enormous value to any project or process in which they are involved. QA professionals have been trained to focus on building quality into products from the beginning, not just looking for errors at the end. In addition, the QA group will be responsible for validating the requirements against the resulting solution at the end of a project. They will be planning how the resulting solution will be tested right from the beginning of the project. Involve the people in the QA department in your projects as early as you can. Invite them to your project scope or initiation meetings. Include them in as many of your requirements reviews as they can attend. Give them drafts of your requirements deliverables anytime they are willing to look at them. QA people are trained to look for inconsistencies, incorrect requirements, and descriptions that are too vague. Because the QA group will often be responsible for testing during a project, they will be reviewing each requirement for testability. If a test cannot be designed for a particular requirement, then the requirement is not specific enough. The classic example of "software should be easy to use" reminds us of how easy it is to write a requirement that is not testable.

You will probably act as a liaison between the QA analyst and the SMEs. The QA analyst is going to ask questions that are extremely detailed and an SME may not understand why the detail is necessary. Also, in many methodologies, the QA analyst is a mandatory sign-off on the requirements. This means that you must write a requirements document that satisfies not only the SMEs but also the QA analyst.

The skills required to be an excellent BA are very similar to those required for QA work. Both professions focus on accurate details and have a continuous improvement mentality. Many individuals work in both areas or transfer from one to the other. QA analysts are typically interested in contributing to the quality of a product by anticipating (noticing) potential problems. The BA should get to know the QA analyst, just like all of the other stakeholders. Try to determine the analyst's motives, interests, strengths, and weaknesses. As with any stakeholder, the better you understand the QA analyst, the more you will be able to help her be more productive on the project. Play into that person's strengths, especially if they are your weak areas. Many BAs like to start a brand new document, draft it, organize it, etc. A strong QA analyst typically enjoys reviewing, rewording, and revising and would therefore be a great partner for a BA. Together they can produce an excellent requirements deliverable.

When QA Is a Bad Word in Your Organization

The term *quality assurance* has been used in many different ways. Unfortunately, some organizations have given this title to people who do not have the appropriate training or experience. Those on the QA team may not have been given very clear direction about what they should be doing or may be assigned to too many projects at once. They may be given the responsibility to sign off on project deliverables, but given no authority to manage the process. This common situation has caused some negative feelings about the QA function. Some people think a QA person is constantly looking for fault in other people's work so that they can report all of these defects to management. This perception creates a negative attitude toward the QA department—causing project teams to avoid contact as much as possible. They conveniently forget to invite QA to project start-up meetings and reviews. The more QA people are made to feel unwelcome on project teams, the angrier they are likely to become, thus developing a negative attitude which can feed on itself.

If your organization treats the people in the QA department like lepers, do not join the crowd. Anyone who reviews your work can give you helpful suggestions if you are open minded. Make the QA people your friends and they will help you. Invite them to every meeting, review, walkthrough, etc. Provide them with copies of every relevant deliverable. Work hard to convince QA representatives that you are different and that you do value their opinions. A second set of eyes on any task can help catch potential issues, prevent re-work, or even find opportunities that otherwise would be missed.

Usability Professionals

There are various titles and roles that focus on solution usability, including human factors, usability engineering (which is a subset of human factors), user-experience design, and user-centered design. A usability professional (UP) is a specialized type of business analysis professional. Individuals in these roles are experts in designing products that are easy to use. They work with users, performing task analysis and eliciting requirements to assist in the development of prototypes. The structured, proven techniques of usability testing are then applied to the prototype and design changes are made based on the results of testing.

UPs have become valuable to organizations for a couple of reasons: (1) the creation of e-commerce, external customer websites, and mobile technology have made usability a competitive advantage and (2) the realization through metrics-based analysis (i.e., Six Sigma, Lean, etc.) that a usable application significantly improves productivity and data integrity.

When a UP is assigned to a project, the business analysis professional should meet with that individual to determine their respective responsibilities. UPs are typically skilled in requirements elicitation, stakeholder analysis, and communication. In addition, they excel at screen design, prototyping, simulation, and usability testing. These skills allow them to focus on the human-product interaction and work with designers and developers to create a highly usable product. UPs will also be excellent resources for requirements reviews.

When a project does not have access to a UP, the BA is expected to play this role. It is important that every BA be aware of the main concepts of usability and, most important, be able to look at each project and determine if usability engineering is critical for success. Alerting the sponsor and PM to this need as soon as it is recognized may facilitate the acquisition of the needed resource or may give the BA time to learn more about usability as it relates to the current project.

Scrum Master

Depending on the project methodology of your work, you may find yourself on a team following agile principles—and here you will find the role of Scrum Master. At the foundation, this is the person who is responsible for ensuring that agile practices are followed on the team. These include but are not limited to removing obstacles, ensuring that the team is functioning at its peak performance, creating the environment for the performance to thrive, getting the product owner fully engaged, and helping to ensure the team is not distracted or derailed from delivering valuable solutions in a rapid manner.

As a BA on an agile team, you would need to have open and frequent communication with the Scrum Master on what is required to help the development team quickly move forward with delivery of solutions. BAs provide the analysis on requirements (including the possible risks) and issue resolutions to help the team quickly build and test solutions. The BA is part of the team reporting to the Scrum Master as to what obstacles might be hindering maximum value delivery. Your clear communication skills and ability to work with the team to quickly define challenges and offer recommendations are crucial to support this high productivity environment.

Your analysis skills are further valued by the Scrum Master by presenting risks and impacts on options so that decisions can be made quickly by the product owner to keep the team moving. These risks often include the lack of presence or failure of ownership by the product owner to quickly prioritize and approve requirements for development. You will need to quickly and succinctly state what the current situation is, what the recommendation and alternatives are, and what impacts the decisions have on the overall solution and value to customers, the organization, and other stakeholders.

Solution Architects

Solution architects are people who understand how the enterprise works at the highest levels and they work to design solutions that fit into the overall architecture of the organization. They are usually familiar with the business and technology strategies of the organization, along with the current internal and external environment in which these solutions must exist.

Their breadth and depth of knowledge helps to ensure the solutions being designed will integrate with current operations, infrastructure, and even personnel. Solution architects should be involved with projects at their inception. They will review the high-level business objectives and requirements to help with the ideation processes on how to best solve the business problem and assess the feasibility of solution alternatives. They ensure all requirements are identified that allow for development, integration, deployment, and maintenance of the solution. They also validate that the resulting solution being produced is actually contributing to the overall enterprise as expected, updating architecture artifacts as appropriate to accommodate the changes.

A BA will often work with the solution architect to ensure all requirements have been identified to describe the solution in such a way that it can be developed and produced. The BA often helps communicate the design recommendations to the project team for project sponsors to approve and advance.

Solution architects are great to work with when developing the testing plan and validating the results to ensure all integration and support factors are fully addressed. Solution architects also pay close attention to how the solution contributes to the organization's architecture after being deployed. They provide acceptance and evaluation criteria for the BA to use as part of requirements analysis. The PM, BA, and solution architect form a key project trio that help the team drive toward powerful solutions.

Real World Example: Working with a Solutions Architect

I was lucky enough on one project to have a solution architect assigned to the team where I was the BA and there was a PM to coordinate the work. It was a challenging project to say the least, as this was a good example where the business had already picked a product without clearly identifying beforehand the need that the product was solving. We were told to simply implement the product (software in this case) that the business had purchased.

Naturally, we had challenges because the business bought what the vendor had sold them and not necessarily what worked well with our environment, current technology, or even security policies. As the BA, I worked hard to get requirements from the business owner that eventually came in the form of use cases, explaining scenarios in which the business was picturing using this software. The solution architect wanted my diagrams, process maps, requirements, full use cases, and acceptance criteria. He continued to push for the capabilities of the software and technical requirements from the vendor while I clarified the use cases and expected outcomes from the business. The more the solution architect understood the software, the more he worked with the technical teams to come up with ideas, validate assumptions, and craft a solution that could be supported by the organization while still appeasing the business owners. As solutions were designed, I helped to capture them since there were pros and cons with each approach that the business was required to understand before making decisions. These walk-throughs of the designs that I did with the business owners really brought understanding (risks and impacts) and set expectations of the team that would not have come from a basic project plan. I, however, could not get to these decision points on solutions without someone looking at how to integrate the software with not only the IT infrastructure, but also the support model and overall technical strategy of the organization. The solution architect confirmed that all functional areas of IT had a say in the solution with the understanding they would have to support their respective areas while still working to ensure that the overall solution performed as the business expected. The solution architect also received a commitment from the functional heads that the resulting solution would be captured and integrated into daily support materials for the continued success of the application well beyond the scope of the project.

IT Developers and Various IT SMEs

As a BA, you will often see the opportunity to use emerging technologies to solve business challenges, while also being put in a position to clearly articulate which needs are not being met and where perhaps a technology solution might be possible. With this perspective, you will often find yourself working with IT developers and various IT SMEs, even if you do not report to the IT business unit.

IT developers and IT SMEs are simply subgroups of an IT department. Sometimes your solution architects will also be in the IT department, helping to craft the technical design of solutions. IT developers build IT solutions. They are often the ultimate consumer of requirements and will be the people who make your solution vision a reality. IT SMEs often include the various specialties that represent the infrastructure and operations that are required to fully integrate, implement, and support the solutions developed. These include—but are not limited to—hardware, networking, security, support desks (or help desks), data management, business intelligence, and even communications. Just as with any other business unit that you might have to work with to support the solution, you should familiarize yourself with the general functionality and responsibility of the roles of the IT department and the terminology and concepts that are most prevalent within the business area—in this case, awareness of the technology that is available inside and outside of the organization. You should also be familiar with technology development life cycles and approaches (see Chapter 5). BAs who have an IT background will be able to easily converse and work with IT professionals. Technology is changing so fast that awareness of the latest and greatest capabilities is not required by the BA—leave that to those SMEs with whom you will work—rather, the BA should be aware of the concepts and the methodologies that are driving changes and development and that affect the longer term value of solutions. This knowledge will help you ensure that you are working to deliver solutions and not simply technology products.

IT professionals are people who are very interested in making, building, and improving things. They enjoy coming up with ideas for both new and existing products, and they enjoy seeing those ideas come to fruition. Some technologists are more interested in building new products, while others enjoy fixing/improving old ones. Some would rather design, while others would rather code. A few rare individuals enjoy doing both. As a BA, get to know your IT people individually and understand their interests. The better you understand these technical stakeholders, the easier it will be for you to explain the business needs and work with them to design effective solutions.

Some developers will want to understand the business reasons for the solution that they are building. These individuals may eventually choose to become BAs themselves. If you find yourself working with a developer who is frustrated with working in a technical requirements' vacuum, include that person in meetings if possible. View this developer as a BA-in-training and mentor him on effectively communicating with the SMEs. Do not feel threatened by this direct communication between the SME and the development team. The role of the BA was invented because some developers do not communicate well with business people, but you should not assume that all IT people are poor communicators. A goal of the BA is to enable the organization to work well together and deliver valuable solutions. To really help with this, aim to evolve your role beyond simply being the translator of technology terms to business terms. Learn to step back so that the teams communicate together. Facilitate this collaboration to ensure everyone is considering the larger picture in the design and that business goals are being achieved.

Variance in Technology Expertise

If you are a *technical BA* or find yourself reporting to the IT organization, your focus should be on the analysis of solutions that fit within the entire business architecture (not just technology architecture). You want to maximize the value of every effort and investment. As technology work is involved, you will often deal with people who perform analysis work and are *generalists* who know best practices, terminology, and enough about the technology to be an effective communicator and work well with technology teams. You will also be working with people who have chosen to be specialists and have taken a deep interest in very concentrated subject areas, staying on top of the latest innovations and technology changes in their area. Regardless of their perspectives, you need to see the value in their area as it relates to the bigger picture. What elements are required for the design of the solution? What do they need to consider about maintaining any creation or product after it is implemented? A BA provides the lens through which others can see how the specific area of interest contributes to the overall goal.

Keeping this in mind, you will work with very passionate specialists who see the world from a very different perspective and are constantly looking at old things in new ways. These individuals are valuable resources in organizations where cutting-edge technology is a critical success factor. The challenge for BAs who are working with these extremely creative individuals is in understanding their feelings about requirements. Creative IT people often appear to ignore requirements, which can be very frustrating for the BA, because they are so excited about the technology possibilities. In actuality, they see the requirements as guidelines. Giving them a detailed set of requirements is like putting them in jail. You are limiting their creativity and preventing them from doing the thing that they are really good at and enjoy the most. A BA can add immense value by approaching this challenge from two angles. First, you need to ensure that the IT people understand the true business need so that you can work with them to stay on scope for the challenge you are trying to address. This supports project work by keeping it on time and budget without overloading the solution with features that are not required at this point in time. Second, you need to communicate openly and often with IT and understand what additional ideas they have on leveraging the technology. There may be opportunities to optimize and enhance current operations or features that actually support other initiatives that are going on simultaneously. As you understand what the value of these enhancements could mean to the organization, you must then focus on how you articulate and present these options to decision makers for consideration. Being able to present short business cases to management for quick decisions enables and supports the IT SME to move forward with exciting features and enhancements that they will passionately devote their time to. At this point, you not only become an advocate for the business, but also the IT SME as well. Also, you often make a great business ally with the IT SMEs because they feel you understand where they are coming from and help garner them support they may not be able to obtain on their own.

However, at the other extreme are IT SMEs who design, develop, code, and test to requirements or specifications *exactly*. They will not add any additional functionality, even when it seems obvious that something was simply missed in the specs. These individuals will not make suggestions for better approaches or ask questions about possibilities outside of the requirements. Often, IT SMEs who are working on contract for outsourcing companies are instructed to deliver exactly to specifications.

This can be a challenging situation for BAs since the requirements are supposed to be complete and accurate and should provide everything that the developer needs to know. Realistically, no requirements specification is perfect, so having an IT SME who thinks logically about the solution that he is helping to create and who asks questions when potential holes are found is ideal. The best way to handle an IT SME who builds blindly to specification is to have structured walk-throughs on each requirement deliverable and discuss the needs regularly. Try to get the IT SME to ask questions and find the missing pieces right away so that you can amend the requirements before the work is started. Ultimately, the business needs must be supported by the solution, so if changes are required after developing because of errors in the specifications, they may have to go through the project change control process. Again, the open communication and understanding of both technology and business needs is what helps to ensure valuable solutions the first time.

Most developers specialize in a particular set of technical skills that are independent of a particular business industry. It is not uncommon to meet a developer who has worked in a manufacturing organization, followed by a telecommunications company, and then a financial services or health care business. Developing software for business functions that are not well understood is possible when developers work with BAs and system architects who understand the business domain. Some developers are not really interested in what the organization sells or services as much as they are interested in using the latest technical tools and approaches. The less a developer knows about (or is interested in) the business domain, the more dependent they are on complete, accurate requirements. The business terminology will not be known, so the specific design components, such as screen labels and error messages, must be explicitly stated and followed.

Alternately, some developers have experience/knowledge in a particular industry or business domain. For example, there are developers who specialize in commercial off-the-shelf applications such as SAP© or PeopleSoft™. These developers may be very familiar with a set of terms that are unique to the application or business domain. They will provide less of a communication challenge because they know the language of the business. Just be sure that the developer knows the language of your particular business. Your organization may use terminology in a different way than other businesses in the same industry. For example, in the training industry, there is inconsistency in the use of fundamental terms like class, course, and seminar. If a developer with industry experience joins your organization, make sure that they do not assume that all terminology is used in exactly the same way. Again, detailed requirements avoid ambiguity.

Data Administrator/Architect/Analyst

Data administrators and data architects utilize many of the same analysis skills as BAs. Often you can find data specialists with titles that include *analyst* in their role. These data experts are responsible for the organization's data—from data definition, to management, to use, to reporting. They might maintain a data dictionary, data warehouse, and/or other repository of descriptions of the pieces of information that are important to the organization. The data expert helps project teams reuse existing corporate data—and use it consistently. Having one central view of business data helps an organization provide accurate answers to questions that are posed by its customers and its executive management.

These data roles have often been found in IT teams. However, more organizations are recognizing the value of utilizing data for decision making and driving the business forward. A BA may work with data analysts in risk departments, finance departments, and even information management groups, depending on the organization. Regardless of the location that the data expert may report to, understanding the value of reusing data assets, integration into daily processes for decision making, and utilization in automation and driving strategy is vital for the BA.

If your organization has a data administration team and a corporate data repository, it is critical that you become familiar and comfortable with them. This is a great resource on every project and will allow you to gather and analyze requirements much quicker. As discussed in Chapter 1, business requirements are made up of data, process, and business rules. When data has already been defined and documented for your organization, then possibly a third of your requirements definition is done before you start. In that case, the already available, quality, consistent view of data requirements allows all projects to be completed faster and the resulting solutions to be more easily integrated and interconnected.

At the beginning of a project, meet with the data analyst and ask for background about his or her particular business area. Learn about the data that has already been identified and documented. Learn which pieces of information are currently stored in a database, in which databases and systems they exist, and who maintains them. You are eliciting requirements from someone who has already done the difficult work and can give you the requirements in their purest form. Take advantage of this jump start on your project by learning everything that you can before you meet with the data analyst. You will be able to formulate more intelligent and detailed questions for your first interviews and will be able to allow this data expert to talk almost exclusively about process (which SMEs love to do). Your work will be to make sure that the processes being discussed can be supported by data that already exists. The data analyst will also tell you about data that has been identified but has not been thoroughly documented and organized. These are areas where you will need to spend more time focusing. The data analyst will be a great resource to assist you as you develop these requirements.

As much as possible, have the data experts review all of your requirements, not just data. They may see process and business rule inconsistencies with existing data. As strong analytical thinkers, data analysts can be peers to help find weaknesses in your requirements as you go along. They will also be a great resource when you move into design, working with the technical team to determine where new data elements should be stored that provide the value that stakeholders are expecting.

Many business stakeholders misunderstand the data experts, especially when they report to IT or risk management, because they feel that the data team is either difficult to work with or is simply an unnecessary expenditure. This is often because the data administration function is not well understood as it relates directly to organizational strategy and can be underfunded and/or underappreciated. Many organizations that created a data administration group in the 1990s were very excited about the data repository when the stock market was booming and business indicators were up. But when an economic downturn was predicted and companies began tightening their belts, the data administration group was an easy area to cut. Many data repositories were left incomplete and only partially maintained. This led to a situation where not all corporate data had been defined and described, so new projects could not always use the common information. With fewer people in the data administration group and incomplete data definitions, it was easy for BAs and project teams to skip the data experts' reviews and just create their own data requirements. This often caused more redundant, inconsistent data sources. The data teams that were left felt that their authority was undermined and their importance to the organization diminished. The more the BA understands about the data team in the organization, where they report, and the capabilities they can provide the business teams, the more the BA can communicate to others the value of these groups of experts. BAs need to do the same upfront introduction and learning sessions with the data experts to understand not only their responsibilities, but also the individual value-added insights and talents they bring to the table. The BA communicates this back to the PM and project team so their inclusion and active collaboration on project planning, design, and implementation brings home a successfully delivered change effort. The BAs will find a lot in common with these fellow analysts because they are concerned about reuse, efficiency, and long-term value—and those are key to any change implementation success.

Database Designer/Administrator

A database designer is responsible for determining where data should be physically stored, how it will be accessed, how it will be protected, who will have access to it, and where it will be used. These are critical decisions that have long-term effects on the efficiency and quality of information systems for an organization. Database designers and database administrators also maintain these data stores for the life of their use, not just the project timeline. They maintain backup and disaster recovery procedures and correct problems with data values when errors are introduced.

When a project involves creation or storage of new information, the database administrator must be involved. Even if you are going to use existing data in a new way, it is a good idea to discuss this new usage with the database team. Creation of and access to data can have large performance impacts for technology users, and providing inaccurate data from a technical application is the quickest way to sabotage trust in your work. Have the database administrator review your requirements and designs for feedback—especially considerations that might affect your requirements' long-term success. Make friends with the database administrator and check with him even when you think you do not need to. As with all stakeholders, when you establish a good relationship always act ethically and keep the database administrator informed. This will create a valuable ally when you need one.

> "Always act ethically, and keep your stakeholders informed."

Testers

Regardless of whether the work is on a specific project, a small task, or a major initiative, BAs will find themselves working on defining and delivering change. During the course of the work, especially on projects that include technology, as the changes are developed, stakeholders will want to test, verify, and validate that the solution is achieving the intended goals.

There are multiple levels to testing on projects so the first task for a BA is to understand what *testing* means to the organization and how is it viewed. Is this a dedicated activity with assigned resources on every project that has a formal change control? Or is this something that is frowned upon because the people who do the testing are too busy with their "day jobs" to take additional time to test something they feel does not impact them? Regardless of the scope, understanding the risk tolerances of your teams, sponsors, and the organization as a whole is necessary when approaching a plan for testing.

Often, BAs are involved with the creation of test plans. Some organizations will have staff that are experts on creating test plans to ensure that requirements are validated through specific test cases. A BA can best support these test plan creators by having detailed requirements with clear use cases and information that clearly provides customer expectations so that the appropriate test cases can be created. Make sure that these people are included in the project work, especially the requirements analysis and design planning so that they have a clear picture of the solution being envisioned, specifically the business owners' expectations of the resulting change. The BA will be a partner to ensure those who are creating test plans are supported with the information they need in order to provide quality test plans that are easily understood, executed, and documented.

If there are dedicated testers for the project, the BA needs to make sure that they understand the goals and vision of the project and the expectations of what is to be delivered before they dive into executing the test plan. BAs often help articulate not only the changes that the project is introducing but also how it fits within the organization. Again, the BA should support these team members so that they will feel included as key members by providing them the information that they need to know—even if they do not participate in the planning and design work of the solution. Often, where the BA provides the most value is in deciphering the test results—if the result of the test case is a true defect, did it result from an incorrect design or was there a misunderstanding on the test case? Test cases too often are reported as *failed* only to be analyzed and found that the requirement was built as specified, but user expectations were not captured that now need to be addressed. BAs who work alongside testers to really understand the results when they do not come out as expected help to ensure that the solution can be addressed in its entirety. BAs bring user expectations to the team to determine if they are within the scope of the project and, if so, how they can be addressed and worked into the solution. BAs can also communicate options with which to address these testing results; for example, the training and communication materials need to be updated to reflect more clearly the use of the solution.

The current best practice is to have a person execute the test plan who did not also create it. Some organizations have dedicated testers who have time allocated to execute the prescribed test plan. Those who have experience can usually execute test plans on schedule without incident. The BA's role is to stay aware of the status of the test plans, not for the progress (that is the PM's role), but rather to be a resource to do the analysis where any questions or inconsistencies arise. This requires analysis to understand what is happening and to decide if the use case was appropriate, if there were additional features that were incorporated but not captured, or if there is an actual defect that needs to be resolved. This is where a BA adds significant value to the team by defining the nature of test cases that do not pass. The BA will not only need to do a strong summary of the situation, but also articulate the risks of accepting or addressing the issue. This is then provided to the PM and the sponsor to decide the course of action.

Often, BAs will find themselves responsible for not only creating the test plans but then also executing them. BAs need to make PMs aware of the risks associated in this approach. A BA (or any stakeholder for that matter) who executes the same test plan that they create often looks to only test what they think they have written. Things are easily missed, items are passed incorrectly, or there is an inclination to only find a certain kind of error. Providing mitigating actions or ideas so that those testing are not the ones who created the test cases is important to clearly communicate to the PM. While the BA should work to collaborate with the stakeholders involved to create solid test plans, the BA should always work to be clear and specific on marrying the test plans with each element of the test case. Further risk can be mitigated by collaborating with the stakeholders when reviewing test plans and getting acceptance criteria from the decision makers. Knowing the definition of a successful test case is often more important than the test case itself.

Again, knowing the organization's structure and approach to testing is important in BA planning since there are often QA personnel assigned to help with the validation of test plans and test plan executions. Understanding the role that the QA person will play and where their responsibility ends is key to defining how much analysis work the BA will need to do on the change effort.

Unfortunately, some teams will prioritize the project schedule and, in order to hurry it along, will accept risks by skipping or downsizing the amount of testing conducted. If this happens, the BA's role is to help with the analysis of the prioritized items that should be tested and to articulate the risks and potential impacts that could occur without the additional testing. The BA delivers this analysis to the PM in order to get the stakeholders' opinions on expanding the schedule to test or move forward with the risks.

Many people feel that testing mostly applies to technology projects; however, there is a lot of work that does not involve technology but does include testing. Testing on a change effort may include focus groups or surveys with potential customers or building prototypes for team feedback on usability and experience. Many of the techniques used for analysis are the same techniques used for testing and validation (see Chapter 6). The business analysis planning work will need to include understanding stakeholders' expectations of testing and what they find value in validating before releasing changes. From here, the BA can plan the analysis work for defining the testing approaches and appropriate test cases.

Trainers

With the incredible pace of change in today's organizations, understanding and awareness of these changes need to be supported with more communication than simply notifying people of the implemented changes. Trainers help to make sure that not only are the end users able to utilize the changed solution, but they also verify that the teams that support the solution are knowledgeable and comfortable with the changes.

Training requirements should be captured as part of the overall requirements—typically identified as part of the transition requirements. The BA will need to work with the trainers to understand what requirements are necessary in order to make sure that the solution can be successful when it is delivered. Some organizations have dedicated trainers within the organization, while others have trainers assigned to different business functions. Invite the trainers to listen in on what changes are coming, perhaps not at initial requirements review sessions, but at later sessions where the requirements are more formalized or complete. Give them information early so they will be better prepared and can start planning the work needed to enable a successful solution and discuss their own requirements when you meet with them.

Vendors and External Consultants

Vendors, or external consultants, are companies from which services or products are purchased. There is typically a contractual relationship between the purchasing organization and the vendor organization. There are many types of vendors with which a BA may work. These could include but are not limited to technology, training, marketing, financial, and audits. There is work done by analysts to determine the *build-versus-buy* question. Does the organization have the capabilities to build the solution or does the organization need to look elsewhere to obtain it? Once the analysis has determined that the organization needs to look externally to achieve the solution, the scope of the project or change effort is modified. Figure 2.2 shows the typical life cycle of a vendor relationship. As a BA, you may be involved from the beginning of this relationship or you may be brought in at any point. Chapter 3 will discuss requests for proposals (RFPs) in more detail.

There are two key points in this life cycle where a BA can add great value: at the beginning (sales, demos) during creation of an RFP and when reviewing the responses to an RFP. A skilled BA will help the organization select the best solution available and expose the gaps with any package solution.

Sales and marketing people in technology companies are very good at their jobs. They create outstanding descriptions of the wonders of their technology and describe how it will make your company more successful and your workload lighter. The demonstrations are slick and polished and make the software

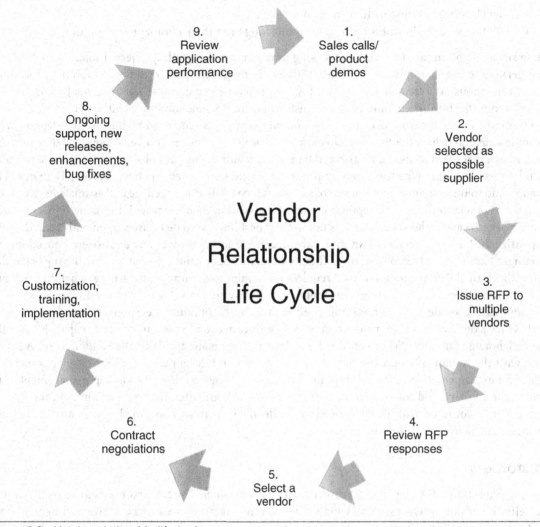

Figure 2.2   Vendor relationship life cycle

appear easy to customize and easy to use. All of these wonderful claims play right into the frustrations of users and their management. Everyone wants to believe that if the company just buys this technology package, all of their problems will be solved. But BAs know that there are no magic wands. In truth, buying and implementing technology and other products does not guarantee a better chance of success than developing the solution internally. There are different issues and challenges, but they are no less critical than the issues that arise during development. The experienced BA is aware that just because technology and products are purchased does not necessarily mean that:

- It will be implemented and deliver value faster
- It will cost less money than developing a solution internally

- It will be easier to support than an in-house solution
- It will provide the business more value in the long term than a homegrown solution

These key assumptions are too often the driving forces in decisions to buy external solutions before truly considering the internal options available. Without thorough analysis of the organization's capabilities, these assumptions are often wrong. As the BA, you should evaluate these assumptions by eliciting and understanding the business requirements, brainstorming for possible solutions, and working with the solution team to estimate the true cost and time—not only to purchase and acquire, but also to integrate, train, communicate, and deliver the solution. Go back to the project objectives and assess how well they would be met. An external solution should be assessed back to all requirements and project goals the same way a BA would assess any solution the team comes up with internally. Only when you have thoroughly analyzed the business and solution options will you be able to assess the viability of a package and estimate its true value.

In terms of relationships with representatives of the vendor, treat them with the same respect as other stakeholders. Be aware, however, that it is not in their best interest to be entirely open with you. They will emphasize the positives (*features*), minimize the negatives, and gloss over any unanswered questions that you might have asked. Overcoming the difficulty of really understanding what you are buying is handled well with a formal RFP process. The RFP requires the vendor to document, in writing, what they will provide and what they will not. Careful development of RFPs and careful review of vendor responses is the best approach to rendering a fair and unbiased verdict on the purchase decision as part of the planning work. Once a decision has been made to move forward with a vendor as part of your project, be sure that you collaborate with your PM to confirm the roles and responsibilities with the vendor. The BA should work with the vendor often during requirements analysis and design discussions. These are crucial for successful implementation of the solution for the business. However, the relationship management of the vendor, the contract, and adhering to performance standards are often the responsibilities of the PM and should not be confused with the BA's need to get detailed, clear, and specified information to help the business team deliver the solution.

Customers

In some projects, the BA may interact directly with the customer. The BA first needs to be really clear on the definition of customer—meaning whether the customer is simply external to the department or external to the organization. The term *customer* typically refers to someone external to the organization who purchases goods and services from the organization and are a key piece in the business model. However, on projects where the goals are to improve internal processes, systems, and products, the customers in these situations are often employees in other departments who will utilize or be affected by the solution. The BA works to help ensure the customer journey with the solution is clearly defined and aligned to customer needs. Articulating to the team as to whom the change is meant to be valuable for is a key skill the BA brings to the team.

STAKEHOLDER ANALYSIS

The relationship that you will build with each stakeholder on a project is unique. Some people will be easier to communicate with than others, and you will like some stakeholders better than others. It will be beneficial for you to think through what you know (or have heard) about each person in order to plan your communication and collaboration techniques and your project tasks. In thinking about an individual stakeholder, there are probably hundreds of things that you could consider. In the context of a work environment, only a limited view of each individual is available. Having acknowledged that complexity, there are several concrete characteristics of each individual that you should consider and plan for:

- Do you already have a relationship with the stakeholder?
- Is it a good working relationship?
- Do you think the stakeholder trusts you?
- What is the stakeholder's relationship to the project? (Will the project have a significant or a minor effect on the stakeholder's work?)
- What is the stakeholder's attitude toward the project? Are they excited about it or dreading it?
- How knowledgeable is the stakeholder about the business area?
- How many years has the stakeholder been with the organization?
- At what level in the organization is the stakeholder?
- How does the stakeholder communicate? Do they explain concepts clearly? Are they detail oriented?
- How does the stakeholder learn?

Obviously, you will not know the answers to all of these questions for every stakeholder on a project. The more you know about a particular stakeholder, the better you will be able to tailor your communications. For stakeholders with whom you have not worked before, you will be adjusting your communications as you get to know them. This is a good example of an area where a BA must be flexible. Try a particular communication technique, and if it does not work, try something else. These are all key considerations that a BA takes into account when conducting business analysis planning.

BALANCING STAKEHOLDER NEEDS

When there is more than one stakeholder on a project (and there almost always is), stakeholder needs must be balanced. This is an important and challenging part of the work of the BA. The BA's role is to help ensure that overall organizational needs are being addressed. But what if the stakeholders do not agree on what their needs are? This requires the BA to be a strong facilitator, consensus builder, and even a negotiator at times.

"This requires the BA to be a strong facilitator, consensus builder, and even a negotiator at times.

To balance stakeholder needs in the way that benefits the enterprise as a whole, the BA must first understand the goals and strategies of the enterprise. This will be discussed further in Chapter 3. Second, the BA must understand which stakeholder or group is funding a particular project along with the specific goals the project is trying to address. The project goals should be in line with and support enterprise-wide goals. If not, it will be difficult for the project to be successful for the organization. If the BA does not see a clear alignment, it should be mentioned to the PM and sponsor to clarify, not only for the BA to best align his or her efforts, analysis, and solution support, but also to ensure a clear message for all of the stakeholders who will be participating in the project.

Even when the project and enterprise goals are aligned, different stakeholder needs may arise. Enterprise and project goals can be accomplished in various ways, and different stakeholders will have different ideas on how to accomplish them. The BA's role is to listen carefully and work to understand each of the different stakeholder issues. If there is a conflict, the first step is to clearly understand both sides. This will often be difficult because you may personally agree with one side and have a difficult time being open minded about the other. Work hard to maintain your neutrality. If the differing groups have difficulty discussing the issue together because they are emotional or impatient, talk with them individually. Work to really understand their perspectives and their motives. Do not try to change their minds or convince them of another way. Be sure that you completely understand the person's perspective and concern before moving forward with discussing possible solutions. Consider ways you can generate positive outcomes for all sides, such as the win-win approach (Covey 1989).

Occasionally, when you truly listen and understand each side of a conflict, you will see common ground. This is the important area on which to begin your consensus building. Help both sides see their shared knowledge, goals, and desires, especially as applied to the good of the entire enterprise. Consensus does not mean that everyone agrees; it means that everyone can support the solution.

When the two sides have large areas of disagreement, be open and honest in acknowledging the issues. Let everyone know that reaching a consensus may be impossible. Ultimately, the project sponsor will be the decision maker and all stakeholders should understand this reality. Help each side present information (keep them to facts and not opinions) so that the project sponsor can hear the perspective of all the team members and make an informed decision.

Real World Example: Working Together with Stakeholders

A business owner had a clear idea of the solution that he needed in order to deliver high-quality services to his customers. As the BA, I worked with the technical SMEs to help develop the designs and to scope out the estimate for the costs—including purchase costs as well as installation, configuration, and management. When the business owner was presented with the recommended design solution and the implementation costs, he was immediately outraged at such an astronomical cost estimate for such a "simple" solution. As a best practice, when there are questions on such designs or solutions, I set up an estimate review session, inviting multiple business area stakeholders along with the technical team and their leadership (decision makers for IT). My role was not to say whether the design or estimates were good or bad. My role in this facilitated session was to clarify the business owner's requirements and then explain the options that would allow that requirement to be delivered, including costs. As we worked through each item individually, it enabled the business to validate their requirements. This validation allowed discussion with the technical team to provide solution explanation and options to the business. The explanations on both sides brought more understanding and awareness of the scope of the effort to all those attending. Some items were changed such that the outcome was less about fulfilling the expectations of each stakeholder and more about collaboration and defining a shared solution vision that everyone could support.

Understanding the Political Environment

Navigating organizational politics can be tricky. BAs face challenges where there seems to be decisions being made based on personal preferences and relationships than unbiased facts. As a guiding principle for BAs, regardless of the environment, the focus should remain on solutions that create the maximum value for the smallest costs or investments. Whenever there is a discussion, focus on clearly identifying the need, which customer the solution or decision is for, and what benefits are expected, as well as any alternatives. Remember, the BA is not the decision maker, but is responsible for bringing a clear picture of the situation and the options that are available to those who must own the decisions and resulting solutions. Holding to this approach will also give the BA comfort when they report to a single line of business such as IT or finance, along with work on cross-functional projects. Regardless of the reporting line, the BA should remain focused on solutions that provide maximum business value. Think about organizational results, not individual business areas, in order to help you present your data in a way that helps make it easiest for decision makers to move forward and see the entire picture.

And yes, sometimes decision makers will still make their own "odd" decisions, regardless of what the data shows. As the BA, avoid feeling like you are stuck in the middle and continue to focus on the data that you know and what information is needed in the discussion. When presenting, focus on where the most value for the entire organization can be achieved versus a single business area. Ask good questions—but do not challenge—as to what goals are anticipated to be achieved and what expected experience the decision makers want to attain from the solution. It would be best to have a center-of-excellence structure with a BA who comes in to work as a trusted advisor to the project teams. However, if you find yourself reporting to a single line of business on cross-functional work, maintain the perspective of the overall enterprise and do not limit your report to only your functional area. Utilize your communication and listening skills. Sometimes simply listening and asking questions will help disparate groups to reach a common vision. In the *Additional Reading and References* at the end of this chapter, there are some good references on how a person can gain credibility and assert influence without having any official authority.

WORKING WITH DISPERSED TEAMS

Many organizations assign project team members who are geographically dispersed. Working with stakeholders in different locations poses unique challenges for the BA—whose main work involves communication. Face-to-face communication is usually the most effective because the BA can listen to not only the spoken word but also the tone of voice and see the body language, which can convey as much as 55% of the message. Personal relationships are much easier to build face-to-face, which can more quickly translate to trust. Misunderstandings are more easily identified and resolved using direct communication.

A BA who has to communicate with stakeholders remotely must be aware of the techniques and approaches that are available along with the advantages and limitations of each technique. Plan extra time to ensure accurate and complete information is not only collected and shared, but also confirmed.

Planning communications with dispersed teams requires the BA to consider the physical distance, time-zone and work-hour differences, nationality and cultural differences, language issues, and the communication options that are available at each location. However, the same challenges of working with stakeholders still exist—whether you are working with a dispersed team or not—when it comes to making sure that the project goal is well understood and supported, articulating clearly the desired outcome of any meeting, and working to ensure that you have the right people present to accomplish your goals. Be clear on defining these before you jump in and start working on your business analysis techniques or approaches.

Physical Distance

Today's digital world often has teams working across physical distances. Even separation of a few miles adds a challenge to communication. While taking into account the time required to travel and meet team members and key stakeholders in person, the BA should still aim to meet in person with as many stakeholders as possible—*at least once*—to build these valuable business relations. You get to put a face to the name, see body language, and learn from their manners, work area, and in-office behaviors. Of course, all meetings should be well planned with the appropriate techniques selected and desired outcomes in mind so that no time is wasted. Doing an in-person meeting with a stakeholder as early as possible in the project will begin to build a relationship that will result in easier access and an open flow of information as the project progresses.

Go into the stakeholder's environment as much as possible. This will not only make it easier for the stakeholders to participate and be forthcoming with valuable project information, but it will also allow you to understand the situations surrounding each stakeholder in greater detail. You show your direct support to the stakeholder while, at the same time, developing a better understanding of the environment and additional stakeholders who are affecting or are affected by the proposed changes.

Time Zone Differences

When stakeholders work in different time zones, scheduling conference calls and virtual meetings can be challenging. Typically, project teams will agree early on what hours work best to get the team on a conference call, along with the procedures that are necessary to get everyone together. As the BA, you may need to schedule additional meetings outside of these project meetings and thus, will need to confirm the same ground rules as the PM does with the team. A best practice is to find the schedule that works best for those you need to associate with—not necessarily your own schedule. You are the one asking for *their* time away from their daily jobs to contribute to the project so be sensitive of that time. Additionally, during the meetings there is the need to clearly define the objectives and be very focused. Make sure that you are inviting all those who need to be in the meeting in order to achieve the objective—and *only* those members who *need* to be in the meeting. Clearly stating what you are hoping to achieve helps team members prioritize their time and adjust their schedules so that they are able to attend.

Try to avoid being a go-between where you meet with a few individuals earlier in the day, meet with another group of stakeholders later in the day, and then have to communicate between the two groups because this behavior only adds duration to the completion of your tasks. If you feel you are inconveniencing some stakeholders in order to accommodate others, then be sure to alternate between different times if possible so you are not always inconveniencing the same group. Remember, you are trying to help them achieve a larger goal and are there to support them in their efforts with their solution rather than the other way around. Be a support resource and not a burden or additional stress as much as possible.

Nationality and Cultural Differences

When you are assigned to a team with members in a different country or from a different cultural background, do some research to learn about their communication styles. As businesses become more global, there is universal recognition that working with people from other cultures presents unique challenges. Project onsets should include a discussion of expected team behaviors and set ground rules on how the teams will engage with each other. Even if this occurs, you may still work with others who are not on the core project team; so, just as you would with any stakeholder in your own office, you should continue to strive to understand the member and their background before demanding their time to work with you on the project.

Be mindful that it may be culturally insensitive simply to ask the other person how they work or what they want from you in regard to meeting and sharing information. Try learning from the other team members who have worked with stakeholders in these various regions. Leverage your professional network for insights and recommendations on their experience. Visit websites or take a class to learn the basics about the country where your stakeholder resides. Find out when national or religious holidays occur because that may affect stakeholder availability. Find out about working-hour norms (e.g., if people put in overtime before or after their regular work hours or on weekends, or if working on a Sunday is completely unacceptable, etc.). And remember that *working* also includes responding to e-mails. Be clear on expectations, such that if you send an e-mail, are you expecting a response in 24 hours or less regardless of the work schedule—or not until the agreed upon next business day?

As a BA, you often find that you learn the most by observing and experiencing first-hand the team member's environment. Asking at the onset of your project to schedule time to travel to meet with team members in person is a great way to not only learn about their environment and elicit additional requirements, but the earlier on in a project this can be done, the more trust can be built. A site visit will require the same preparation as any meeting, but additionally will require you to learn more about the history and current issues of the location you are visiting. You build more trust and credibility as you learn more about their customs, communication styles, and dress code—almost the same way you might prepare by booking lodging and learning the best transportation methods. The same research and planning effort needs to be built into planning your meeting with the stakeholders the first time.

Also, bring your own culture with you and be ready to share (but do not push it upon them). Meeting with team members from other countries allows you both to learn about each other beyond a simple project. If your country believes in bringing gifts or in the sharing of traditions and activities, then ask if it is appropriate to share these during your time visiting. Just as you are learning as much as you can about your team members' country and work environments, they may have the same interest in you. And the more knowledge and understanding that people have between each other, the more successful the engagements often are. Consider meeting in person as an investment in not only the current project's efforts, but in establishing a foundation for future work.

Language Differences

Most global organizations choose one language for their internal business communications. If the BA and a stakeholder do not speak or know a common language, a translator or tool must be employed to manage all communications. This is rare but, when necessary, will add both cost and time to the business analysis processes. More often, the project team members will share a language, but some team members will be more fluent than others. Setting ground rules at the beginning for your communication plans and styles is an important investment activity to help the project tasks run as smoothly and efficiently as possible while minimizing any issues with language differences.

Consider for example that if English is a second language for a team member, they may have a smaller vocabulary than native English speakers. And even for native English speakers, remember that words in English can have different meanings in different locations. Reinforce the team ground rules so that should someone not understand a key element, they are encouraged to promptly inquire as to the meaning. Additionally, acronyms should be avoided during any discussion until agreed upon by team members—the BA may start a glossary to be shared and updated by the team during the project to facilitate discussions (see Chapter 6 for more details). Also, be mindful of any slang or colloquial terms that are used. Clear, consistent business language should be utilized as much as possible. And if you are unsure whether or not everyone knows the meaning of a situation or element, it does not hurt to take a few extra seconds to clarify a topic before beginning.

Team members may speak English but have a strong accent, which could make them more difficult to understand. Talk with each stakeholder as early as possible, and listen for vocabulary usage and accent. If you determine that one or more stakeholders are less fluent, plan more time for elicitation sessions and follow-up communications. If possible, exchange written communications (e.g., e-mail messages) as soon as possible to assess writing skills. Often, people who have learned a second language in school are better able to communicate in writing because pronunciations are not involved. Choose your communication techniques based on your assessment of each stakeholder.

Using Team Collaboration Tools

A BA working with team members who are located in different areas of the organization—let alone in another geographic area—will benefit greatly from using collaboration tools. Coordinating the massive amounts of information that needs to be shared, communicated, and developed on a project can be very challenging and is exponentially harder when you have the physical separation as well. Becoming more adept at managing information will not only generally help your overall collaboration efforts, but will help you be successful—especially when working with dispersed teams.

Always begin by finding out which tool(s) the team members or those you are working with are most familiar with and comfortable using. Like all of your other engagement activities, researching your audience and understanding how they share information helps you plan your approach. You may have used tools that they have never used before, and even if you see the value in these other tools, using a new tool with team members means you are adding additional training and communication needs to each of your facilitated sessions that must be planned and taken into account. Remain focused on the goals of your meetings and interactions rather than on the fancy abilities and features of the technology—use the appropriate tool for the situation at hand. Even pencil and paper can be very effective collaboration tools for some stakeholders. Build the *buy-in* and get the information you need to complete project tasks while seeking the opportunity to improve communication through the gentle introduction of technology. Of course, if the team is already fluent and quite comfortable in advanced communication networks, you will need to do the same research and even self-training to bring yourself up to speed so that you may keep up with the team.

This is a key aspect for any BA: remember to always be learning. Learn how the stakeholders communicate today, and also learn how they did in the past and what successes and challenges emerged. If they are using newer and advanced collaboration tools, then take the time to become comfortable with them so that you may adapt to the team. If no tools are used, research what is available within the organization since not all tools are free, secure for storing sensitive information, or simply compatible with the standard technology available to an organization's employees. This is the additional planning work that the BA role needs to build into all of their meetings and facilitated sessions in order to be a successful, value-adding team member.

Real World Example: Utilizing Collaboration Tools

Microsoft's collaboration tool, SharePoint, was deployed in the organization where I was assigned to a project. The PM used SharePoint for project documents, but told me that none of the team members liked it because it was too hard to use. Thus, it was more her backup repository of what she had done since she would e-mail all of the team members any documents as attachments. I had used SharePoint at a prior organization and knew of many of the capabilities it could offer in terms of facilitating collaboration; however, during my first few meetings with key stakeholders, I never even mentioned the word SharePoint. As we began to get into the project, there was documentation I would send out—asking for their review. I would e-mail one copy only to get 10 different versions back; and it began to be quite time consuming for me to consolidate them and still analyze the results. With the next item that I needed collaborative feedback on—basically a single working copy of what we were all using—I utilized the SharePoint collaboration tool to post the document. I verified that I had set up the tool's permissions so that all the team members could have the appropriate access. In an e-mail to the team members, I clearly laid out the instructions on how to collaborate on this single document with simple instructions that never named the tool, but rather focused on the user's instructions—i.e., "Here are the three simple steps to add your feedback to this team's documentation." I then sent the e-mail with a single link in it to the team members so that a single document was being used to collect the team's feedback and come to consensus. I also made myself available to answer questions or give further explanations. The first time I did this, I did have to send it as an attachment to a few people who had trouble; however, as the project went on and we continued to use the tool, the easier the collaboration began to get for the team members and the less support I had to give to individuals. As the project came closer to completion, I was even asked by team members how they could get the same *repository* tool (as they called it) for their own department teams. Only then did I share more about the name of the tool and the supplementary features it had to offer. Yes, it did require additional time up front, but it was also an investment in myself, my technology knowledge, and my training skills—and ultimately, it was a greater value for the organization whose personnel were finally starting to take advantage of IT's investment in collaboration tools.

Using a Shared Presentation

When you have information to present to a group for review or approval, a shared view of the information can be very helpful. You should prepare your presentation materials just as you would for a formal, in-person presentation. This formality is required because your listeners are remotely located and you may not have the advantage of watching their body language in order to determine their understanding. Continue to follow the same best practices that encourage clear and succinct presentation topics (i.e., do not read the displayed text to the audience, but rather explain what the content means and why the listeners should care or how it impacts them). Presentation-style meetings require even more planning to be successful, so also consider whether you need to send information prior to the meeting to help prepare the attendees to participate. Taking a few extra minutes to think through the presentation from your attendees' perspectives can be the difference between success and failure. Do you want everyone to participate? Then perhaps you plan the questions so that you can ask specific people to respond versus asking everyone to simply agree, such as, "John, would you agree or disagree with this conclusion?" Are there people who will attend who may not know why their manager invited them, but have chosen to attend regardless? Then perhaps some time should be taken at the beginning to highlight why each attendee is valuable to achieving the decided outcome of the presentation.

With many tools, you can not only present material but leverage their participation. Think beyond simply asking questions and looking for responses, especially if the audience is very large and the topics are controversial or contested. Consider what engagement is required to achieve your goal(s) of the presentation and then structure your interaction accordingly. If you are looking for consensus, consider utilizing the presentation tool to collect the votes of attendees (this is great if looking for anonymity of votes or reducing bias). If you are presenting a topic for further discussion and feedback, allow the use of chat or whiteboard tools to collect thoughts as you are going through the materials. Of course, the greater the engagement, the stronger your facilitation skills are required to be, so consider getting someone to assist in managing the actions of the meeting. For example, use a moderator to collect questions that are being submitted as you are presenting and then will read them aloud one at a time during pause points for you to respond to the group. Like all other BA activities, start to plan your presentation by defining the presentation goal, explain why each person attending is required, and clarify the technology and format that you plan to use to collect and communicate feedback and decisions. Often, successful presentations are a result of the actions taken before and after the meeting itself so that all stakeholders are on the same page and working toward the same goal.

SUMMARY OF KEY POINTS

The most important skill of a BA is effective communication. To be effective, communication must be tailored to and for the audience. Understanding all of the people in your project is the first step to being an effective analyst.

- People who are involved with a project are commonly referred to as *stakeholders*.
- To tailor communications, BAs must really know their audience. They should get to know each project stakeholder and develop a relationship of trust and open communication.
- Understanding the background along with the skill sets of the stakeholders that a BA may engage with allows the BA to determine how to best elicit and present requirements and other project tasks.
- The PM and BA should work together very closely. Ideally, two different individuals who are appropriately trained in their respective areas are essential to project success given the amount of communication that must take place.

- BAs will typically find themselves working with stakeholders who represent many different roles, especially on project-based work. Understanding the strengths and potential challenges that the BAs may have with each of these roles helps them to determine the most appropriate approach for successful engagements.
- BAs plan, design, and deliver communications in order to balance all stakeholder needs and to manage the challenges of dispersed team members.
- Working with disbursed teams requires even more planning and forethought to ensure that communications are clear and consistent. This triggers the need to take into account the additional planning and communication time when completing BA work activities.
- BAs should constantly learn about not only their stakeholders but also the technology and organizational resources that are necessary to best leverage interaction with team members—particularly disbursed team members—and focus on meeting outcomes versus the process and techniques utilized.
- The more a BA understands the stakeholders, their environment, and the context of the project, the more successful a BA can be at facilitating communication, identifying requirements, and helping to design and deliver valuable solutions.

BIBLIOGRAPHY

Agile Alliance. (2018). "Agile Glossary." https://www.agilealliance.org/glossary.

Covey, Stephen R. (1989). *The 7 Habits of Highly Effective People*. Free Press: New York, NY.

International Institute of Business Analysis (IIBA). (2015). *Business Analysis Body of Knowledge® (BABOK® Guide)*. IIBA: Toronto, Ontario, Canada.

IIBA. (2017). *Agile Extension to the BABOK® Guide*. IIBA: Toronto, Ontario, Canada.

Layton, M. (2017, September 5). *Agile Project Management for Dummies. 2nd Ed*. Wiley Publishing: Hoboken, NJ.

Project Management Institute (PMI). (2017). *Agile Practice Guide*. PMI: Newtown Square, PA.

ADDITIONAL READING AND REFERENCES

The American Society for Quality (ASQ). "World wide organization focused on quality. Includes information on quality certifications, including Six Sigma and Lean." https://asq.org/.

Cohen, A. R. and D. L. Bradford. (2017). *Influence without Authority*. Wiley Publishing: Hoboken, NJ.

Hill, G. (2013). *The Complete Project Management Office Handbook. 3rd Ed*. Auerbach Publications: Boca Raton, FL.

Kirkwood, J. (2018, January 31). "The 9 best online collaboration tools for remote workers." https://www.invisionapp.com/inside-design/online-collaboration-tools-remote/.

Lojeski, Karen Sobel (2008). *Uniting the Virtual Workforce: Transforming Leadership and Innovation in the Globally Integrated Enterprise*. Wiley Publishing: Hoboken, NJ.

Londer, O. and P. Coventry. (2016). *Microsoft SharePoint 2016 Step by Step*. Microsoft Press: Redmond, WA.

Miller, J. (2017, October 19). "What Is a Project Management Office (PMO) and Do You Need One?" CIO.com. IDG Communications. https://www.cio.com/article/2441862/project-management/what-is-a-project-management-office-pmo-and-do-you-need-one.html.

Neilson, J. (1993, September 23). *Usability Engineering*. Morgan Kaufmann: Burlington, MA.

The Open Group. (2009). "Architecture Framework TOGAF®." http://www.opengroup.org/TOGAF-9.2-Overview.

Osman, H. (2016). *Influencing Virtual Teams: 17 Tactics that Get Things Done with Your Remote Employees*. CreateSpace: Scotts Valley, CA.

Quality Assurance Institute (QAI). "Consulting and workforce development organization focused on *operational excellence*." http://www.qaiusa.com/.

User Experience Professionals Association (UXPA) International. "UXPA International supports people who research, design, and evaluate the UX of products and services." https://uxpa.org/.

Withee, R. and K. Withee. (2016). *SharePoint 2016 for Dummies*. Wiley Publishing: Hoboken, NJ.

CHAPTER 3

YOUR THIRD STEP—KNOW YOUR PROJECT

Most of the work assigned to business analysis professionals is within the confines of a project. A project is a temporary endeavor that is initiated in order to achieve very specific goals. It is critical for the business analyst (BA) to thoroughly understand the project to which they are assigned. The BA must be aware of the parameters set for the project, the individuals involved with the project, and most important, the purpose of the project. Without clearly knowing the goals of the project, an analyst will not be able to focus elicitation and analysis activities in the right direction. Knowing *why* the project was initiated is the first step in business analysis planning.

To help understand the goals of each project, a BA should be aware of the organization's strategic vision and long-term goals. The enterprise strategic plan is the organization's road map to long-term success. Each individual project supports a piece of the strategic plan. The BA's work during project initiation is to understand its alignment with corporate goals and to plan analysis activities that will best support those goals.

> "The enterprise strategic plan is the organization's road map to long-term success."

WHY HAS THE ORGANIZATION DECIDED TO FUND THIS PROJECT?

It is critical for the BA to understand why the organization has decided to fund the project. The BA must be sure that analysis work is always aimed toward accomplishing the business objectives and is aligned with the organization's mission. Project work always costs money, even if a project involves only internal resources (such as employees). Employees are expensive resources and need to be used wisely. Everyone on a project, especially the project manager (PM) and the BA, should be constantly evaluating the expenditures against the expected benefits. Is the effort—including costs, resources, tools, and even prioritization over other project work—returning benefits that are at least equal to, if not greater than, the intended results?

While neither the PM nor the BA is typically the decision maker, the responsibility to clearly analyze the current situation and the perceived benefits and then present the findings to key stakeholders, especially to the PM and project sponsor, rests on the shoulders of the BA. Whenever the perceived benefits do not line up with the original decision to move a project forward, bringing this awareness to the major decision makers is key and part of the successful working relationship between the PM and the BA.

For many projects, the benefits to the organization are obvious. But some project benefits are not so tangible or apparent. The successful BA must know the underlying rationale for funding a project (from the viewpoint of the project sponsor) before they can dive in and begin analyzing and understanding the requirements needed to implement the change.

Business Case Development

The decision to start a project comes from defining the business value that the change is expected to achieve. This is found in a business case. For a BA to know a project, they must understand the business case, which is often done during enterprise planning sessions. This is where the vision and mission of the organization are assessed against the current industry environment, competition, digital innovations, internal capability analysis, and other strategic analysis in order to identify where the organization is and where it needs to be. The business case is the justification to do a project to deliver the change. Enterprise analysts often work with sponsors, subject matter experts (SMEs), and other planning team members to ensure that the benefits are analyzed and properly articulated so that value-adding solutions can be considered. Understanding the importance of developing business cases is a key skill. We will talk more about strategic analysis later in this chapter, but understanding where the business case came from and what a person should expect to find in it is a crucial BA competency.

"The business case is the justification to do a project to deliver the change."

Have you ever tried to convince someone that you need a new car? Did you ever try to justify driving your own car over riding public transportation? Whenever you are working to persuade someone (even yourself) to act, you are building a case. You think through all of the positive results that will occur if the request is approved and prepare to counter any objections that your decision maker has. You evaluate the potential benefits and weigh those against the anticipated costs/effort. You consider what risks may occur and address the value of alternatives. When it appears clear that the benefits outweigh the costs, the request is often approved. Companies have to make these same types of decisions all the time. They are presented with ideas and opportunities and need to evaluate the potential value that could be achieved.

A business case is an explanation of why the organization has decided to go forward with a project. The word *case* comes from the legal profession and means an argument for or against something: "We are building a case for. . . ." Business cases, which depict the value of an endeavor, have become more common as organizations realize that projects may be expensive and sometimes do not deliver the expected results. A business case documents the project's justification for executive decision makers and provides a mechanism to evaluate the success of the project at its completion. You have probably had to write mini business cases when you requested time off of work or to attend a company-paid training session. What were you requesting and why? What details did you provide so that your manager had the necessary information to determine the value of granting your request?

Other projects are started after performing feasibility studies and cost/benefit analysis. A feasibility study determines the practicability and workability of a potential solution before a project is approved. It answers the question: *can it be done*? Cost/benefit analysis focuses on a financial analysis of the potential solution, using economic calculations to project the potential return on investment (ROI) and payback period. It answers the question: *what are the costs versus the benefits of the change*? Some costs and benefits are not easily measured. Benefits like goodwill and positive public relations are referred to as intangible. Costs that are easily measured are referred to as tangible. Many business cases for larger projects include both a feasibility study and a cost/benefit analysis, referencing both tangible and intangible benefits. Be aware that the project you have been assigned to may be the feasibility study itself—or what is often called a *pilot* project to validate the concept and approach. A good BA understands not only why a project was started, but also quickly recognizes what stage the solution is in at any given point since not every BA is brought on at the beginning of a project.

BAs are often asked to write and present a business case for a project or potential project. This is a very important skill for a senior BA who is interested in moving into consulting, strategic and enterprise planning, or corporate management. Building a business case for a project can be challenging because it requires significant research, analysis (logical reasoning and financial estimates), and strong communication skills. In addition, business case development requires creativity and big-picture thinking.

Business case development and cost/benefit analysis are important skills for business analysis professionals to develop early in their careers. Although a formal business case document is not created for every project, someone in the organization should always consider a project's worth before funding is approved. If you are assigned to a project where a formal business case was not created and approved, it is best to practice this skill by drafting one that you and the PM can use with team members. Because business cases contain the project's ultimate goal and objectives, they are great documents to help not only keep the team motivated but also on scope and, therefore, on track for successful project completion.

The *practice* of writing business cases can also continue outside of your project work. On your teams and even with your family, whenever you find yourself trying to guide others toward a specific decision, practice your business case skills. Take a few minutes to think about the costs and benefits. Try to break down your thoughts and analyze your decision-making process. You can start by looking at the pros and cons of the decision, as shown in Table 3.1.

Be sure to list everything, regardless of whether or not it can be measured or quantified. Cost/benefit analysis often includes items that are intangible or difficult to measure—ones that are often very customer focused—such as *ease of use* or *excitement factor*.

Next, look at each pro and con to determine if there is some way to quantify it. The more quantifiable the analysis, the more objective it will be. If you can show your spouse that a new car will require a smaller monthly cash outflow, then you would probably have a pretty good business case. When you are considering a job change or career move, there are a number of factors you weigh against each other—and salary would presumably be one of many factors. The

> "The more quantifiable the analysis, the more objective it will be."

Table 3.1   Decision-making considerations

Pros	Cons
Profitable	Costly
Easier	Takes a lot of time
Faster	Not supported
Simpler	Complex
Done before	Never have tried
Happier customers	More responsibilities
Visually appealing	Competition

same approach is to be taken with change efforts, whether big or small, since you are spending company resources to achieve some sort of result.

Research anything that may have a tangible cost in order to help represent the most accurate picture possible. Remember to include not only the cost spent on the effort, but the time spent on resources used—and if you have proper access, examine the cost of not doing other projects. When you estimate, always document the assumptions upon which you based the estimate. This helps capture the timeliness of your estimate because things can change from the time you do your research to the time a person is reviewing it. See Table 3.2 for examples of some of the one-time costs and recurring costs that might come up for a technology solution. It is important to separate one-time costs from recurring costs for payback period calculations (the length of time required for the organization to recover its investment). In looking at these examples, BAs need to consider the entire solution impact rather than simply the project or implementation costs. Some example considerations include:

- *Operational maintenance and support*: Who does the upgrades? Who helps users when there are issues? While 24/7 support can be costly, it may be a benefit that is worth the cost to the organization—which is why it is identified as a risk mitigation option.
- *Security*: Who has access to the organizational data? It may not be an organizational desire to have data shared with other firms when it comes to technical designs (such as those for hosted solutions).
- *Training*: Who does the initial training? Is this for end users? What about the business teams? What about ongoing training for end users? The organization may want training as part of the implementation plan, but may not have resources ready or available to do any training beyond the project scope. This is an important consideration for solution cost versus project cost.
- *Marketing and communication*: Are there marketing needs beyond initial rollout to communicate the solution? How are materials and other marketing resources updated in the future in the event that the solution changes? Is there dedicated support from the marketing teams to answer end-user questions after the implementation?

The answers to the previous questions will affect the scope of the solution.

BAs should also enlist help from financial professionals, when necessary, to help lay out the complete financial picture among the quantitative benefits. The business must understand what benefits are being received for the costs—in both time and money—that are being dedicated to the effort. While some organizations may use a template for presenting project proposals, know that there are many ways to represent costs and benefits. BAs must utilize communication skills and always tailor the presentation of the

Table 3.2   Ongoing and one-time costs examples

One Time	On-going
Hardware	Licenses
Software	Maintenance
Peripherals	Support
Networking	Security
Consultants (i.e., implementation)	Employees (i.e., staff support)

information to the audience to which the business case is being presented. Sticking to the facts and reliable information helps the presentation remain objective and focused on organizational value, building greater credibility and ultimate value to the BA role.

For cost and benefits that cannot be quantified, describe each intangible aspect, articulating possible metrics and how it could possibly benefit or negatively affect the organization. Some examples are listed in Table 3.3. Really consider if the entire picture is captured, showing both immediate and long-term value and then for what costs and effort, especially if there are additional costs in the future in order to keep the solution providing maximum value.

A key aspect to also consider in business cases is providing alternative solutions. Many expect that the person who is presenting the business case will have strong points for their solution. But as an unbiased advisor, the BA is always trying to present the most valuable information needed at the time for the decision makers. Presenting alternatives helps decision makers see the situation more clearly and gives the solution you are recommending more context and credibility. Alternatives should be presented in the same manner (considering costs and benefits). The overall recommendation, though, should highlight how the selected solution provides the most value. The alternatives should also include the option of doing nothing. Calling out the costs and potential benefits of *not* moving forward with a project allows the bigger picture to remain in focus, rather than getting excited over something that might feel like it is too good to be true. Presenting alternatives helps demonstrate the credibility of the analysis work while enabling the decision maker to reach an informed decision.

Table 3.3 Ongoing costs examples

Qualitative Measure	Possible Metric(s)	Impact to Organization
Customer satisfaction	Customer surveys	Increases can lead to increased revenue
Employee satisfaction	Employee retention Employee surveys	Decreases can lead to higher costs and inefficiencies
Customer loyalty	Length of customer relationship Purchase history of customer	Increases can lead to increased revenue
Ease of use	Time taken to complete tasks	Decreases in time can lead to greater productivity and, therefore, revenues
Efficiency	Number of tasks completed in a given time frame	More tasks completed in less time decreases costs

Real World Example: Presenting Business Cases

As is popular in large organizations today, business areas will come to the information technology (IT) department to implement the products and software that they want to purchase to enable their lines of business. At the large organization in this example, business cases were presented to a cross-functional team to review the cost/benefit analysis and make decisions against other projects and organizational

continued

initiatives. The financial team presented a project that proposed significant cost savings over a five-year period. Many team members wanted to quickly approve such a valuable project, but there were others who asked for more information before approving. The costs were focused solely on implementing new software to streamline manual processes. Further information was requested concerning the training and communication to staff that would be required to ensure a successful rollout. Additionally, the IT team had questions about whether or not the organization actually owned software solutions already that could perform the same functionality. I was assigned as the BA to research these very questions and help present a more thorough picture since, while the value was high, so were the costs. Multiple options for achieving the goals of the project were then added to the business case that not only included the presented solution, but additional solutions such as utilizing current systems as-is, hiring consultants to customize existing systems, and purchasing other third-party software similar to the one proposed. With this clarity, the business case came back to the team with greater emphasis on a hybrid approach that utilized some of the software features the finance team was presenting, but combined with existing software systems utilizing in-house IT resources. The additional research and analysis helped provide the decision makers with a clearer picture of how to move forward that best fit the needs of the entire organization.

There are several common reasons why an organization decides to fund a project:

- A problem
- To reduce or eliminate costs
- Outside regulation
- An opportunity
- For marketing or advertising
- To align business processes
- To deliver organizational strategy

Project Initiated Because of a Problem

Many projects, small and large, are quickly initiated because there is an immediate problem that needs to be solved. It is important during project scoping to make sure that you really understand the problem that is to be addressed. This sounds very simple—and many times it is. Sometimes the problem as stated by the project sponsor is exactly the problem that needs to be addressed. But sometimes the stated problem to be solved is not really the problem. There may be a deeper issue. You don't want to try to solve the wrong problem. Understand the true business problem before trying to solve it.

Technique: Root Cause Analysis

The technique that is often used when trying to discover the source of a problem is *root cause analysis*. Root cause analysis involves identifying the known symptoms or effects and looking for the cause of each symptom. The reason for the analysis is to make sure that the solution solves the fundamental issue that is causing the effects, rather than trying to address each effect. You can use functional decomposition to help break down processes or systems from complex items into simpler parts so that you can analyze each piece individually. This helps you see where the actual issue is or what it is affecting. See Figure 3.1 for

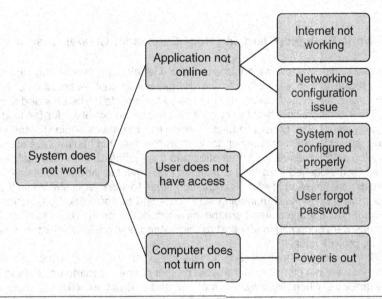

Figure 3.1 Functional decomposition example

an example of decomposing a technical issue. BAs can also use the *5 Whys* technique to help identify the root cause. This approach encourages you to ask *why* again and again in order to clarify what is occurring. Repeatedly asking why something is not working allows the specifics of the problem to become more evident with each why. For example, a user may tell you a system is broken. Before you run off to talk to the system administrator, ask the user why they feel that way. Why do they know it does not work? Asking why a few more times may reveal user error versus the actual system being broken. Knowing the root cause of an issue ensures that you are solving the actual problem.

Root cause analysis is useful for addressing projects in which the goals are to improve something. This technique helps when there are issues preventing the organization from getting the most value for their time and money.

For example, a company's customer service satisfaction scores may be low in one area. A project is then approved in order to help improve these scores. The project begins by understanding what is causing low satisfaction scores in the first place. Now, if the organization has already defined a *solution* to the issue and the project is to simply implement the solution that will solve that predefined problem, the BA needs to be careful and validate that the solution selected does indeed address the root cause of the problem. The project needs to clearly articulate the problem statement before the team begins to work on the solution. Too often a solution is chosen that does not fix the problem and then the project team or vendor is blamed. Asking early on for clarification of the issue at hand is a key skill set of the BA. Asking *why* is an easy way to initiate a discussion with the business about the ultimate goals they hope to achieve by breaking down the issue. You would rather find out early on if the selected solution does not address the intended issue prior to spending significant time and money.

> "The goal of the project needs to clearly articulate the problem statement."

Real World Example: Clarifying Root Causes for Clearer Change Goals

At the organization in this example, the maintenance and repair teams were struggling to keep up with their work order requests and were often losing the paperwork that recorded all of the information. Additionally, the managers would constantly get asked for reports and status updates on the maintenance work. The managers said that the current processes did not allow for the kind of traceability that was being requested. The project to help address this issue was originally started as a need to purchase mobile tablets for the teams. A vendor was preselected that had the type of software that the organization could use to organize the information and then utilize on the mobile tablets. The maintenance and repair teams pushed hard for a significant investment in mobile tablets as their solution to increase their response times and reduce completion times to work requests. While the PM was very good about controlling scope and managing schedules and budgets (as the business continued to increase the number of tablets required from the initial request), I, as the BA, researched the scenarios where these issues were occurring in an effort to understand how the implementation needed to work in order to ensure project value.

Understanding the working environments where these work requests were completed exposed process issues that were not captured in the initial project scope. Repair teams believed their managers notified the requester when tasks were completed and thus did not follow up. New staff members did not receive any training that explained the work order forms and that often led to the requests being thrown away (literally). However, many of the team members had heard about the project and viewed the tablets as their solution to all the work challenges the team faced surrounding efficiently and effectively addressing work orders. Clarification was needed to explain that the *inefficient processes* were what was being addressed, not the need for tablets. I explained that there were many ways—beyond the tablet suggestion—to address this need, such as new-hire training and the use of spreadsheets to track data and process changes. The fact that someone had already made a decision to purchase tablets was only one solution. So, first we clarified the project goal of streamlining the maintenance and repair process, which included accurate reporting features. At that point, the actual project goal was acknowledged by the team who reinforced the fact that it was more than simply setting up mobile tablets, and that there was communication, training, and even technology validation that also would need to occur.

Project Initiated to Eliminate Costs (Jobs)

Often, the project objective is to save money by cutting costs. Unfortunately, one way to cut costs is to decrease head count—in other words, reduce the number of people working in the business. While many companies work hard on their talent-management strategies in order to keep the valuable skill sets in-house, reduction of positions is not uncommon and is a situation that you should be prepared to handle. It will present you with some of your most difficult communication challenges.

Technology innovations (digital transformations) continue to disrupt business models that change the staffing perspective. Kiosks and self-service stations replace in-person service personnel. Mobile applications and online chat services reduce the need for physical company locations that are accessible to their customers. And even physical mail services are decreased because of the reliance on digital services. Be aware that these types of *innovations* are also seen as disrupters.

When you are assigned to gather requirements for a project with the objective of cutting personnel, be clear on the business case and rationale for the approach. Often, cutting staff is only one solution to a bigger need. While the BA (or even the PM) is not a decision maker who gets to select the specific solution approach, like any project, knowing what business need you are solving is still the most important aspect. You need to fully understand this need, especially as you work on a project that reduces the number of staff. Try to get as much information from the management team as you can before you start talking with the SMEs. Questions that not only articulate the business needs that are being solved, but also *why* they feel that staff reduction is key to the solution should be posed to the PM, executive sponsor, corporate management, human resources management, and any other executive-level people who will be involved in the workforce reduction. You may personally feel otherwise; however, you must ensure that you check your own feelings and remain unbiased, objective, and dedicated to overall organizational success. Asking difficult questions with the goal of more understanding not only helps you have a sturdier foundation for when you speak to stakeholders, but it also helps to ensure that the executive and decision-making stakeholders truly understand the scope and impact of the solution approach that they have chosen. These questions may include:

- What challenge are we solving or opportunity are we taking advantage of?
- Are there other changes that are included in the scope of the work (process changes, role descriptions, organizational changes)?
- What alternative solutions were considered? Why were those not selected?
- Are there options to reduce costs in other areas? Reduce non-personnel resources?
- Do you anticipate additional changes in the near future that are related to this work?

As you ask these questions, you may discover that not all of these questions have been discussed thoroughly to a point of common message. This shows the BA's value by helping ensure that needs are being addressed rather than diving directly into solutions. Remember, cutting staff is simply one solution. The need to reduce costs, however, could have many solutions.

If the decision makers have already done the analysis at the point you are assigned the project, then make sure that you have all of the information clearly defined before you dive in and start the redesign processes. The requirements for successfully reducing a workforce often include more than simply the elimination of positions. The BA will be gathering numerous requirements that may address such items as:

- The criteria and selection of the positions being eliminated
- The transition process for these positions
- Communication requirements for the individuals in the job roles, the teams, and the organization— and quite possibly to support external public relations
- Changes to the processes to accommodate the lack of positions
- Updates to remaining job descriptions
- Additional impacts or changes to the organization as a result of the reduction

Reinforcing the strategic ties of the project will help define the scope of requirements—the same things that a BA would do for any other type of change. This is also the foundation that the BA relies on when finding it hard to get answers to a number of the previously mentioned questions since it is also possible that decisions about personnel changes cannot be determined yet because a business solution/change has not yet been defined. In these cases, it is important for the BA to be aware that whatever solution design is recommended, it will have a direct impact on people in the business area. It may be difficult for BAs to be objective if they see a solution design that will automate someone out of a job. You must remember that you are working for the organization's long-term success. Ignoring a good solution that will increase organizational effectiveness just to save someone's job will make the organization less competitive and may decrease its long-term viability. It may be an extreme thought, but if you save one or two jobs now, you may contribute to the failure of the entire organization in the long run—resulting in a much larger loss of jobs. You must keep an objective perspective and remain grounded in the goals and strategic alignment of the project.

With these kinds of projects, the keys to success lie in your communication skills in clearly articulating the situation. Whether decision makers specifically say up front that they are reducing workforce or you feel that reduction is the direction they want (and are utilizing the project to prove it), keep your own personal thoughts out of the discussion and stay focused on what the organization needs in order to be successful. Facilitated discussions still require you to understand your stakeholders and prepare any engagements for successful, defined outcomes that support achieving the project's goal. If you are gathering requirements and are unsure of the alignment with the original project's goal, then clearly and without bias articulate this to the PM to clarify—or raise your concerns to the project sponsor. This clarity helps you continue your support of a shared and consistent understanding among the project team members as you collaborate on solutions with them.

At times, the stakeholders you have to work with may be difficult when it comes to sharing information or even when trying to coordinate a meeting time (and may even exude passive-aggressive behavior), but do not let it keep you from listening and trying to understand their opinions and suggestions. Just like any other project, go to your stakeholders and collaborate *with* them to help share their voice and articulate how they see that value can be added to the organization. They may even have innovative ideas that senior decision makers are unaware of. Clearly capturing, articulating, and sharing the requirements that are identified and analyzed as a result of your meetings with stakeholders remains your goal. Bring the information that has been gathered to help define the solution and be sure that the solution that is selected shows the potential to achieve the executives' intended results. The trust you build with stakeholders and your commitment to honest and unbiased facts contributes to being part of a successful project, but also builds your own credibility for further analysis work.

Project Initiated by Outside Regulation

Many projects are initiated due to outside regulations. A regulation may be imposed by a government agency, industry watchdog, or standards organization. New regulations may be created, existing regulations updated, or an organization may be changing (i.e., growing) such that it will soon be affected by regulation. Many government regulations are only enforced for large companies, so if your company grows, it may suddenly be required to follow a rule that did not apply in the past. Many companies do not think about the true cost of a regulation. They may consistently prioritize regulation projects as mandatory without performing any cost/benefit analysis. A value provided by the business analysis professional is to ask the *why* questions, even about these projects. Ignoring regulations is not recommended, but each organization that is impacted by regulations should make a choice about whether or not to comply. Noncompliance usually results in negative consequences like penalties, bad press, or elimination from some markets. An organization should develop a business case, including a cost/benefit analysis—weighing the cost of the regulation against the *benefits*—which may simply be the avoidance of negative consequences.

Understand that a change in mandatory regulations requires the organization to analyze the value of the change. Rarely are any changes simple—even if the change does not affect the technology that the organization is currently using, training, communication, and updates to existing organizational artifacts may still be required. All of these changes cost the company (even if not spending dollars, remember that it costs an organization money whenever they take people away from the work they would normally be doing). If a regulatory change comes out in which noncompliance within 12 months results in a $100,000 fine, compliance may seem like a priority project. However, if this regulation would take $500,000 in new technology hardware and an additional $500,000 in organizational resources, then is the $1 million change worth the risk of a $100,000 fine? The business may decide to take the time and research additional options, including whether the regulation will change again in 24 or 36 months since it would take 10 years of fines before costing the organization more than the actual change. Of course, if these changes affect brand reputation or represent a major safety risk, then those are other costly elements that need to be estimated and weighed against the benefits. All this analysis work should be done before any decisions are made. These decisions benefit greatly from analytical BAs helping the strategic decision makers see the entire picture.

In contrast, another major strategic consideration is to change the organization so that the regulation no longer applies. When the U.S. government enacted Sarbanes-Oxley financial reporting regulations for publicly held companies, some companies decided to buy back all of their shares and reorganize privately to avoid the costly regulation. Blindly deciding to comply with every rule or guideline is not always a good strategic plan. Each relevant issue should be examined and analyzed for its true cost and value. This is why always trying to present fact-based, objective, and unbiased information in the analysis work is the best way that a BA adds value to an organization and supports decision makers.

Cost/benefit analysis, alternatives analysis, and risk assessments are all crucial activities that need to be completed during strategic analysis of regulatory issues. BAs performing these strategic analyses leverage their communication skills to ask in-depth questions in order to get to the root of an issue and truly understand the need and possible opportunities. The value of change efforts is maximized by understanding what has to change and also what should not.

Project Initiated by an Opportunity

Many projects are initiated to support a new business opportunity. For example, a new product design may be appealing to potential customers who have not purchased existing products. Advances in technology could help the organization reach markets they have never been in before. When an opportunity is identified, the organization decides if the opportunity is worth pursuing by considering what value the opportunity could present to the organization.

Analyzing an opportunity is the same as any other project—the costs and potential benefits that might be achieved have to be assessed to determine how much potential value could be added to the organization. An estimate of what it would take to modify the organization to incorporate the opportunity and the costs, time, and resources involved is first identified. Then those numbers are balanced against the potential value that would return to the organization. Different implementation options may need to be assessed as part of the analysis to truly understand the opportunity. The additional perspective of considering what value the organization would get for *not* taking the opportunity, but rather continuing *as-is* or simply waiting until a later time also needs to be considered.

Opportunities do not simply arise from the executives coming up with new ideas in a closed room. These opportunities may start from customer feedback and interaction, employees talking about how easy (or hard) their work processes are, or may come from looking at what competitors or the industry are doing. What is even more exciting today is that opportunities are now coming from looking at *different* industries and leveraging their approaches in new and different ways. Opportunities are arising from asking, *what if . . . ?*—and then considering what could be possible.

Some opportunities are large, like offering a brand-new product or redesigning processes, but many opportunities are smaller, incremental changes to existing products or processes that will improve customer service, increase quality or efficiency, or decrease costs. The small opportunities often can have a huge impact in an organization. Suppose a supermarket chain identifies a change in its distribution process that would save two cents on every dairy product sold. The savings could quickly reach millions of dollars. On the other hand, a *simple* edit to an online form may actually require significant technology, process, training, communication, and marketing changes.

When opportunities are identified, a business case should be built. Most executive-level managers are looking for the benefits to outweigh the costs before they will give approval to go forward and fund a project. Positive cash flow or ROI is typically required because pursuing an opportunity is purely optional to an organization. A regulatory change or problem resolution may be considered mandatory, whereas an opportunity is a choice.

Projects for Marketing or Advertising

Projects requested by marketing or advertising departments differ from other projects in that they are usually focused on selling more products and/or services. These projects are often driven by an expected increase in revenue. Marketing and advertising projects include queries for direct marketing campaigns, enhancements to screens to capture additional data, new product support, customer relationship management systems, and specialized reporting. Many tend to be short projects that are needed immediately. Because they are often small projects, the BA frequently plays the role of PM and quality assurance analyst in addition to being responsible for the requirements.

These projects often make use of existing data, exploring it for sales opportunities (referred to as data mining). The marketing group may want to target existing customers for repeat purchases or other product offerings. Marketing requests typically contain complex criteria. For example: "We want a list of students who have attended class A, have not attended class B, live close to one of our public class locations, and have requested a catalog in the past year." Analysts need to first ask the *why* question and then probe for even more criteria because marketing stakeholders frequently assume criteria without realizing it. The more an analyst knows about the data available, the better the questions that will be asked to completely detail the request. For example, the analyst might ask: "What about students who have tested out of class B?" Answer: "Well, of course we don't want to market to them!" When you hear a stakeholder say, "Of course," you are discovering an underlying assumption that the stakeholder has made that should be captured in the requirements.

For complex query requests, the analyst should not only ask questions to reveal *all* of the criteria, but should also review the results before providing them to the marketing stakeholder. Initial query results often expose problems or challenges within the request that the analyst may be able to catch. Providing inaccurate data to the requester diminishes credibility and frustrates the requester. Carefully capturing the query criteria and reviewing the results will ensure the request is completed quickly and accurately.

For these new products and opportunities, do not be afraid to ask about or confirm the business cases for the organization. There is often excitement surrounding the launch of a new and exciting feature to your customers—especially when concerned with competition and wanting to stay up with the latest trends. However, business value to the organization should always be the top priority. The BA can help by either creating or validating the business case to demonstrate the estimated ROI. An exciting new project is only exciting if it returns value to the organization. And yes, many marketing metrics could include qualitative factors such as customer satisfaction; however, these still need to be quantified and measured in order to justify the expenditure of organizational resources.

Projects to Align Business Processes

As mentioned, there are many functional aspects to business that have standard approaches and practices across a wide range of industries such as human resource management, financial management and planning, customer relationship management, and enterprise resource planning. As organizations look to optimize their operations to focus on customers and products, projects sometimes emerge to utilize industry standards to streamline these business processes.

As with other projects, always start with a clear understanding of the goal. Knowing the difference between a project aimed at improving customer relationships versus a project to simply implement purchased software is important (one is a need, the other a predetermined solution). The BA needs to help articulate that the software itself does not solve the organization's issues. It is how the organization changes in order to utilize the software's streamlined processes that brings the value.

The BA would begin by confirming that the process being "fixed" by the software solution is a standard one and not a customized function of the organization's niche market. If the function was tied directly to customized services or products that the organization provides, then the project might best utilize a customized solution that is tailored specifically to the organization. If it is a common business process, then the organization can consider solutions that utilize commercial off-the-shelf (COTS) components. There are considerations to each option that the business needs to weigh against the desired outcomes to determine the best approach. These might include greater costs and longer timelines with a customized solution versus the COTS options that are quicker to integrate but offer less customization.

With the approach determined, the search for the *best fit* begins. There are three common techniques used to aid in the selection process: request for information (RFI), request for quotation (RFQ), and request for proposal (RFP). These requests are prepared by the organization that is interested in purchasing solutions from vendors. They are sent to vendors that offer solutions in the requested area. Each request is a formal petition asking vendors to respond.

These formal requests are used to make sure that all vendors are given an equal opportunity in the bidding process. This procurement process of sending a formal request and receiving formal replies was first used by U.S. government agencies and private companies that were concerned that employees were showing favoritism to a particular vendor; they wanted to have a well-documented explanation and justification for the selection process. It is not uncommon for vendors that are not selected to question the fairness of the selection process, which then raises questions about discrimination. To avoid these accusations and possible legal action, most large organizations follow a structured process and have rules that strive to make the process as objective as possible (e.g., employees are not allowed to accept gifts from vendors over a small dollar amount, employees are not allowed to talk with vendors during the proposal process, all vendor inquiries and answers are written and published to other vendors, etc.). The BA role begins here by providing the analysis that clearly articulates the needs, goals, and requirements of the organization and what it hopes to achieve. The analysis then continues with a review of the responses and how well each response addresses the stated needs or requirements in order to make a recommendation on how best to proceed.

An RFI is a document that outlines the business problem or opportunity that a company is trying to solve and asks vendors to provide initial, general information about product offerings. This is a great tool to use first if the business is unsure as to how to proceed or to see if the solution is even physically or technically possible. The RFI may be sent to numerous vendors, giving as many as possible a chance to participate in the bidding process. Often, some vendors will choose not to reply because their solutions do not meet the need or they do not think that they can support the customer on an ongoing basis.

The second type of request is an RFQ. This is a document asking vendors to provide a formal price quotation. These are often very formal and are used when it is explicitly clear what the requirements are and the specific solution being requested.

The third and most frequently used type of request is the RFP. This is usually a longer document that describes, in detail, the needs of the company. It asks vendors to describe specifically how their solution will match the needs of the organization. An RFP is effectively a requirements package (this is discussed more in Chapter 6) that describes the needs of the business area without defining the solution. The vendor is expected to propose a solution approach and define how it meets the requirements that will include implementation, the solution itself, and continuing support. This may include customization of features, training for software users, consulting on implementation or rollout plans, development of interfaces to other applications, and ongoing maintenance changes. Creating an RFP and reviewing vendor responses is often key business analysis work. An RFP may contain requirements related to the contract (written by the legal department) or the procurement process (written by procurement) beyond simply technical requirements. Often the PM will be responsible for pulling all the requirements together along with other documentation for the formal engagement and contract work with the external vendors. The BA will review the documentation to ensure that the needs are fully articulated through the requirements and then work to help validate that the solution is delivered as defined and agreed to.

Projects to Deliver Organizational Strategy

Projects that address organizational strategy are often less about single solutions and more about how to change vision, perspectives, and ultimately, attitudes of organizations. These projects often require a BA with advanced analysis skills where the focus goes beyond the *as-is* definition and requires analysis of the *to-be* strategy. Analysis work will often include competitive analysis of what other organizations are doing in the industry as well as exploratory research into business trends, technology, and methodologies that may or may not relate with the industry or the type of work the organization commonly performs. This is because the organization is looking for a new shift in focus and can no longer get by with "how it has always been done." The information brought by the BA gives greater breadth to the decision-making process such that a much wider view is considered. Many senior BAs are now experiencing these kinds of projects to build more business agility for the organization rather than specific products or processes.

Typically, these projects include upgrading legacy technology to current standards or redesigning to leverage industry standards to be more compatible with external elements. These projects help prepare the organization to be ready to take advantage of those opportunities as they arise and will require significant understanding of current state systems and environments coupled with a more externally focused analysis on technology and industry trends. The BA does not need to be the SME on the technology or solution, but remains responsible for the analysis where information is reviewed with the SMEs to allow the BA to bring options, design ideas, and recommendations to decision makers. In order to make these recommendations, the BA needs to consider those external factors of industry trends and technological advancements—either as part of the solution design or articulated in risks and impacts.

Designs may end up being revised more than once since these projects can begin as more of an exploratory discussion, which then leads to projects being generated. The team dynamics are often much more collaborative when working together and considering what changes are possible that would drive positive outcomes. The BA role often facilitates discussions to identify clear goals that align to organizational vision. BAs collaborate with the teams to define descriptions and measurements of what success would look like at the initial onset of these projects. A great amount of analysis occurs throughout the project regarding alternatives and risk analysis in order to help the team and decision makers consider what else is possible that will benefit the organization beyond what processes are followed today. The BA helps bring in the perspective of how to achieve value before, during, and after implementation.

STRATEGIC PLANNING

Projects are initiated for very specific reasons, and those reasons can be traced back to an organization's strategic plan. Strategic planning is an important activity for every enterprise. It is the development of a cohesive, long-term plan for the organization. It helps articulate how the organization will work to achieve the organizational vision. Strategic planning may be performed at the organizational or department/

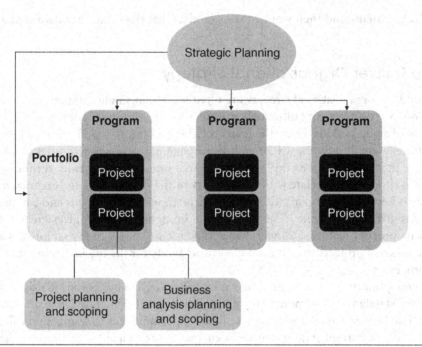

Figure 3.2   Strategic planning decomposed

divisional level. In some large firms, there are entire departments dedicated to strategic planning and measuring the organization's adherence to the plan.

Most junior to mid-level BAs will not be involved in strategic planning, but it is an important activity for all BAs to comprehend. You need to be able to read and understand the plan because it sets the direction for the organization. BAs should ensure that project work is moving the organization forward in achieving its strategic goals. Many senior-level and experienced BAs participate in strategic planning activities. This is often part of the progression of advancing your analysis activities from targeted-solutions analysis to project-based analysis to more enterprise-level analysis. If you wish to grow in your analysis career, maturing to support enterprise-level analysis is a natural progression beyond project-based work. This type of analysis provides the information that will help the firm choose which projects to undertake in the first place—by looking at not just one project, but rather all projects and how they blend together.

Figure 3.2 provides an overview of the relationship between strategic planning and individual projects. In large organizations, strategic planning leads to the identification of programs within which most projects operate. Many organizations also use the concept of a portfolio of projects that are managed similar to the management of a portfolio of assets.

Portfolio and Program Management

A portfolio refers to a collection of projects and programs that an organization has identified and prioritized to support the strategic plan. A program is an ongoing strategic business initiative that supports multiple related projects. Programs and portfolios are two different ways to group projects together logically; however, the perspective is part of strategic planning by looking at the enterprise efforts rather than individual task-based work, an essential element of strategic analysis.

Portfolio and program management are important terms that every business analysis professional should learn. These disciplines have grown out of the project management profession and represent high-level management of projects. Small to medium-sized companies may not have formal portfolio and program management groups, but the ideas are still important. Projects in a program may be in various stages: some may just be ideas, some have been approved and funded, and some have been started and are in the process of being completed.

The goal of portfolio management is to review all of the projects on a regular basis to confirm that the organization is making the best use of its limited resources. Projects are prioritized, and higher-priority projects are assigned more resources based on their needs. Analysis is needed to ensure that the projects are delivering the intended value of the portfolio to support the organization. The decision makers need to be aware of changes that affect this value since they constantly review and reprioritize to keep the organization driving toward its strategic goals.

How Does Your Project Relate to Others?

It is important for the PM and BA to be aware of other projects that may be related to their project. Learn about completed projects and the impact they had on the same stakeholders or business processes as your project. Learn about projects that are currently under way. Projects should share as much *corporate knowledge* as possible. Sharing information always results in a higher quality product and often speeds project completion. This is one of the primary benefits of a corporate business analysis center of excellence or community of practice. BAs share corporate knowledge, including an understanding of the detailed business processes that are performed, descriptions of the information needed by each business process (data), business rules, guidelines, policies and constraints of the business, information systems (software), hardware and equipment, and detailed procedures and workflows. Consider reusability with your project deliverables so that they are easily used, accessed, and even updated as you or other BAs access them to help on future project work (see Chapter 6). Spending a little time at the beginning of a project researching available corporate knowledge will pay off in time savings later—and more important, in solutions that are consistent and in sync with the rest of the organization.

Enterprise Architecture

One of the activities that may take place during strategic planning is the development of an enterprise architecture. The enterprise architecture is a description of the enterprise and how the organization plans to achieve strategic goals. It describes the current business and technology components that are required for the enterprise to operate and it needs to be understood before trying to drive forward any successful change effort. Enterprise architecture can be thought of as the overarching architecture containing everything about the organization (see Figure 3.3). Often, the architecture is modeled so that stakeholders can visually understand how a change would impact and be impacted by the enterprise's structure and outlook. Figure 3.4 shows an example of some of the elements to be considered when modeling an organization's enterprise architecture.

	WHAT	HOW	WHERE	WHO	WHEN	WHY
Scope	Data	Processes	Events	Organizations	Locations	Goals
Enterprise Models	Semantic models	Business process models	Master schedule	Workflow models	Logistics network	Business plan
System Model	Logical data model	Application architecture	Processing structure	Human interface architecture	Distributed system architecture	Business rule model
Technology Model	Physical data model	System design	Control structure	Presentation architecture	Technology architecture	Rule design
Implementation	Data definition	Programs	Timing definition	Security architecture	Network architecture	Rule specification
Functioning Enterprise	Usable data	Working functions	Usable network	Functioning organization	Implemented schedule	Working strategy

Figure 3.3   Enterprise architecture example

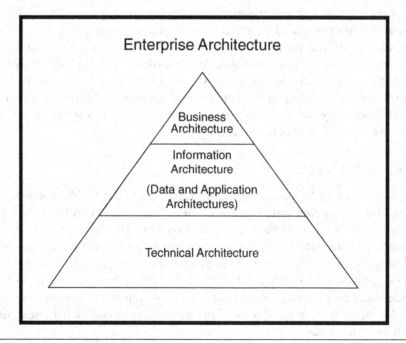

Figure 3.4   Architecture hierarchy

Technique: SWOT Analysis

With an enterprise architecture perspective, it is easier to perform activities such as SWOT analysis, which asks participants to list the company's strengths, weaknesses, opportunities, and threats. Strengths and weaknesses are identified for the organization itself; opportunities and threats are identified for the outside environment in which the organization operates. These components help to clarify where the company should look for growth opportunities (e.g., areas where the organization has strengths and there is an external opportunity). For example, if a company's strength is providing consulting services in the insurance industry and there is an opportunity to work in the banking area, the senior executives may decide to go after that market. Once you do the original SWOT analysis, it becomes necessary to determine how to use those strengths and weaknesses in order to take advantage of those opportunities and minimize the threats. Table 3.4 shows the format of a SWOT diagram.

Table 3.4 SWOT analysis

	Strengths	Weaknesses
Opportunities	*What strengths can be used to take advantage of opportunities?*	*Is there an opportunity to eliminate a weakness?*
Threats	*What strengths can be used to minimize threats?*	*What threats should we avoid due to our weaknesses?*

Business Architecture

Business architecture is simply a subset of the overall enterprise architecture where the focus is on business functions and processes and the assets that enable these operations. Whether at the enterprise or business level, the architecture is important to understand to bring context to the environment in which the solution or change must be successful. Do you understand the goals of the organization? Do you understand how the products and services not only drive revenue but value for the business or how the organization structures the roles and people? Are you aware of where the physical and virtual locations are? These are all considerations when analyzing a future-state idea. The business architecture is a way to understand current states and articulate many of the business and stakeholder needs that a BA will utilize to ensure that the requirements of the change produce a solution of value.

Information Architecture

Information (or data) is a valuable asset of every organization. Over time, an organization collects billions of pieces of information about customers, vendors/suppliers, products/services, expenses, etc. The value of the information is directly related to how quickly a particular piece of data can be retrieved when needed. An information architecture is a plan for where the organization will store information so that it is safe, secure, and easily accessible by the right people at the right time. As you work on a project, you should always be aware of the information used by the project and where it belongs in this information architecture. Some organizations have trouble articulating this across the entire enterprise, while others are much more mature and have strict guidelines that fall under the information management plan.

An example is the *requirements* architecture. Before a BA starts collecting and analyzing requirements, the planning includes identifying how the BA will structure requirements and designs to support not only achieving the project and organizational goals, but also how all of the different information will work collectively together. Will you be analyzing different types of requirements such as *business* requirements, *solution* requirements, *technical* requirements, etc.? How do you plan to structure your results such that the requirements that are identified for the solution not only align with each of the different types, but also still support the organization? By defining a requirements architecture, you help to ensure that requirements are complete and consistent. An example of a model of the requirements architecture for a technology project is displayed in Figure 3.5.

Figure 3.5 shows that business requirements will be broken down to identify the functional and non-functional requirements as part of solution requirements. These will break down further into technology requirements. What it also captures is the relationship back to the information architecture and enterprise. Business requirements come from the project objectives and deliverables (information architecture). Then these project objectives and deliverables align with the enterprise strategies (enterprise architecture).

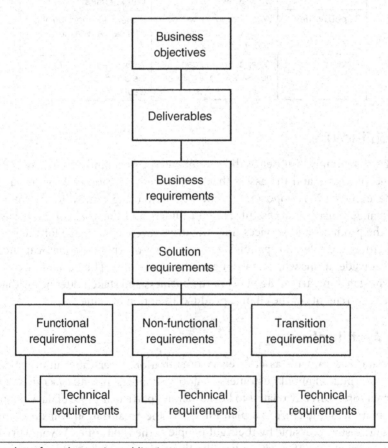

Figure 3.5   Examples of requirements architecture

This approach allows the traceability to occur that helps validate the *right* requirements have been identified. No technology requirement should emerge that does not support solution requirements. And the business requirements will make sure that the project objectives and deliverables are achieved. This is the requirements traceability that is discussed further in Chapter 6. Also, from this perspective the analyst can align the project with the enterprise and see what other elements might be affected by these requirements.

Real World Example: Working with the Different Architectures

A business case I was working on aimed to upgrade an existing technology that the company currently had in use. Business requirements had emerged that included both collaboration and communication requirements. In the initial analysis, we identified that we could deliver these requirements by upgrading the existing platform. When talking with the technical team, they also wanted to address some limitations of the current setup by including additional technical requirements as part of the upgrade approach. These addressed the needs of reliability (disaster recovery), scalability (storage, software, and hardware), and accessibility (networks and security). While each requirement was easily traced to the business needs from the simple requirements perspective, these topics led to bigger conversations with the IT team. The IT team was currently redesigning some of the backup and disaster recovery configurations. Not only was this business case going to have to be aligned and timed with these other projects, but the architecture decisions of backup and disaster recovery needed to be made by IT *before* we could validate our requirements. We needed to be sure that we aligned with the architecture of the organization.

While more technically focused, this is a great example of how being inquisitive with SMEs as to what approaches are ideal and should be considered for long-term organizational success is a key trait that BAs need to possess. Make sure you know the capabilities of your organization—not simply the technical capabilities, but also the ways your organization exists, profits, and thrives in its industry and communities.

Technology Architecture

While all areas of business operations should have a view of the architecture they need in order to be an effective component of the organization, the technology teams often have a clearly modeled view on the technology architecture for an organization. This is similar to the enterprise architecture, but it only focuses on the technology—such as types of hardware, software, operating systems, networks, programming language, database management system, etc.—that will be used by the enterprise and what tools are required to support the success of the enterprise. When thinking about technology architecture, think beyond simply a project. The technology architecture considers the day-to-day operations and what capabilities the technology must provide to enable the organization. By having a long-term plan, IT departments are better able to obtain beneficial purchasing and licensing agreements with vendors and then plan for periodic upgrades of equipment. This *IT road map* often includes an inventory of an organization's current equipment and software. This information is incredibly useful when brainstorming for possible solutions. Teams often need to first consider what already exists versus what needs to be created or acquired, especially as part of project work. It also helps identify what requirements are needed to ensure that the resulting solution of the project-based work can continue to operate and provide value in the enterprise once the project is completed.

Real World Example: Considering the Technology Architecture

A simple example that comes up often when considering technology purchases is finding out when the IT teams plan to upgrade software or hardware. An organization wanted to update their external website, so they worked with an external vendor to address their needs. Part of this discussion included the vendor proposing the use of a common Microsoft tool for the application. Before the marketing team moved forward with having the vendor build and host the new website, the BA took the requirements and ideas to the IT team to review for feedback to confirm that this was the right approach. The IT team noted that they already used the same application in the organization for internal collaboration. While IT was not planning to upgrade the application to the newest version for another 6 to 12 months, the IT team actually wanted to reconsider and discussed upgrading sooner so that the single application could support both the existing internal collaboration as well as the future external customer portal. This would be easier for the organization to support and provide consistency of infrastructure as well as alignment with their current IT plan to consolidate applications. While the marketing team was not fond of waiting for the upgrade, the change in solution to utilize the organization's own application after it was upgraded offered the enterprise more value and easier integration than simply purchasing another technology.

Communicating Strategic Plans

Unfortunately, in very large organizations (and sometimes even medium-sized ones), corporate goals and direction are difficult to communicate well. Corporate executives may have spent days or weeks working through a strategic planning session to develop these goals. Then they try to communicate them to thousands of employees throughout the world in just a half-hour employee meeting. Most employees have never really thought about what their organization's high-level goals might be, or more important, how each employee plays a crucial role in achieving them. These messages can often lack the direct impact the executives hope for—making communication one of the biggest challenges in organizations.

To be a superior BA, you should work to see the organization from the perspective of the corporate executives. Learn as much as you can about the strategic plan and direction of the company—truly listen at those company meetings and ask questions. It is important to consider how your projects, no matter how small, will support the strategic goals of the company. As an analyst, you can sometimes more easily break things down (i.e., functional decomposition—mentioned earlier in this chapter) and understand how these corporate messages translate to your daily work. You impact the bottom-line goals of the organization—every employee does. The more aware you are of these goals, the more focused your work will be and the more on target your requirements elicitation will be. You will also help your stakeholders keep the correct perspective when they have conflicts about how to handle specific problem areas. Figure 3.6 is an example of how a BA directly impacts the success of an organization. The tasks the BA does and the deliverables produced are in direct support of completing the project. The project is then traced to business solutions or capabilities, which in turn, are traced to the business goals. The BA knows that by

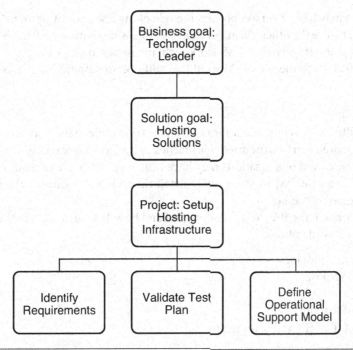

Figure 3.6   Example of a BA's impact on an organization

completing the requirements, test plans, and operational support models, they are helping the organization achieve its business goals.

Project Identification

Once strategic direction is determined, tactical or short-term goals are determined. These short-term goals will support the long-term strategic plans. Projects to accomplish these tactical goals are identified and prioritized. As those on the planning team complete the strategic plan and business architecture, they begin to see where the major problems are with the organization and where the biggest opportunities lie. These areas are where projects are often identified and outlined. BAs can assist in this project identification by examining the business architecture and strategic plan. They provide the analysis on the organization's current capabilities and what is lacking to achieve the business plans. The BAs can help stakeholders by suggesting projects that are of a manageable size and that address the needs, gaps, or opportunities that arise from understanding where an organization is and where it wants to be.

PROJECT INITIATION

Ideally, a PM and BA are assigned to each project at its inception. These two highly skilled professionals work together to assess the project request, talk with the sponsor to understand the objectives, and bring the team to consensus about the scope of work to be done.

Realistically, there may be one person playing the role of the PM and BA or one of the roles may be assigned to the project before the other. Business analysis professionals must be flexible and be able to come onto a project at any point. If you have a PM, work with him or her to scope the project. If you do not have a PM, be sure to initiate the project as a PM would, in addition to scoping the analysis work.

Initiation

When a project is initiated, it is important for the team to truly understand and agree upon its definition. Organizations with more formal, structured approaches to project management may provide a full business case, whereas more fluid organizations may have little more than a user request or idea. Regardless, the BA should work with the PM to more finely detail their understanding of the project, the project's goals, and their expected outcomes.

Key to project initiation, the BA should understand and be able to articulate to the team for validation the following project considerations:

- Approach or methodology
- Statement of purpose
- Objectives
- Problems/opportunities
- Stakeholders (all SMEs and team members)
- Business risks
- Items out of scope
- Assumptions
- Scope of the business area (external interactions and high-level processes)

Project initiation work and the resulting documentation will vary depending on the importance and size of a project. A small enhancement project may only require a few minutes of thought and a few sentences. But even on a small project that may appear simple, a few minutes spent at the beginning doing some planning and definition will be well worth the time. Even if the team says they know what is going on, doing this as the BA helps to ensure your own understanding of the initiative, allows you to do better business analysis planning, and supports your efforts in the BA role. The goal of project initiation work is to make sure that the project makes good business sense and that everyone on the team has the same expectations about what will be accomplished.

Approach or Methodology

This is simply an acknowledgment/description of how the project work will be done. It is a paragraph or two describing the overall approach that will be taken by the team and can be as simple as articulating an iterative or agile approach to development of the solution (see Chapter 5 for more on this). Organizations may have a standard software development methodology with analysis guidelines, a project management methodology, or a structured analysis road map to leverage. The BA should review these and note any variations or challenges that are anticipated. The approach may also include a description of requirements management software that will be used. The purpose of this analysis is to confirm with all project stakeholders the approach to getting the project done. The project initiation documentation may also include the next steps for the project.

Statement of Purpose

This is a short description of the project that is focused on explaining why the project has been initiated, approved, and/or funded. It is the *elevator speech* that can be given quickly when someone asks you what you are working on. It should be written in business language and be at a fairly high level so that everyone in the organization understands the project goal.

Do not discount the importance of formally writing this description. It may be more difficult to write than anticipated, so several revisions may be necessary. The act of writing something down, reading it, and revising it forces analysis. Try to do this with your teams. This will not only help you complete the definition but will also build buy-in through collaboration. Think about each word being used. Does it truly convey the meaning intended? Is it accurate? The project *statement of purpose* should not describe how the project objectives will be met, but it should clearly describe what will be accomplished. It may also include a sentence on the current environment or situation and should describe the main problem or opportunity being addressed. This is the one component of project initiation that must be formally documented. Even if no other document is produced, a project must have a clearly stated reason for its existence. This description may be referred to as the problem description, vision statement, or project request.

Objectives

An objective is a specific goal or outcome of a project. There are many great resources and tools to help PMs and BAs develop outstanding project objectives. Spending time clarifying these objectives with the business stakeholders is a valuable task. Objectives should be SMART—specific, measurable, achievable, relevant, and time-bound.

Having written, clear, and accurate objectives is important because they define the success criteria of a project. They help to articulate what *done* looks like. They also give the project team clear direction for project work. Project objectives, once approved by the sponsor, should be shared with everyone on the project team and reviewed frequently throughout the life of the project. This is a great resource for the BA if they start to experience *analysis paralysis* (discussed more in Chapter 7) or get overwhelmed by the work of eliciting, organizing, and analyzing requirements. Take a few moments to reread the project initiation documentation and focus on the objectives. Remind yourself why the project was started and what goals are to be accomplished. As previously discussed, your requirements should always trace back to supporting the goals of the effort. Taking a step back from the details (seeing the forest, not the trees) is an excellent way for a BA to regain perspective and to refocus on the most important requirements work that trace directly to delivering the objectives.

Problems/Opportunities

As discussed earlier in this chapter, projects are typically initiated in response to a business problem or opportunity. At the beginning of a project, the business stakeholders often state a number of things that they want from the project (opportunities) or problems that they currently have. In many organizations,

Table 3.5 Problems and opportunities

Problem	Opportunity
	Our competitors have websites selling their office supplies via mobile technologies. We need to compete in this area.
Customers complain when they call in and customer service has no record of them calling previously about the same issue.	A large organization in another industry uses technology to keep track of the status of all their clients so that any team member can help the client at any given time. We need to consider this approach to our customers and the service we provide.
We get many calls about store locations, product prices and availability, and order status.	
Our delivery department is not being utilized to full capacity.	Deliveries of both web and phone orders could be combined.

these are referred to as the high-level business requirements, but these items are not necessarily requirements yet. They are raw and unrefined. They have not been analyzed or approved. These problems and/or opportunities should be clearly stated and included with the project initiation material. This is the place to give more details than those found in the statement of purpose regarding why the project work is important and how it will benefit the organization. Table 3.5 lists some sample problems and opportunities you might hear. Note that every problem does not necessarily lead to an opportunity and every opportunity is not identified as a result of a problem.

Stakeholders

As discussed in Chapter 2, identifying and understanding project stakeholders is a fundamental task of the PM and BA. An initial list of stakeholders should be included in the project initiation documentation. An important component of scoping the project is knowing who will be involved and how many individuals will be participating. At initiation, while some individual members may not have been assigned yet, articulating the roles that need to be filled to help ensure project success is key to showing the estimated breadth and depth of the effort. Know, though, that this can always be refined (and often will be) as the project moves forward and specific requirements are defined that drive which expertise the team will need to access for delivery of the project. And be mindful that there are often multiple stakeholder lists. Primarily there will be the project stakeholder list that identifies the core team members assigned to the project who are responsible for delivering the change. Then often there is the analysis stakeholder list that the BA will put together. While many stakeholders will be included on both lists, be aware that there will often be additional stakeholders that the analyst needs to work with to define, verify, and validate requirements and designs that the project team does not identify as included in the work. One example is having the marketing manager be part of the project team to ensure the appropriate messages are getting created and the vision is clearly communicated throughout the change effort. The BA, however, may sit and work through the website designs with the company's website administrator. The website administrator discusses the opportunities and challenges on the specific requirements and design with the BA, but rarely, if at all, attends a project meeting. The BA then reviews and validates the requirements and design elements with the marketing manager (and the rest of the project team) as they move forward with implementing the requirements.

Business Risks

There are two types of risks to be considered for a project: project risks and business risks. Project risks are potential problems or events that may impede the success of a project. These are typically identified by the PM and include things like a resource not being available when needed. Business risks are potential problems or events that may impede the success of the business with respect to the project. These risks could be solely focused on ensuring that the product of the project generates value (i.e., revenue) for the organization or they could be as large as disrupting current operations and industry position. These risks should be identified by the BA when working with the SMEs. This is often one of those areas where having a separate PM and BA is important. The PM can remain focused on the successful delivery of the project while the BA continues looking at the project both internally and externally to ensure solution success. It is important to understand these business risks because they help to prioritize requirements, test cases, and implementation plans.

It is worthwhile to think about risks and to formally document and communicate them, especially on large-scale projects. Each risk should be clearly stated, along with the potential impact and a risk strategy. Risk strategies are recommendations on how to approach each risk. Table 3.6 lists risk strategies and considerations for each. Notice here that not all risk is negative. There can be positive impacts that were not considered but that may lead to additional opportunities and greater value. See Table 3.7 for an example of a business risk assessment.

Table 3.6   Risk strategies

Risk Strategy	Explanation	Approach
Avoid	Eliminate the risk	Decline the option that has the risk
Transfer	Have another party accept the risk	Insurance is a great example
Mitigate	Reduce the risk	Lesson the impact of the risk by taking a smaller amount or only partially investing
Accept	Recognize risk but do not change course of action	Acknowledge the risk and continue to move forward
Leverage	Capitalize on the risk	Increase the risk

Table 3.7   Business risk assessment

Business Risk	Probability	Risk Response	Impact
Students who want to attend a class will not be able to register due to full enrollments	High	Mitigate: By automating our registration process, we will have time to schedule more classes	High: Loss of primary revenue
Students who are registered fail to show up for class	Medium	Mitigate: Send a reminder e-mail a few days before class	Medium: Class requires payment prior to start, but instructor is already scheduled
Instructors who are scheduled to teach fail to show up for class	Low	Avoid: Accurate, up-to-date schedules will always be available; administration personnel will talk with each instructor before each class	High: Loss of revenue and reputation due to canceled classes

Items Out of Scope

This list provides a place to notify all stakeholders of specific items, requirements, features, objectives, and anything else that will *not* be addressed by the project. It is important to get clarification on what is *out of scope*. This section is necessary when there are specific topics or items that seem to be very closely related to the project scope and could easily be assumed to be included. Explicitly stating that particular items will not be addressed clearly sets expectations about these items and also tells stakeholders that the items and requests were heard rather than ignored. Items are identified for this list during initial project discussions with the project sponsor and key SMEs. The PM and BA work together with the business area to develop a project scope that can be accomplished in the desired time frame while still delivering the necessary business value. Business people are not always aware of how long a particular requirement will take to develop and implement. They need to understand the organizational cost of each request, along with the expected time required to complete it. When armed with this information, they can make good business decisions about what to include in the project or each iteration and what to leave out.

Assumptions

Another section of project initiation is assumptions—essentially, facts that are assumed to be true and will remain true for the duration of the project. A false or missing assumption can steer the project team in the wrong direction. People and projects always make a lot of assumptions, and the PM and BA—having experience—will be able to discern which assumptions should be explicitly stated. For example, the external vendor is assumed to provide *training* as part of the deliverables on the project. Until confirmed and validated in the requirements, the BA may want to explicitly state the assumption that the organization's training team will still be expected to provide classroom-delivered end user training on the new solution. This reveals to the organization that there are assumptions on the organization's training team and their level of competency, participation, availability, and overall understanding of the effort.

Some organizations also include constraints with assumptions. Constraints limit the solution, whereas assumptions are underlying circumstances within which the solution will operate. A constraint can be as simple as the availability of a resource or it could be a more complicated, larger, industry constraint.

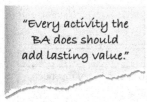

"Every activity the BA does should add lasting value."

Like risks, assumptions and constraints should be identified according to the methodology, organizational standards, and overall information management plans and architecture. Not every risk, assumption, and constraint needs to be identified and documented—this would take too much of the BA's and the team's time and not produce much value. As the BA, look for key elements that would directly affect delivering a valuable, long-term solution. Staying focused on the goals and objectives of the change effort helps you target the areas where you should concentrate the most analysis.

Scope of the Business Value

The most important part of project initiation work for the BA focuses on understanding the business and how the project is generating value. Regardless of the type of project or methodology, doing some planning work and sharing with your PM is essential for helping you to provide the most value in your analysis role. A great tool to help you capture and think holistically about the changes that are being implemented

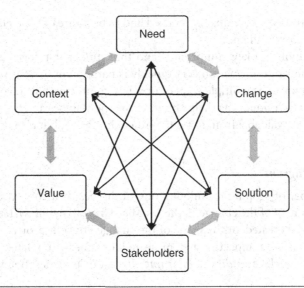

Figure 3.7   Business Analysis Core Concept Model™ (BACCM™)

by the business is the Business Analysis Core Concept Model™ (BACCM™) (IIBA 2015). Figure 3.7 shows the BACCM elements and how they impact each other. To use this approach, begin by answering the following questions:

- What is the problem or opportunity being addressed?
- What ideas exist for the solutions to the problem or opportunity?
- What changes are occurring or need to occur to make the solution successful?
- Who is affected by the changes? Who could impact the solution or change effort?
- Within what environment, circumstances, and other context must the changes occur?
- What is the value the project or solution is delivering?

When you *as the BA* have brainstormed these questions, the next step is to consider how they are related. If you change the solution, what impact will that have on stakeholders and the value proposition? If the context of the environment or organization changes, does that affect the scope of the problem or opportunity? When you consider the holistic view of the project from the business perspective, it helps give a better understanding as well as ensures that overall value is being addressed. If you have trouble answering any one of these questions, you need to discuss it with the PM and the project sponsors or business representatives in order to clarify before moving forward. This is a great way to acquire the understanding of what is going on before you dive headfirst into the details.

Context of the Change

Once you have a good understanding of the value and how it is considered in the organization, the focus centers on the work of the project. While the PM is focused on the budget, the tasks, and the schedule, the BA looks at how the team is going to complete the work. Having a clear understanding of what is changing helps the BA and the entire project team stay focused and to be aware of what effects the changes are having on the organization around them.

As a BA, communication is a key competency and thus, understanding that visual models can help articulate massive amounts of information very quickly is paramount to your professional success. Business analysis work often includes multiple ways of presenting information so you should get comfortable with modeling tools and techniques that help you describe the changes and the value of the work you are doing. These are extremely valuable from not only project initiation, but also throughout the life cycle of the project.

Technique: Context Diagram

While there are a number of scoping techniques, one of the best is a context diagram (see Figure 3.8). Begin by placing the key area of the change in the middle. This can be the system that is being upgraded, the deliverable that is to be created, or the name of the change effort or project. Then brainstorm the elements that are involved, will be impacted, are connected, or otherwise related. Then connect them and identify the relationships, such as *sending data* or *impacted by* or *utilizes* (often verbs). Also add elements

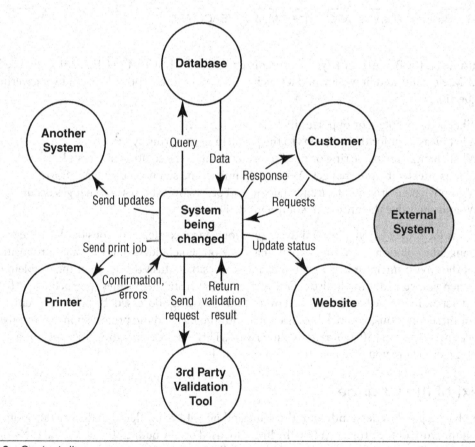

Figure 3.8 Context diagram

to the far corners and purposely not connect them to show that these elements are not simply out of scope but, more important, have no relationship to the change. This starts to paint a picture for the stakeholders on the design and delivery of the solution.

Do not worry about being *right* or complete at this stage; it just lets you articulate what you know already (or do not know) about the project so far. The PM can help fill in details as you get started. Also, think of this as a working document that you will utilize as a tool to engage with stakeholders and get their perspectives.

Real World Example: Working with a Context Diagram

On a project where the organization was upgrading its workflow system, the project team kept discussing all of the systems that were going to be affected. There were serious debates about whether those systems affected were included in the project work. As I came in after project initiation, I was forced to come up to speed quickly in order to be helpful to the team. I started a document where I put the system we were upgrading in the middle. Then every time another system was mentioned, I added it as a new entity around our main system. As I learned about the other systems' relationships to the workflow system, I would connect the two systems with a line—labeling the line with the nature of the relationship (such as "sends data," "receives data," "produces report," and other integrations). I would then show the updated diagram to the project team. I would bring the diagram to every project meeting, either to add more systems as we discussed other topics or to have it ready to validate the discussions on the scope and work levels. It became such a great visual model to aide discussions that we started to color code the depicted entities to more clearly articulate where changes were occurring. I did not have to worry about being *right* at meetings. Rather, I utilized the drawing as an elicitation tool when working with the stakeholders. It helped everyone get on the same page (literally). In fact, they would often tell me to "add another bubble" when they found another system, even when we were well into the project. It was an incredibly valuable tool to keep the project team focused on where we were working (and where we were not) for our project scope.

This seemingly simple diagram requires the business stakeholders to answer several key questions and clearly articulate what part of the business is to be studied. BAs should be familiar with this technique and be able to use it at a moment's notice. Even a project that appears small may have hidden complexities that will be revealed by using this analysis technique. The power of the diagram is in its simplicity. Anyone reviewing the diagram can quickly learn and understand the scope of the work to deliver the change and, more important, how the change works within the whole of the organization.

The context diagram can serve to give the BA boundaries around which to analyze and understand. Obviously, no one has the time to learn everything in an organization, so some limits need to be put around the analysis work. A clear scope helps the analyst stay focused and not get overwhelmed with business modeling (see more on staying focused in Chapter 4). The context diagram provides the analyst with a clearly defined area of study but should not prescribe any particular solution or answer. It should simply guide the analyst and business SMEs in their learning about business needs.

Remember that the true value in using this technique lies in the development of the diagram, not the diagram itself. By asking questions about who is affected by the project and what relationships they have with the solution, the team thinks about the scope of the upcoming work in more detail. Traditional project scoping performed by the PM does not usually include discussions about relationships, information flows, and external entities and processes. This is necessary specifically to define the scope of the analysis work.

Revisit Scope Frequently

An important aspect of business analysis is being flexible. Even if the scope and the requirements are formally approved, the scope of analysis could change. As the project progresses, greater understanding is gained by the BA, the PM, and the entire team as to what the change truly embodies. Ensuring the solution is producing full value is important to any analyst, especially on project-based work. It is possible to get so focused on the solution that your thoughts go well beyond the project scope and what is achievable by the organization in a timely manner. The PM will keep the project on scope, but the BA must do his or her part and keep the analysis work on target. The BA always needs to ask if the task being performed is not only moving the project toward its goal(s) but also providing value to the organization.

When the BA focuses on continuing to communicate the scope, it not only keeps the teams focused, but also helps address changes to scope. The PM is responsible for making sure that no change in scope occurs without acknowledgment and approval—better known as scope creep. And this can be a challenge since too many projects start off with one idea and the resulting products and solutions are not only different from the original idea, but also do not provide the desired value. This is often due to not properly managing changes. Changes are a natural part of any project, regardless of methodology. Analysts should be keenly aware that project work will evolve over time. So, re-evaluation of the given direction, approaches, and requirements is necessary to ensure the project is still driving toward a powerful solution. Even after you confirm the analysis work and the understanding of stakeholders' expectations on the solution and value, know that the stakeholders will leave that meeting thinking of more ideas. The key stakeholders may be changing their minds without realizing it and then become disappointed when the resulting solution does not match what is in their head. BAs combat this by continuing to review and confirm goals, direction, requirements, and solutions. And this can be accomplished by simply bringing your context diagram to meetings. This is important because when there are desired changes, they can be more formally acknowledged and recognized so that the overall project work stays on track. The PM will help ensure that the budget and schedule are re-evaluated (re-baselined) to incorporate the change. The BA will need to ensure that the change in requirements, scope, and especially in the solution is accurately recorded so as to adjust the analysis work appropriately.

Now, even though change is natural on projects and should be accounted for, do not automatically accept every change. BAs need to consider how they will handle the new information and how much change to the plan should be supported in their recommendations—that is the real question. Just because new information comes to light does not mean that it must be acted upon. It should be carefully considered and its impact forecasted into the project. How would the project change if this new knowledge was incorporated? What will the impact be if the knowledge is ignored or not included? Does this new information mean even more new information will be discovered as the project continues?

The approach used when considering why to do a project in the first place is the same approach that a BA should take with changes. The BA provides the analysis on not only what the effects would be on the project, but more important, what the impact would be on the business. This is why the BA needs to constantly be looking at solutions and how the project work will affect and produce value for the organization, not simply the project scope. A regulation change that costs $1 million in system changes to the organization may be worth waiting a few months and paying only $50,000 in fines while the organization reconsiders its strategic plans. Having a project scope managed by the PM and an analysis scope managed by the BA helps to truly articulate the effort and what considerations the business will need to address to bring lasting value.

SUMMARY OF KEY POINTS

It is critical for the successful BA to understand and be able to explain why their project is important and why stakeholders should be excited about the lasting value the *solution* provides. Knowing the ultimate objectives of a project will drive the direction of the analysis work. As BAs learn about the reasons for project initiation, they may be asked to develop a business case, a cost-benefit analysis, feasibility studies, and to provide general analysis on risks and impacts to the organization. BAs should also understand how their project aligns with the organization's strategic plans. They may not be involved in creating strategic plans or business architecture, but they must be aware of them and make sure that all of their work aligns.

Much of the work performed by a BA is within the context of a project, so keep these key points in mind:

- You should always know what you and your team are doing to help the organization achieve its long-term goals.
- There are many reasons why a project is initiated, including a government mandate, response to competitive pressure, or a clearly cost-justifiable change. It is critical for you to understand why the project is important enough to be funded and occupy valuable organizational resources. The most important word here is *why*.
- Project initiation involves working with the project sponsor and PM to define the boundaries of the project and plan for its completion. This analysis work is then required to be communicated and reviewed often with the project team to ensure alignment and focus on the desired goals and outcomes.
- When you are faced with a situation where someone is recommending a choice that would not be aligned with the high-level strategic plan, you should be able to explain why this is the case and how it would negatively impact the organization as a whole. This is a great opportunity for a strong BA to shine.
- Consider the power of visually representing the work to be achieved so that stakeholders and the business clearly have the same concept of the work required to bring organizational value.

BIBLIOGRAPHY

Green Car Congress. (2011, April 11). "NIST Prototypes Framework for Evaluating Sustainability Standards." https://www.greencarcongress.com/2011/04/nist-20110427.html.

International Institute of Business Analysis (IIBA). (2015). *Business Analysis Body of Knowledge® (BABOK® Guide)*. IIBA: Toronto, Ontario, Canada.

Project Management Institute (PMI). (2017). *The PMI Guide to Business Analysis*. PMI: Newtown Square, PA.

ADDITIONAL READING AND REFERENCES

Business Architecture Guild. (2017). *A Guide to the Business Architecture Body of Knowledge® (BIZBOK® Guide)*.

Business Architecture Guild. (2018). *The Business Architecture Quick Guide: A Brief Guide for GameChangers*. Meghan-Kiffer Press: Tampa, FL.

Business Architecture Guild. (2018). https://www.businessarchitectureguild.org/.

MITRE. (2018). *Enterprise Architecture Body of Knowledge (EABOK)*. http://www2.mitre.org/public/eabok/.

The Open Group. (2018). *The Open Group Architecture Framework (TOGAF®)*. http://www.opengroup.org/subjectareas/enterprise/togaf.

Project Management Institute (PMI). (2009). *The Practice Standard for Project Risk Management*. PMI: Newtown Square, PA.

PMI. (2013). *The Standard for Portfolio Management*. PMI: Newtown Square, PA.

PMI. (2015). *Business Analysis for Practitioners: A Practice Guide*. PMI: Newton Square, PA.

PMI. (2017). *A Guide to the Project Management Body of Knowledge (PMBOK® Guide)*. PMI: Newtown Square, PA.

PMI. (2017). *The Standard for Program Management*. PMI: Newtown Square, PA.

PMI. (2018). *The Standard for Organizational Project Management*. PMI: Newtown Square, PA.

CHAPTER 4

YOUR FOURTH STEP—KNOW YOUR BUSINESS ENVIRONMENT

The title *business analyst* (BA) is so named to emphasize the importance of the business in analytical work. Understanding the business requires that business analysis professionals understand the organization's business model, products, and services offered. They need to know why the organization exists. To perform detailed analysis, they need an overall understanding of the business and the context within which they are working. BAs must understand how all of their change work ties back to the high-level corporate goals and overall strategy.

As a BA, from the moment that you start work at a new company, take every opportunity to learn about the organization from the top down. Use time between projects to brush up on new products and services. Encourage your BA community of practice to highlight different organizational divisions and share information about various business areas. A BA is never without work; if you find yourself with spare time, use it to learn something new.

To learn about your business, start with the company vision and mission statements. A vision statement is an enduring reason for being and energizes stakeholders to pursue common goals. A mission statement describes the operational, ethical, and financial guidelines of the organization. Most organizations, including not-for-profits and service organizations, have a vision and/or mission statement. These statements have been developed by company owners or key stakeholder representatives and tell an enormous amount about the business as a whole. In a well-run organization, every project should tie back to the corporate vision; otherwise the organization would not fund the project. Everyone in the organization should always be working toward the organizational vision and mission, making sure that all work is in line with those goals (see the section on strategic planning in Chapter 3).

> "Every project should tie back to the corporate vision."

Real World Example: Mission Statements

Vision and mission statements help drive the excitement and energy of the organization and give teams who are introducing change to an organization a reason why their work is so important. These are high level and often inspirational to encourage activity, drive, and passion for the tasks to be undertaken. Microsoft's mission is "to empower every person and every organization on the planet to achieve more." Southwest Airline's mission is "dedication to the highest quality of Customer Service delivered with a sense of warmth, friendliness, individual pride, and Company Spirit." Virgin's mission is "to embrace the human spirit and let it fly." These statements clearly set the tone and direction of each organization.

BAs should also understand the industry in which their business operates. Knowing the competition, competitive pressures, innovations, and market forces will put the BA in a better position to make recommendations for long-term solutions to business problems. The BA should know where the industry is headed, what the popular trends and major organizations are, what technologies are being used, and what vendor packages are available that support the industry and business.

Part of knowing your business environment is being aware of the job roles of the stakeholders working in the business area. Do these workers have specialized training or certification to do their work? Have they been trained by the current organization or did they learn their skills in another organization? Understanding the background and experience of the business stakeholders improves your communication.

The BA must not only be aware of how the organization structures itself, such as specialized departments or cross-functional teams, but also how these departments support the organization as a whole. Is a department a mission critical area or is it a support area? Is it a profit center or cost center? Understanding the priority that the enterprise places on each particular business unit involved with a project helps BAs choose how to spend their time and drives what types of recommendations to make. Review the corporate organizational chart and learn the reporting structures of the organization. Remember, the BA skills of listening, observation, and inquiry are some of your most valuable assets to drive value for the organization.

HOW DOES A BA LEARN ABOUT THE ENTERPRISE?

All organizations and industries have unique complexities. Business analysis professionals work to learn as much about their industry and their specific organization as possible to enable them to provide the most value. Some industries require specialized knowledge (e.g., engineering, investment banking) and some BAs specialize in a particular business area (e.g., accounting, human resources). BAs can learn about their businesses by:

- Reviewing marketing materials
- Reviewing financial reports
- Reviewing the corporate strategic plan

Read the Organization's Marketing Materials

There is no better way to get a foundational understanding of an organization's products and services than reading what marketing materials say about them. Marketing materials have been designed by expert communicators who have a specific goal in mind. The goal of a particular brochure may be to create brand awareness or to reinforce the organizational image. Another marketing piece may be aimed at selling a particular product. Marketing materials show how the organization positions itself to potential customers, against competitors, or its role in the community. Study your organization's website and visit it frequently to review new content. The more BAs know about the marketing message that has been developed for external customers, the better they will be able to communicate with business stakeholders about products, services, and customers. This knowledge is critical for BAs who are assigned to represent business areas like sales, marketing, product development, and customer service.

This suggestion also applies to BAs who are working as external consultants. Before you walk in the door of your next client, visit the company's website and read everything that you can about its products and services. There is nothing more annoying to business executives than an outsider who is hired to come in and help and does not even know the product or service around which the company is built.

Read the Organization's Financial Reports

Publicly held corporations and nonprofit organizations are required to provide financial statements to the public. These reports contain a wealth of knowledge, not only for accountants but also for anyone working with or inside the organization. A BA should know how to review the basic financial reports and know their purpose. These reports include the profit/loss or income statement, balance sheet, and cash flow statement. A great way to build rapport with your stakeholders and learn as much as you can about opportunities to help the organization is to find individuals who are knowledgeable in this area and would be willing to sit with you and explain some of these basics. A great elicitation technique for any analyst is to ask others to share and clarify their world to you.

Look at how well the company is performing in terms of profit, market share, shareholder value, and amount of debt. Knowing a company's immediate financial history and their current financial situation tells you an enormous amount about how the business stakeholders will feel and behave. When a company is doing well, you will typically find an upbeat and optimistic attitude in most business areas. Employees feel secure in their jobs, they are being rewarded for their work, and their ideas are welcomed by management. Most project stakeholders will be glad to spend time with you because new projects are perceived as building the future of the company and they want to be a part of that work.

When a company is struggling financially, understand that this can significantly impact the mood of the staff and the general morale of the organization. Uncertainty in the organization can be translated into uncertainty in their roles, reducing willingness to help. You must be perceptive of the environment—be honest, open, and willing to listen and genuinely show your concern for the organization and its employees. These skills are all key to helping you build rapport and earn people's trust.

You can also gather beneficial information by reading between the lines. Look at the overall size of the company compared to the size of your project or change initiative. If the company has annual revenues of $40 million and you are working on a project budgeted at $100,000, your project is a small part of the organization's work. Alternately, if your project budget is $1 million, it will have a significant financial impact on the company as a whole. Knowing how your project or change initiative compares to the organization's size tells you about its importance (priority) and will give you the facts you need to convince stakeholders that their time spent on the change is important. If your change is specifically mentioned in the financial statements, shareholders will expect to see progress and may pressure senior executives throughout the initiative. Announced projects or change efforts are highly visible and have high business impact.

Review the Corporate Strategic Plan

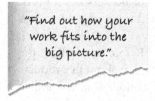

"Find out how your work fits into the big picture."

Read all of the documents that you can find about the company's strategic vision, mission, and plan. Often, high-level plans are mentioned in the financial reports. They may also be available on an employee intranet system. What is the company mission? How is that implemented? Your project, no matter how small, should be traceable back to a high-level strategic goal of the organization—investigate, ask questions, read, and try to find out how your work fits into the big picture.

SEEING THINGS FROM THE BUSINESS AND CUSTOMER PERSPECTIVE

Experienced BAs put themselves in the business stakeholder's position and try to see things the way the business sees them. This is especially important for projects that need the collaboration of cross-functional teams in order to be successful. Business people often have a very different perspective than information technology (IT) people, and marketing can have different ideas and concerns than finance. Until you can put yourself in their shoes, you will never be able to really connect with them.

Many people within the organization may not be intimately familiar with the fundamental concept of a *project*. For many business areas, most work is done on a continual, operational, or ongoing basis, or the changes are simply considered day-to-day tasks that are assigned. Defined *start and end* points with measurable deliverables may not be typical for the business units. The BA needs to ensure that they tailor their vocabulary to help the teams understand the change at hand.

Real World Example: Understanding the Business Perspective to Change

Each day, customer service representatives (reps) come to their desks, wait for their phones to ring, and then answer the questions that are posed. Most questions are ones they have answered before. Some may require looking up an answer, but in general the call comes in, they answer, and the call is logged. As each call is completed, the rep has finished the task and is ready for another. There is no work at the end of the day and they come back the next day to perform the same tasks.

Suppose that Jan, a BA, arrives to discuss the development of a new customer relationship management (CRM) system that the organization is thinking about implementing, that not only better tracks customer data and their interactions but also helps to report on employee activities. Jan wants to schedule interviews with all of the customer service representatives to discuss their needs. When would be a convenient time? The reps acknowledge that call volume is low on Friday afternoon, but the rest

continued

of the week it is pretty steady. Jan quickly learns that she will need to tailor her schedule around the reps' daily schedule in order to not only get good, focused feedback, but to also get their support for the change effort. She realizes that every time she asks a question, she prevents the reps from doing their job and making customers wait goes directly against the department's goal of low customer wait times. If she plans to talk to the reps, she will need to do some planning work so that she can ask all her questions in one session.

Also, Jan should engage managers and team leads and explain that she is working on a project that is supposed to make the reps' daily activities easier and give them more time to spend with customers. This will help gain some immediate support as leadership buy-in is a key success factor for all projects. These leaders can then help articulate the value to the team members and why a few minutes with Jan will ultimately help them in the long run.

> "Leadership buy-in is a key success factor for all projects."

This example points out a fundamental difference between project and operational work. Many business people respond to customer needs immediately while project work (solutions) takes much longer to implement and may not produce immediate results. This task-based work approach and prioritization is not the same as a project-based work approach. Project prioritization is much different, and often is what leads to project management offices that prioritize project resources, timelines, deliverables, and internal and external influences. Be aware that just because the organization prioritizes your project does not mean that the individual stakeholders may see your work as high priority. Taking this into account in your planning work (see Chapter 7) will help you define ways to be more successful.

HOW A BA LEARNS THE BUSINESS AND CUSTOMERS: ELICITATION TECHNIQUES

There are many techniques that business analysis professionals use to learn about the business, including:

- Document analysis
- Observation
- Interviews
- Context diagrams
- Surveys and questionnaires
- Facilitated sessions
- Focus groups
- Competitive and market analysis
- Collaboration games
- Job or persona analysis
- Process modeling

BAs should learn and practice as many of these techniques as possible. Experience will help in determining which technique is the most appropriate for each situation. BAs should think about making the best use of their stakeholders' time in their BA planning work. Choose techniques that are the most efficient and effective based on your understanding of the individual stakeholders and what goals you have to achieve from your interaction with them. Always try to minimize taking people away from their work as much as possible. Rather, aim to incorporate your analysis work into operations and the growth of the business.

> "Focus on under-
> standing the
> situation rather
> than worrying
> about getting the
> right answers."

Take note that when you are eliciting here, it is important to focus on understanding the situation rather than worrying about getting the *right* answers. Elicitation means to draw out information so that you understand it from the given point of view and context in which it was provided. It is important to see the whole picture—understand the solution, the requirements, the user, and the needs—so conduct more than one interview and/or use multiple elicitation techniques. Practice and experiment with these techniques (and even others not mentioned in this book) to uncover what techniques draw out the most information based on the type of scenario. The previous list is only partial—the references and additional reading sources at the end of this chapter will supply you with many more techniques that you may want to try. Make sure that any elicitation technique begins with a goal that you hope to achieve through your actions. Then afterward, reflect on whether you achieved that goal and modify your plan to continue moving your change effort forward.

Technique: Document Analysis

Reviewing existing documentation is often the easiest and cheapest analysis activity with which to start. Reviewing existing material helps the analyst by introducing the terminology used by the business. It also helps the analyst formulate questions to ask stakeholders. You should read system or software documentation, employee procedure manuals, policy handbooks, etc.—anything you can find that might give you some insight into the business and, most important, the workers. See what online resources (internal and external) are easily available that you can read through. A BA should not waste stakeholder time by asking questions when the answers to those questions are readily available in existing documentation. When reviewing documentation, be aware that not everything you read will be 100% accurate and up-to-date. Your BA activities should include additional verification and validation of your analysis work, so at this point, just be open to simply understanding more about the organization.

Real World Example: Reviewing Documentation

Documentation can prove invaluable for introducing key concepts and concerns of stakeholders. On one project, I was completely new to the subject matter at hand, whereas many project team members were well experienced. One of the key deliverables was training documentation for the client's team. While many of the staff had lots of information and knew in general how things worked, the goal of the project was to standardize and streamline training for a more positive customer experience. There was an extensive user manual on the system that the IT leads had created that they were quite proud of. However, the business area admitted that not only did they not read it—many of them did not even know it existed. Our goal was *not* to duplicate this manual, but rather leverage the work already done by team members to improve the processes.

continued

> I took on the task of going through the existing system's user manual to help validate that the required training competencies had been accurately captured. I read the manual as written and without bias, and then made sure the concepts or processes defined were articulated in our competency models. I did not judge whether the process was customer-centric, but rather looked for whether the topics that were documented in the system's how-to manual should be part of the training materials.
>
> In going through this massive document, I observed how the material was written from a system and functionality standpoint. I could quickly see why someone who is servicing a live customer may have trouble using it. I was able to identify key functionality of the system, but also noticed where and how validations and approvals occurred that could easily lead to bottlenecked processes. It gave me a chance to learn a process and identify some opportunities for improvement—all without having to ask any stakeholder for their time.

Technique: Observation

One of the most enlightening ways for a BA to learn about a business area is to work in or observe the work as it is being performed. This is easier for some types of businesses than others, but it is always worthwhile for BAs to physically see where their stakeholders and customers work to best understand context and scenarios.

Basic observation can be as simple as watching stakeholders in their traditional office setting. The work setup and general environment in the most basic of settings still offer quite a bit of useful information. Does each employee have an office? This implies that the work requires individual or quiet time. If a one-on-one interview is warranted, there is a space to do it. If employees have their own spaces, they may not interact with each other frequently. This implies that talking to one person about your project will not necessarily mean that everyone else will know about it. When workers interact frequently and can hear each other's conversations, word of the project will spread quickly—both good and bad news. Be aware that when you ask a question of one employee in collaborative environments, others will know about it. They will anticipate you asking the question of them and may be more prepared.

Consider who is in the office. Are a number of offices empty but message boards or notes are left that say "on site" or "at (customer) location?" This implies there is a lot of work directly with end users of products. This would allow you to ask questions of these stakeholders who could give you awareness into the customers. Are employees using chat and virtual office tools? If so, many of the employees may be able to work remotely and thus may be comfortable with virtual calls and online meetings. All of this information will help you to better understand how best to solve their business problems.

For workers in warehouses, factories, mail rooms, distribution centers, clinics, outdoors, and other environments outside of a traditional office, observation will be an extremely important source of information. Often, these employees are doing the primary work of the business that all other employees are supporting. If you work for a shipping company, spend time observing the movement of packages (sorting, moving, and delivering) to get in touch with the core business. If you work for a manufacturer, observe the assembly line or production process. An understanding of the core business work helps you think about how users could be better supported by solutions, and prevents you from suggesting changes that will negatively impact the work environment.

Real World Example: The Power of Observation

Even as the world goes to more digital and paperless solutions, there is still significant work being done manually. During a visit to a legal department at a major financial organization, I was invited to a space that was not only lined with bookcases, but the office area was filled with desks that had papers stacked on them almost a foot high. As one worker called to another, I could hear comments of, "I'll print that out for you" and watched people with hard copy papers walk to each other's desks. There were laptops on each desk docked to workstations, but I never saw anyone pick one up. This led me to believe that these team members might not be comfortable using online collaboration tools. I might need to guide them on how to access and update a shared document versus e-mailing the information—or worse, printing it and bringing it to me. This observation was done in a matter of a minute or two. Simple, but it gave me insight into what was the comfortable *practice* with these stakeholders.

Observation may reveal that there are variations in how a process is performed. This is another reason why it is an important elicitation technique. There can be three "descriptions" of a single process: (1) the way the process should be performed (usually documented in a procedure manual), (2) the way an employee describes his or her process, and (3) the way an employee actually performs the process (seen through observation). When a worker performs a process, you may notice that he or she makes assumptions or performs steps that are not in the procedure manual. The worker may forget to tell you about these steps when describing the process because they have become second nature and the individual is not even aware that he or she is doing them. Be aware of the possibility that employees may behave differently because they know that you are watching. Workers may follow an established procedure only because they want you to think that they follow it. Encourage employees to perform their work as they normally do.

Observation requires patience on the part of the BA and the worker being observed. The BA should limit questions during observation because interruptions may prevent a typical procedure from being followed. If you think of questions or comments during an observation, write them down and save them for a follow-up interview. If employees feel that their work is not very interesting, remind them that you are trying to learn as much about the business as possible, that their work is very interesting to you, and that they should try to work as they normally would.

There are additional alternatives to in-person observations that you could consider. Ask the stakeholders if you could take some pictures or even better, record some of the activity, especially when you are trying to understand a process or interaction between groups. This allows you to play back the interactions slowly to see what subtle clues are being missed on any discussion you might have with the stakeholders. Did they smile as they greeted the customer? Did they walk back to their computer more than once during the transaction? Did they scribble information on scratch paper versus typing it into the computer in the same room? This visual approach lets you see more than what you may see in a quick site visit.

Planning for observation often takes more work than simple document reviews. When planning for observation, consider timing and business activities. Be aware of daily, weekly, monthly, annual, and seasonal fluctuations in work volume and requirements. Are there access or security restrictions for observation or the information? Does the team rotate locations or have changing schedules that would impact what you see? A little planning helps you to make sure that the time being spent is valuable by having the right people ready to observe when you show up.

Having a goal in mind as to why you are observing in the first place also allows you to validate that you are watching the most appropriate stakeholders and customers for your change effort. Do you need to observe different skill sets or managerial levels? Determine what observation options would help you validate some assumptions quickly—such as observing more than one employee perform a task to see variability. It may not be possible to observe everything, but covering a broad range in a quick but efficient manner while not disrupting current operations should be your goal.

Technique: Interviews

When we think of elicitation and drawing out information, the main tool in the analyst's toolbox is conducting interviews. Interviews are systematic ways to use questions to elicit responses from your stakeholders. These are often the quickest and most convenient form of information gathering, especially when working with one or two stakeholders at a time. These conversations allow the analyst to learn about the existing business and/or talk about possible improvements. For an interview to be successful, the analyst must carefully plan the questions and the focus of the conversation. An interview can be any length of time, but should always be balanced according to the amount of stakeholder time you are taking compared to the quality of information you are receiving. The analyst must estimate how many questions can be covered in the allotted time while staying focused on achieving the goal of the interview. Having reviewed existing documentation, the BA can develop very pointed questions to confirm understanding of overall business functions. Alternatively, the BA can utilize open-ended, probing questions to expand on an unknown area. Then they can follow up with more detailed questions on a particular topic and narrow the scope, as required.

While interviews can vary from fully structured questions to free flowing, there always needs to be a clear goal or objective to the interview—that is, what you are trying to accomplish during the session. For example: *I would like to come away from the interview with a clear understanding of why the accounting department categorizes vendors and obtain a list of the categories that are currently used.* Without a clear objective, an interview can turn into a conversation, meandering in many directions and not meeting project needs. When a

> "There always needs to be a clear goal or objective to the interview."

subject takes longer than the allotted time, ask the stakeholder for another appointment. Do not assume that he or she can spend more time with you than originally planned. However, do not rush through your interview either because this is a great chance to build rapport and trust with the stakeholder. Allow the conversation to flow at a good pace, but stay focused on the objective. If you ever feel like you are meandering too far from the original subject, simply restate the objective to bring the stakeholder(s) back to the topic.

To prepare for an interview, the BA should become familiar with the individual being interviewed. Where does the stakeholder report in the organization? What is his or her title? How involved has he or she been with the project? Will his or her work be significantly impacted by the project? Is this person a decision maker? Understanding the position of the stakeholder will allow the BA to develop questions that are at the proper level (see Chapter 2).

Consider how you plan to capture the results of your interview. Just like planning the questions, there are a number of techniques to consider that each have their strengths. The simplest is taking notes as you talk with the stakeholder. Get in the habit of writing down short statements and key words rather than writing full sentences. Stay focused on your objective and capture the information that is directly relevant—the key elements that are related to the change and the context around it. Taking notes during the discussion may seem a little rude to your stakeholders if you appear more interested in your notes than in the person you are talking to, so consider getting a scribe. This is a great opportunity to bring another project team member along to learn more or even a junior BA to watch you in action, but most important, it allows you to engage directly with your stakeholder and really focus on him or her.

Of course, you could always record the session; however, know that your planning work for these methods can be more involved. You will want to inform the interviewee ahead of time of the format and explain thoroughly why you are using this method—emphasizing the desire to focus on the person and not miss any pertinent information. Clearly emphasize that it is in no way meant to judge or assess the person or their skills. Video recording may require more setup planning to ensure that you are able to get the information appropriately during the session without it becoming a distraction; but again, this is a way to see the body language and facial expressions. Also, you will need to plan additional time after the interview to go through your recordings and ensure that you captured the necessary notes.

Circumstances in today's world may not allow for an in-person discussion, so getting comfortable with utilizing technology that allows for virtual interviews is key for analysts today. The best part is that you can still do the face-to-face interaction with video displays while recording the session for playback and review, as required. Keep the person engaged so they are not distracted by their environment. This pertains to you as well. Be sure that you stay focused and work quickly to gain information regarding the issue at hand. Of course, simply picking up the phone can be the easiest way to ask a question and get the answer. The synchronous interview to explore concepts is one of the easiest and fastest ways an analyst can get information for requirements specifications.

Regardless of your approach, you need to do proper planning. As always, be clear on your goal and what you hope to achieve. Then, once you decide the most appropriate approach to learn more about the business, stakeholders, and general situation, plan out your questions and interview structure. Build in some contingency to explore ideas in more depth or discuss areas that you had not considered before but are relevant to your change effort. Make sure to be comfortable with the technology you are using so that you can focus on quickly getting valuable information and minimize the amount of time that you are asking of your interviewee. The last thing you want to do is come back to the same person with the same question.

As part of your planning, also identify how you plan to follow up with the interviewee. One recommendation is to send the interviewee a copy of your notes as soon as possible after the interview. This allows the interviewee to correct anything quickly, as well as include additional information if they feel so compelled. This can also build trust and grow your relationship with stakeholders since if they see that your notes are objective and task focused, then they can feel comfortable that you are indeed focused on understanding the facts for building solutions. This is a simple and valuable way to verify and even validate your notes quickly and holds more weight the closer to the end of the interview you send them. Showing action also engages the stakeholder to be more proactive than if you e-mailed them a copy three weeks following the interview.

Technique: Context Diagrams

The approach to change that separates BAs from project managers (PMs) and subject matter experts (SMEs) is often the BA's consideration for context. As discussed in Chapter 3, understanding the context of a change and what is affected, influenced, and needs to be considered helps a BA work with the business to deliver solutions that are long-lasting and impactful. When you look at the context of a change or solution, you can start to see what challenges and opportunities might be afforded to the business that leads to this lasting success.

Starting off any engagement or even doing your own BA planning work with a context diagram is a great technique to identify what you know and what you do not. Start with the change or project in the middle and then brainstorm all of the elements that you believe are related around it. Then add the relationships to each of those elements by drawing connections (see Figure 4.1). This is a technique that helps you think about what is truly involved with a change effort.

Context diagrams give you a starting point at which to begin to identify what you know about the environment before meeting with stakeholders. As you talk to stakeholders and learn more, update your

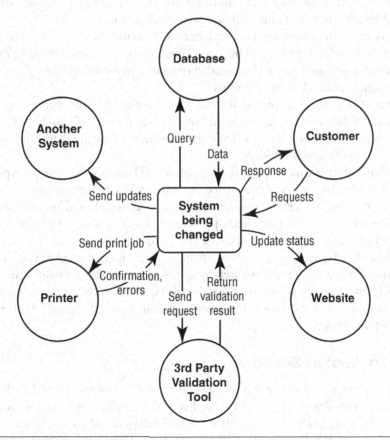

Figure 4.1 Context diagram considerations

context diagram with the information. A great approach is to actually share your context diagram with the business.

There are many context diagram approaches that are free flowing, such as *mind maps*, and others that are more detailed such as *interface analysis* and *data flow diagrams* (see Chapter 6). BAs will often find that their challenge is getting people to understand the solution and what is being affected and that visual images quickly (and literally) get people on the same page.

Technique: Surveys and Questionnaires

While talking face-to-face with a stakeholder is often the most common way to do an interview, do not discount utilizing virtual tools and asynchronous options as well, such as questionnaires and surveys. In-person interviews also give you the opportunity to observe body language and reaction to certain topics that might not be present in asynchronous approaches. However, the strengths of questionnaires and surveys include giving the stakeholder more time to respond and to share their thoughts without the needed burden of coordinating schedules. Conducting a survey or questionnaire can be useful when the sources of information are in different locations or the number of participants answering a given question is large. They can be administered to internal or external stakeholders.

Surveys and questionnaires allow the BA to ask exactly the same questions over a large group of stakeholders, removing any subjective interviewing bias. They may be conducted formally or informally. Formal surveys are usually designed and led by a market research firm or department. The BA will often work closely with researchers to develop the questions.

Informal surveys can be used to confirm the analyst's understanding of a process, assess the impact of a change, or generate solution ideas. Informal surveys are used for a small number of people and require less preparation than more formal surveys. They also may be used for brainstorming ideas or getting an initial feel for the needs of the stakeholders.

Content and distribution are factors that require considerable planning if the BA expects a high rate of return and useful results. The layout of the form or screen sent to the participants must be clear and easy to use. Participants must be told why they have been asked to participate and how valuable their responses will be. The shorter the survey, the more likely participants are to respond. The questions should clearly relate to the survey objective and be focused on, at most, two subject areas.

Typically, closed-ended questions (i.e., yes or no, multiple choice) are used to allow answers to be tabulated and reported quickly. They must be carefully worded to minimize ambiguity. Be aware that you are forcing the participant to choose an answer. Closed-ended questions are limiting and can lead stakeholders to an answer with which they do not truly agree. Most analysts *test* the questions on a few stakeholders before sending out the survey.

Technique: Facilitated Sessions

A business analysis professional who needs to learn information from several stakeholders, troubleshoot an issue, or discuss a new design or product should consider conducting facilitated sessions. Facilitated sessions are generally designed to bring together people from different areas of the business to focus on one particular process or topic. The attendees work together to build a shared understanding of the topic at hand and may also work to develop ideas for problem-solving solutions. This technique was developed around an impartial, trained facilitator who conducted each session with specific rules and leadership skills to obtain a desired goal. A facilitated session can also be referred to as a workshop with the understanding that *work* is expected to be done during the session to complete a product, which is normally the intended goal.

Facilitated sessions and workshops are not meetings. They are structured, planned working sessions where every participant is carefully chosen and has a critical role to play. Planning and preparing for a facilitation session are significant tasks that, if not done well, results in a poorly run session and a waste of time for the participants.

Knowing when to conduct a facilitated session is very important. These sessions can be costly in terms of the number of participants and the time required. They should be scheduled and conducted only when there are more than two viewpoints that must be represented. Every business analysis professional must be familiar with the steps required to conduct a session successfully. Ideally, a junior BA will be able to observe several sessions before conducting one of his or her own.

Facilitated sessions are an excellent technique for project initiation activities. The newly formed project team of business and technical stakeholders can come together to clarify their understanding of the objectives of the project. In addition, the team can help to develop the scope or boundaries as well. Bringing together project participants at the beginning creates team enthusiasm and synergy. Everyone feels a part of the planning and decision making. They *buy into* the project goals and will be advocates for change in their departments. These initial project kickoff sessions are even more valuable when the project sponsor starts the session by telling the group the reason for initiating the project and explaining its important business value to the organization.

Facilitated sessions are also useful for detailed requirements gathering, elicitation, and design planning. A particular business process or set of business rules may be the focus of the session with participants providing content for and review of requirements diagrams or models. These gatherings can also be structured as brainstorming sessions where participants generate ideas for process improvements or new product designs.

These information-gathering sessions are led by a facilitator who is usually supported by a recorder and a timekeeper. The session is carefully planned by this facilitation team. Topics on the agenda, participants, meeting location, and length of sessions are all carefully considered and documented.

It is important to recognize that a BA acting as a facilitator on their own project is not independent or completely objective, as traditional professional facilitators are. The BA brings his or her business area knowledge and understanding of technological options and organizational environment to the session, making him or her not only the facilitator but also a valuable member of the group. Part of the planning work often weighs the value of getting an external facilitator who is unbiased on the project versus leveraging the BA to drive toward the needed business requirements. The facilitator needs to keep the group focused and on track while still allowing the free flow of ideas and conversations.

Why Use a Facilitated Session?

There are several reasons why a facilitated session might make gathering requirements easier:

- *Multiple versus individual input*: as stakeholders listen to other stakeholders describe their requirements, they may all be reminded of additional requirements that might have been missed with one-on-one interviews.

- *Resolution of differences*: individual interviews with stakeholders often result in different answers to the same question. This causes the BA to re-interview people to try to resolve the discrepancy. By using a facilitated session with all parties involved together, the BA can help them discuss their disparate points of view while they are all together. Often, these differences result from something as simple as different use of terminology or different assumptions. When a requirement is discussed by the group, these differences may be resolved quickly.

- *True differences in requirements are identified immediately*: the team quickly becomes aware of issues that will need to be addressed. The entire group recognizes that the ultimate solution must be able to address a variety of needs. When it becomes clear that stakeholders have conflicting requirements, the BA and PM may need to adjust the project plan to allow time to address these conflicts.

- *Balancing priorities*: different stakeholders often have different priorities with respect to requirements. Leading the group through a discussion of priorities will result in everyone understanding other stakeholders' needs. The facilitator can direct the negotiation among stakeholders to arrive at one shared priority list.

- *Scope the project*: a facilitated session is very beneficial at the beginning of a project as a way to develop the scope or area to be studied. This session is planned and prepared by the PM and the BA and can increase the likelihood of project success by having all of the stakeholders understand and agree to project boundaries.

- *Team building*: as with any well-orchestrated group work, team members develop rapport with each other and become more vested in the success of the project. Teams often behave dysfunctionally at the start of a project. Participating in group sessions increases team cohesiveness and helps to create high-performing teams as they learn to understand and then respect the unique viewpoint that each brings with them.

- *Process improvement identification*: occasionally, as people from different departments talk about how they do their work and exchange experiences, one may learn of a different procedure or policy that could solve a business problem right away. These business process improvements often can be implemented before a project is complete.

Technique: Focus Groups

Focus groups are facilitated discussions where a group of participants who have been pre-qualified by some demographic, viewpoint, or other aspect are invited to share their opinions and perspectives on a very specific topic (IIBA *BABOK® Guide*). While quite popular for eliciting external customers' views on consumer products and services, focus groups can be done internally for feedback on how the organization operates, performs, or other specific topics.

Focus groups are led by professional, independent facilitators who are skilled at observation and listening. The facilitator does not participate in the group discussion directly. They do not attempt to influence any opinions. Rather, facilitators structure key questions to start the conversation and then moderate to ensure the resulting conversation stays focused and achieves useful feedback on the topic at hand.

Traditionally, focus groups are often conducted by marketing research professionals. Here, the BA often assists the facilitator with the stakeholder analysis and helps determine the appropriate participants based on the information needs. The BA can also help develop specific questions to drive the session toward the intended goals. The BA is often a key analyst of the resulting feedback as well. If required, BAs can conduct their own focus group as long as they stay focused on the facilitation aspect and avoid trying to analyze any feedback or sway the conversation to a particular outcome. The focus group is meant to get a wide range of feedback on a specific topic, so free-flowing conversations are encouraged. Make sure that the scribe or recorder for the session is comfortable with capturing all of the information being shared so that the BA is not distracted by this task and can focus on the participants.

> "The focus group is meant to get a wide range of feedback on a specific topic."

Real World Example: Utilizing a Focus Group

In one project, changes were being implemented that did not go as planned and caused issues for the organization's customers. While the issues were addressed and the project eventually completed successfully, the organization wanted analysis on why the issue occurred in the first place and what it could do to prevent it in the future (a great example of lessons learned—see Chapter 7). I was asked to help facilitate the session since management wanted someone who was not tied to the project to help encourage open and honest feedback. The session had to be carefully planned to ensure success on this sensitive topic.

The PM helped me identify the appropriate team members to invite to the session. This was a mixed group of stakeholders across different areas of the organization, but all were familiar or had participated with the project. Then I had to coordinate the time and location to get everyone together. A site was chosen away from working areas that was private and would not have interruptions (i.e., not near a common area or frequently used meeting room). I had to choose the format with which to conduct the session and what questions I would ask. I also had to consider how I would capture the results. I decided on a collaborative game approach (see later in this chapter) that would encourage equal participation by all attendees so that I could include feedback from all perspectives.

I got the project business owner to attend the first few minutes and let the attendees know that their time and input was important and truly valued. This was the leadership support that I planned into the session in order to help validate the participants' attendance and, of course, time. I explained the ground rules and emphasized again that the goal of the session was to focus on getting a clear understanding of the situation and what could possibly be done to improve future processes. We then began with one of my planned questions where each member took a turn sharing their views. Thoughts were captured by attendees on sticky notes as comments were shared. I did not participate in the discussion directly. Rather, I occasionally would have to encourage attendees to stay on track or even explain a little more detail with a guiding question or two. In general, the approach of everyone taking a turn to share opinions while hearing from each other helped to get the desired feedback.

At the end of the session, I thanked and dismissed the attendees. I then took the feedback captured on the sticky notes and documented it in an electronic file. As follow up, I e-mailed all of the attendees to thank them for their time and let them know where the feedback was going, in addition to attaching a copy for their reference. My plan also included how I was to present this information to the leadership team. In this case, it involved e-mailing the feedback to leadership team members and then discussing questions or key aspects in a meeting with them the following week.

Technique: Competitive and Market Analysis

Another approach for learning about the enterprise as a whole is competitive and market analysis. A BA should always be aware of the competition and what is happening external to the business, not only for the

> "A BA should always be aware of the competition and what is happening external to the business."

opportunities and threats (see SWOT analysis in Chapter 3) but also regarding how the business responds to these environmental factors. The strategy of the organization (see Chapter 3) should always be considered against these analyses. You need to determine whether those external factors would have an effect on the efforts of the organization and if so, what changes should be considered. Some organizations constantly adjust their strategy based on market reactions and changes from their competitors, whereas other organizations are set in their goals and accept the risks of what competitive factors they might face on the way forward.

Questions to consider include:

- Who are your company's competitors?
- Does your project assignment involve direct customer or product impacts?
- Does the organization lead its industry with state-of-the-art products or is it an industry laggard?
- How does the company differentiate itself from its competitors?

> "BAs should be keenly aware of what the industry is doing, key trends, and best practices and benchmarks of organizations in their industry."

Often, you can find competitors and their products and services by doing simple research. Review competitive marketing materials, just as you would with your own organization. How do they compare? Are there areas for possible advantages?

BAs should be keenly aware of what the industry is doing, key trends, best practices, and benchmarks of organizations in the industry. Asking questions of the business stakeholders and what their thoughts are on these external factors gives the BA insight into where the stakeholders stand and what areas of concern they may have when it comes to the success of the business. The amount of knowledge and up-to-date assessments that an organization keeps on the competition and what their respective industry is doing gives the BA insight into the organization's perspectives and viewpoints that can affect how they approach change work.

There is also market analysis work to be done based on business area. There are industry standards and best practices for HR, IT, finance, risk, and operations, among many others that should be considered. Do the business areas know what these standards and best practices are? Are they following them? These are important inputs to consider when approaching various solutions within specific business areas.

Technique: Collaboration Games

Collaboration games are one of the most engaging and interactive forms of elicitation that many BAs are incorporating into their work. Not only are these more fun than some of the traditional analysis work, but they also capture a lot of end-user feedback and open perspectives that BAs need for delivering successful solutions. The power of the collaborative games lies in building joint understanding of a situation through encouraging all attendees to participate. There are many structured types of collaborative games—such as product boxes, affinity maps, and the fishbowl approach (IIBA 2015)—but really, any technique that incorporates gamification and encourages interaction and collaboration can be considered collaborative games.

Even though these are called games, there must still be a structure for it to be an effective technique. The game should always have a clear purpose. The BA will need to make this purpose clear before starting, emphasize it again during the game, and then reinforce it at the conclusion to make sure that the desired outcome is achieved. Each game should have a process; these can be simple or elaborate, but the BA will focus on making sure the process is clear. Then the BA allows the participants to share and collaborate. The BA will then bring everyone together to close the session, reaffirming the goals. Of course, the most important part is the outcome of all this work. The BA should have a clear elicitation goal and emphasize what was collected. They should also highlight the learning and collaboration of the attendees that often occurs with this type of activity and leverage it as the team moves forward. Often, having the attendees share their thoughts and feedback helps reinforce the learning and secure the buy-in and continued support of stakeholders.

When starting out on a project, these types of sessions are beneficial because you can learn *who* the organizational members are, not just their job descriptions. Collaborative games can allow active brainstorming and visual role playing of what happens in the work environment to give a BA insight that would not necessarily come from the structured work environment. As you get further into a change effort, these sessions are effective for exploring solution options, defining the needs for implementation, and ensuring that solutions are successful.

Technique: Job and Persona Analysis

Like other organizational material, reading through job descriptions or other information from the organization on what job requirements and competencies are required of certain positions can help you understand the function, expectations, and activities of a business area. These materials help bring a BA up to speed on the business expectations of team members. By diving into role definitions early on, the BA will have greater insight into the scope of the change, especially if the change work affects business processes.

Often when a business process is changed, the roles that perform the business process may have to adjust. There may be more or less competencies required and new positions may be created while older positions are reviewed and even eliminated. It is an interesting observation when you read a job description and then watch the employee perform different work than what was described or handle completely different functions. Has the work evolved to meet changing market and environmental demands? Is there lack of alignment of current skill sets that may need to be addressed as part of your change effort? Using multiple analysis techniques can help with this approach to validate what expectations the organization has on the employees and what functions the employees feel they are expected to perform.

Persona analysis is a technique that can be used to understand how processes work by creating a detailed *role* to test process steps and outcomes. Rather than relying on a specific stakeholder, a persona is a very detailed description of a fictional character who would operate in the solution space. You remove the personal attachment of *Joe* or *Linda* and instead focus on the details of the user. This allows you to have free discussions with stakeholders on envisioning the business process and often what it *should be* versus only hearing how it is today because a certain person does it that way. Asking how *Joe* performs a process is different than asking, "If a new financial analyst was hired with a financial background but no industry background, they would first need to . . . ?" This allows the BA to hear more about the process than may be disclosed by someone very comfortable with it.

Personas are exceptionally valuable when eliciting requirements, discussing design ideas, testing solutions, and confirming an implementation. Describing a very specific customer comes into play all the time on market analysis and product discussion. It defines characteristics that shape specific scenarios and help team members visualize the person/solution in question. How your organization markets to a *single male with a good credit score, no children, rents an apartment, and has been employed less than 6 months* may be very different than how the organization considers a *retired couple, married over 30 years, good credit score, 12 grandchildren, owns home with no mortgage, and is receiving social security benefits*. Putting personas into your work with stakeholders can help you gain greater insight into the business and maximize solution value.

Technique: Process Modeling

One of the most popular techniques associated with business analysis is process modeling. It is a graphical way to show how processes work and is often done so that a BA can analyze a process for improvement or troubleshooting. The organization may already have plenty of process models captured and defined for how things work. These can range from high-level value-stream definitions to detailed processes performed daily by technicians. It is a visual artifact of the sequential (or parallel) steps that it takes to complete a process. A fundamental activity for most BAs is to do a process model of the current (as-is) situation and then draw out the future state (to-be) models to help articulate the differences and what it will take to get to the future state. Often during elicitation activities, BAs will model the information that stakeholders share about their processes as a key artifact of the BA work. Process models normally consist of activities, events, directional flows, decision points, and roles or functions. See Chapter 6 for more information.

Getting comfortable with the tools and standards that an organization uses is key to a BA's success. BAs should be able to draw out process models on whiteboards during meetings with stakeholders. They need to be able to take process steps and produce a visually appealing electronic image. If you have not tried these approaches, then those are key areas you will want to practice in order to improve your BA skills.

See Figure 4.2 for an example of a process model. Find out if the organization has any modeling software or tools, especially since process models are great for asking *what-if* questions. Modeling software can provide a number of simulations on your process that will give you great insight into what is possible and how things function.

There are a number of different modeling notations and standards that are available today. Value stream mapping (VSM), Unified Modeling Language™ (UML®), Business Process Model and Notation (BPMN), and SIPOC (suppliers, inputs, process, outputs, and customers) are all common. Data flow diagrams are another type of process model with a specific focus that is discussed further in Chapter 6. See the *Additional Reading and References* section for more information on the types of process models.

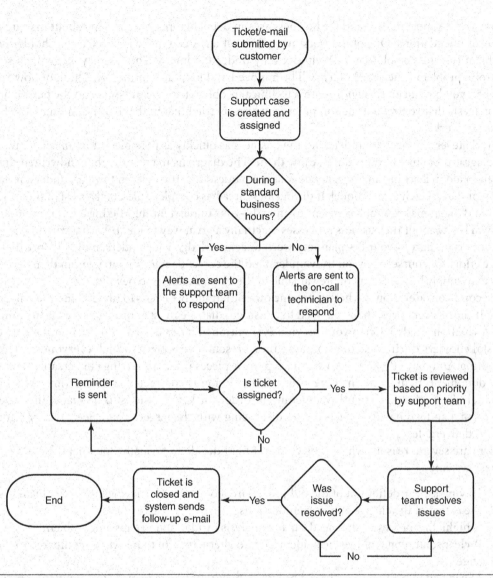

Figure 4.2 Example process model

LEARN THE CURRENT (AS-IS) SYSTEM

A common question among BAs at the beginning of a project is: "should I learn the current business procedures and then document the *as-is* processes before I start looking for a solution to the problem?" This is an excellent question that should be part of the business analysis planning work (see Chapter 7) on every project. The answer is not simple or straightforward and will differ depending on project characteristics.

First, the BA must understand the business area in detail before even thinking about making any solution recommendations. One of the worst mistakes that a BA can make is to tell a stakeholder how to fix a problem (i.e., toss a solution out) without fully understanding it. The BA may be giving a solution to the wrong problem. The stakeholder will be annoyed and lose faith in the BA. Think of how you would feel when you have been struggling with a technical problem for several hours and the person at the help desk suggests that you reboot the computer. You already tried that in the first five minutes and know that it does not work!

Do whatever you need to understand the business as quickly as possible. If that means drawing workflow diagrams of current procedures, draw them. The diagrams may be rough, handwritten drafts—just enough to aid in learning and to generate follow-up questions. If you learn through understanding information or data, sketch a data model. If the business area has complex rules, make a list of them. The documents and diagrams are simply a means to an end—your understanding. Taking a few minutes to capture what you know about the business processes is actually a great way to identify what you do not know and is an important part of your BA planning work to acknowledge your understanding before diving into a change effort. Of course, once you truly understand the current environment, you can then decide if these notes may simply be filed away or are valuable to the change effort and beyond.

A second consideration is whether anyone other than the BA needs to understand the current procedures. If the answer is yes, then you need to consider what the most appropriate way is to communicate the information needed. Often your previously mentioned notes are great for facilitating conversations with stakeholders during meetings because they present a visual with which everyone can picture the same thing. You may edit and redraw and keep these pieces informal during conversation and then formally document them as an outcome after the discussion is completed. At other times you may bring your analysis of what is currently happening in order for key decisions to be made; these need to be more formal and validated artifacts before discussing with the larger group. See Chapter 6 for suggestions on deliverables.

There are several reasons why a project team might decide to formally document the current or as-is business system:

- Having a clear definition of the old procedure along with the new will help the team understand the extent of the change and its ramifications
- It highlights processes that need further analysis by identifying gaps and problems
- A clear solution has not yet been identified, so alternative solutions will be compared to the current state
- During an interim period, the old processes may continue to be used in conjunction with the new process created

When you have the opportunity to brainstorm possible solutions and make recommendations, be sure that you completely understand: (1) the core business requirements and (2) the current *how*—that is, the system and procedures currently used to accomplish the work. Understanding the needs of the core business independent of how they are currently performed allows for creativity in solution brainstorming. Understanding the current procedures prevents you from redesigning the same processes.

BAs will often ask if there are scenarios when you do not need to document the current processes. Again, you need to separate the actual documentation from your *understanding*. BA planning will always push you to understand the environment—external and internal factors—and maintain a general awareness of the organization and how it's operating beyond just business processes. However, documentation of current processes should not be done just because *that's what BAs do*. Documentation of the current business processes is done to aid the change. If there is acknowledgment that there is no process today because the business is considering new products or ventures that it has never done before, then perhaps there is nothing to document for the product/process itself.

"Document the current business processes to aid the change."

Real World Example: Capturing Current Business Processes

In this scenario, a retailer decided to create a mobile app to help engage with customers. This is the organization's first dive into using mobile technology. As the BA, I realized that there really was no current process to capture. The planning sessions were all about brainstorming ideas and ways to design the solution to satisfy business needs and customer requirements. However, in order to help with the solution, I considered what support processes the organization already had. How do we support our websites? How do we engage with customers (i.e., in person) in our stores? I captured these processes to help articulate the scope of change so that we could identify what we had in place already to support the product/change and what would need to be done so that the new product would become successful. The product itself had no documented current processes, but the support models and processes were captured to highlight the changes needed for a successful total solution (not just a product).

WHAT IS A BUSINESS PROCESS?

Many organizations use the phrase *business requirements* to mean high-level goals of the business. Excellent business analysis requires that business requirements, and in particular the business processes, be analyzed at a much more detailed level. Analysts should work to understand as much detail as possible about each business process because these processes often drive the business requirements deliverables that are needed for successful change initiatives. As with all other business analysis activities, planning what amount of detail, formality, and what format is required is dependent on how much value each activity will provide your change effort. However, especially with business requirements and processes, you should always consider the amount of reuse that you can leverage from your activities since business requirements and processes exist well beyond the scope of project-based work and also support ongoing operations and continued change efforts. Modeling these business requirements and processes is discussed in further detail in Chapter 6.

To understand a business, you must understand the work that is performed. This work can be defined as a business process. There are as many different definitions for the word *process* as there are BAs and consultants! Most people agree that a process is an activity—a verb—something that an organization performs. Since the word *process* and other words that are closely related to it (activity, function, task, scenario, and even business use case) are used so inconsistently, the BA must be able to interpret their meaning from the context within which they are used. The terms that are used to describe business activities and processes have subtle differences that are often lost when people do not understand what the original author or analyst intended. Table 4.1 gives the proper usage of terms that are commonly used to describe business processes.

When focusing on understanding the business and what the current state is, sometimes it is most helpful to start by asking what capabilities the business has that can be utilized to achieve the organization's goals. As discussed with enterprise architecture (see Chapter 3), knowing the capabilities of an organization is key to understanding the value stream regarding how the organization is successful and gives you insight into what is required to achieve the success. Once you have learned about the business capabilities, then the *process* is really *how* they perform those capabilities. Part of a good BA skill set is asking probing questions that elaborate on a situation or item—that is exactly the step here. How does the department or

Table 4.1   Business process terms

Term	General Usage	Examples
Function	Generally considered higher level than a *process*. Functions are ongoing activities of the business. Names are usually nouns.	Human Resource Management, Marketing, Finance
Process	This can mean anything from a very high-level activity in the organization (i.e., Sell product) to a low-level, detailed activity (i.e., Record order). Some people use *process* to describe *how* work is done, others use it to describe the goal of the work. Some use it to describe how software is developed (RUP—Rational Unified *Process*). In business process management, it may be a high-level business transaction being managed across the organization. Names are usually verb-noun phrases. Processes should be named from the perspective of the business.	Receive order Validate order
Sub-process	A portion of a major process.	Validate address on order
Activity	Used interchangeably with *process* or *task* or *procedure*.	
Task	Generally considered a lower level, sub-*process*. A task is usually defined as an individual unit of work that can be accomplished by one business worker in a short period of time. Names are verb-noun phrases.	Add new account
Procedure	Procedures are step-by-step activities that define how work should be done.	New Employee Procedure, Hiring Procedure, File a Claim Procedure
Use case	A use case is defined as a **goal** of the business. The term *use case* is used inconsistently—some analysts define very high-level use cases, some define them as very detailed (more technology-oriented analysts), and others create multiple levels. They are named from the perspective of the actor (person for whom the goal is desired). See Chapter 6 for more information.	Place order
Event	Something that happens—and causes the business to react. There are several types of events, primarily: external and temporal. These requirements components are used in a technique called Event Partitioning. This will be discussed further in Chapter 6.	Customer requests product

staff provide that capability or feature to the organization? If you are talking with IT, asking "How do you support the application?" is a good starting point. Have them walk you through what activities need to be completed in order to achieve their goals.

When understanding how business works, asking about capabilities is a good way to keep the stakeholders talking at a high level and focused on the business goals and features that they provide to the organization rather than focusing on details concerning technology or specific individuals doing the work. People and roles will change, so ask questions that center on the activities. Try to focus on the function to be completed when *work-arounds* or other challenges or constraints are discussed, and identify what needs to be completed for business success. Technology should be replaceable, so again, understand what steps are being taken regardless of the technology that is being used when you are still at this high level and trying to understand what the business level does. The systems that a business uses today may be different tomorrow, but the process and ultimately the desired capabilities that are needed to support the organization will still be performed.

When modeling business processes, always start with what *should be* happening or the *perfect world* scenarios first. If "80% of the time the process acts this way," capture that information first, then move to the exceptions. People often spend 80% of their time on those 20% of exceptions that make the minimum business contribution. This is a good time to consider what your time is worth. Like all of your business analysis activities, you will want to weigh the amount of time you spend understanding existing processes, and especially the time spent documenting these items, against the value achieved from your activities. Spending time mapping a process that is not part of your change effort's scope may be valuable to you but may have little immediate reuse and, therefore, minor value. Will the process change by the time you need it again? Is there another process that is directly affected by your change and you plan to show the process at multiple project team meetings so that everyone understands where the impacts are? In this second instance, you will want to spend the time accurately capturing the process in a format that is easy to share and reuse.

Many BAs get excited about starting process modeling for anything they can get their hands on, but they should always remember to ask what the organization already has. If your organization has a more mature business analysis approach, there may be a repository of processes already captured that you can simply review and leverage during your change effort. If the stakeholders know they have already captured a process, you will get push back if they feel you are not valuing their time.

Describing a Process

As each business process is identified and named, detailed questions should be answered about why it is done, what information it uses, and what business rules constrain or guide it. The successful analyst will delve deeply into each essential business process to make sure that its purpose and fundamental value to the organization are captured. Many of these questions may be difficult for SMEs to answer. The analyst must work with the business stakeholders to talk through the *whys* and *whats* of the process because only a deep, thorough understanding will give rise to improvements. By discussing each process in detail, the business SME thinks about the work in a new way. Often during analysis work, the SME comes up with a process improvement idea because the process is being examined from a different perspective. Figure 4.3 shows a template for describing a business process.

Process ID:	1.a.i
Process Name:	Add/update customer information
Detailed Description:	This process accepts customer information and records it in our business area.
External Agents Involved:	Customer
What causes the process to occur?	Customer contacts Customer Service to place an order, change an order, cancel an order, request a catalog, or for any other inquiry.
What happens after the process is complete?	If a new customer has been added, then a new catalog is sent immediately.
Business rules:	• If the customer does not exist in the database, then add all required customer information. • If the customer is already in the database, then verify that the information is correct and make any necessary changes. • If a customer is an organization, then there must be a contact person's name.

Data (attributes):	CRUD	Source
Customer name	CRU	External agent: Customer
Customer number	C	Internally created
Customer contact name	CRU	External agent: Customer
Customer contact phone number	CRU	External agent: Customer
Customer contact e-mail address	CRU	External agent: Customer
Customer mailing address	CRU	External agent: Customer

Additional notes:	
Information source:	Mary Smith

Functional Requirement—AS-IS

List the group(s) that currently performs this process.	Customer Service
How is the process currently performed?	An online inquiry/update screen accesses a customer database.
Who uses the output?	Order fulfillment, Shipping, AR, Marketing

Metrics (only required if the process is a candidate for re-engineering):

How often is the process performed currently? (i.e., daily, weekly, monthly)	Daily
How many occurrences of the process are completed within the above time frame?	100
How long does it take to perform the process in the current environment? (specify minutes or hours)	1 min
Efficiency rating (1 to 5, 1 is lowest)	4

Functional Requirement—Suggestions/notes for TO-BE

Anticipated future changes?	Customers should be able to update their own information via the website.
List the group(s) that may perform this process.	Customer via the Internet.
Desired time to complete process? (specify minutes or hours)	1 min
Anticipate future volumes?	100–200 per day
Implemented in Use Case ID(s):	

Figure 4.3   Process template

Naming processes is important, yet is often done carelessly. Names should be chosen to accurately communicate the activity of the business (verb-noun), so that when the process is shown on diagrams, it is immediately recognizable. Process *names* should describe the *what*, not the *how*. Analysts can use the business glossary to help determine good business names. Strong verbs to use in process names include:

- Accept
- Add
- Calculate
- Capture
- Communicate
- Delete
- Dispatch
- Generate
- Place
- Prepare
- Provide
- Receive
- Record
- Remit
- Request
- Send
- Submit
- Tabulate
- Update
- Validate
- Verify

In addition to a strong, clear name, a description of the process must also be written. A name can only convey the basic information about what type of activity (the verb) is being performed on what type of data (the noun). A few sentences will elaborate on this name, providing all stakeholders with a clear, consistent understanding of the process. This description should explain why the process is important.

During process analysis, it is important for the analyst to ask questions about sequence. What happens before this process (i.e., what triggers it)? What other processes are triggered by the completion of this one? And most important, why are processes performed in this order? One of the common mistakes made by new analysts is assuming that the current order of work is a requirement and must be maintained. This assumption locks the business into its current procedures and leaves little room for creative new solutions.

Each process must also be examined for business rules. There will not always be a rule for every process, but most processes are guided by some type of a constraint (e.g., invoices are paid on the 15th and the last day of each month). As you identify business rules that are used during a process, think about whether each rule may also be used by another process. These shared rules should be defined consistently and their descriptions reused to save analysis time. Business rules will be discussed further in Chapter 6.

For each process, the analyst should think about the individual data elements needed to successfully perform the process. These data elements may (1) come into the process from an outside source, (2) be created by the process, or (3) be retrieved from a storage facility (i.e., filing cabinet, database) inside the business. Businesses store a lot of data so that processes can use them whenever needed (e.g., customer addresses are stored in a database so that customers are not asked for their address every time they place an order). Process analysis includes verification that all of the data elements needed by a process are available to it. The importance of data requirements will also be discussed in Chapter 6.

While analyzing, naming, and documenting essential business processes are important BA work, understanding how a process is currently performed can sometimes be just as important. Often when you ask stakeholders questions about core business activities, they want to talk about the *how*. They feel that it is important for you to know, step-by-step, *how* they perform this business process. Listen carefully and make the notes that you need. Listen for gaps in the process or between processes. If you know that the technology currently supporting the process will be changing, understanding the details about the current *how* may not be critical. Listen for problems and complaints to make sure that the new design will address these issues.

In addition, make notes about metrics. How long does the process take? How many times is it performed? Make sure you also understand who currently performs the process and who benefits from it. All of these things may change as your team brainstorms alternative solutions. Understanding how the work is currently done prevents you from redesigning the same system. Finally, when talking with stakeholders about a process, listen to their suggestions for changes. They may have some great ideas about how the process could be made more efficient.

When the reason for a process is understood, as well as its constraints and data components, different creative approaches to accomplishing it can be imagined. In what ways could the business receive an order? Via a text message? In an e-mail message? On a handwritten note? Suppose the products being sold are car parts. Could the car itself send an electronic message when one of its parts is wearing out and place an order for a new one? This core business activity may be performed successfully in many different ways (different *hows*). When business requirements and processes are documented independent of current technology, they can be reused on future projects in the same business area. This can save the BA a significant amount of time while opening up the business to many new opportunities.

This is where an analyst's creativity can really shine. True innovation occurs when the innovator strips away the current procedures and looks at the base requirements. Then he or she can be creative in meeting those requirements. When you see a new product or service offered, think about how the inventor might have come up with the idea. Was it in response to a problem? Was it designed with the goal of increasing productivity or quality? Was it created to increase sales? Remember the primary business drivers (i.e., increase revenue, decrease costs). Any improvements made to an individual process will end up helping the entire organization.

> "Excellent BAs balance creativity with facts and metrics."

Excellent BAs balance creativity with facts and metrics. Each process should be measured for its resource use, time to complete, efficiency, and number of times performed. Process improvements are evaluated by their improved metrics. Can the improved system get the process done faster? How much faster? Can the improved process allow the organization to handle larger volumes of transactions? How many? Will the improved process result in higher quality products or services? By how much? Effective business analysis professionals ask these questions because they understand that measuring process improvement quantifies the success of a project.

Six Sigma is an approach to business process improvement that relies heavily on metrics. The objective is to eliminate defects and variations in processes. Lean focuses on customer value while eliminating waste or inefficiencies in processes. The 5S methodology looks at organizing workspaces for performing work efficiently and effectively. See the references at the end of the chapter for resources on learning more of these popular process improvement approaches.

Formality of the Capture and Use of Business Processes

Some organizations have very formal business analysis processes and structures and will have specific templates and formats for capturing business processes. Other organizations may still be growing their analysis capabilities and thus, business processes may be found on notes, sketches, or captured in other techniques such as use cases and scenarios (see Chapter 6). Just as you do with other business analysis techniques, approach your analysis work with plans of how to leverage your time spent for maximum value and getting strong buy-in from your stakeholders. Capturing a business process is not about how well you can use a modeling tool (such as Microsoft Visio®) but rather how well your process presents a unified vision that everyone can understand and be used in order to make valuable decisions.

Seeing Things from the Top and from the Bottom

It is critical that a BA know as much about their business as possible. This requires an understanding of the business at both a macro and micro level. In other words, you must be able to see the big picture: Why is the organization in business? How does the organization make money? You also must be able to see the detailed work that goes on inside the business: when a customer orders a product, how is inventory checked for availability? How do products get to the customer?

Being able to see the big picture (abstraction) and the low-level detail will make you a valuable analyst. Most people in an organization cannot do both. Most of the executive-level people in an organization are very good at looking at the big picture. They can see opportunities for growth in the marketplace. They can see trends in the industry. They can envision the organization doing new things with new people. But most executives cannot understand or do not want to know about the day-to-day details of making the organization work. And realistically, they do not have time if they are truly focused on the vision and direction of the organization.

At the other end of the scale, individuals working in the business, performing individual tasks like customer service or claims adjusting, see work at a very detailed level. They know exactly which procedure is required for each type of transaction, but they may not understand how their detailed work fits into the big picture. They know which transaction code sets up the correct account in their software application. They know how to get around an approval requirement if the customer is important. Many of these people are very good at details but cannot or do not want to look at processes from a higher level. They are not comfortable with abstraction. This is where the BA comes in. BAs can listen to the broad, high-level plans and visions of the executives and imagine how the detailed work processes could support those plans. The more you work with different teams at different levels of an organization, utilizing multiple elicitation and process techniques, the greater your skills will be at connecting the dots to define the value streams of the organization.

Implementation Planning

Part of knowing your business environment is truly understanding how the business area will be impacted by the solution that has been designed for a project or change effort. Implementation or transition requirements describe the necessary actions to ensure a smooth transition of the product into the day-to-day operations of the business. This is what makes it a solution. No matter how well-built the product is, a rough, unplanned implementation may be disruptive and negatively impact the business. The BA helps ensure the continued success of the change long after the project or initiative has been completed.

> "BAs are the change agents who are tasked with assessing the impacts of a change and planning the best approach to implement it."

BAs are the change agents tasked with assessing the impacts of a change and planning the best approach to implement it. Implementation planning involves analysis of the current (as-is) business environment against the future (to-be) business environment. The analyst identifies all aspects of the business that will be impacted by the change and then plans each transition. Change impacts may necessitate training, coordination of an implementation timeline with other initiatives, and updating employee job descriptions, procedures manuals, policies, and more. Considerations of these elements should start during the planning stages so that they are worked into the overall change effort or project work. BAs are essential for helping prevent additional work during implementation. Their "solution" perspective versus "project" perspective ensures the solution is received, incorporated, and continues to add value per the given strategy.

SUMMARY OF KEY POINTS

BA professionals must understand business terminology, objectives, and processes of the business area within the scope of each project:

- When the BA is organizationally placed inside the business area, they understand the employee's perspective and can advocate for the business. When the BA is organizationally assigned somewhere outside the business area, in IT for example, this is a more challenging step.
- The BA should be comfortable using various elicitation techniques and should be able to select the most appropriate approach for each situation. Understanding each technique's purpose before engaging in any elicitation activity is key to successful BA planning work.
- Understanding business processes is a foundational skill of business analysis professionals that allows for change ideas to be analyzed and assessed. Having a keen understanding of how things work in an organization is crucial.
- Using BA techniques to capture business processes is what allows the BA to help the organization consider the scope, risks, and impacts of the change effort to design a solution that will provide lasting value.
- The BA must be conscious of the entire scope for a successful solution, not simply a project or product. Understanding the processes around a product or deliverable helps the BA articulate

requirements for implementation, training, and continued support of the product or deliverable for continuous value. This is solution focused.

Business analysis often involves eliciting business requirements from various stakeholders whose viewpoints are different. The BA confirms his or her understanding by learning from various sources, filling in gaps, and developing complete business models.

BIBLIOGRAPHY

International Institute of Business Analysis (IIBA). (2015). *Business Analysis Body of Knowledge® (BABOK® Guide)*. IIBA: Toronto, Ontario, Canada.

Project Management Institute (PMI). (2017). *The PMI Guide to Business Analysis*. PMI: Newtown Square, PA.

Whittemore, C. (2017, October 10). What Great Brands Do with Mission Statements: 27 Examples. *Simple Marketing Now*. https://www.simplemarketingnow.com/blog/flooring-the-consumer/bid/168520/what-great-brands-do-with-mission-statements-8-examples#virgin.

ADDITIONAL READING AND REFERENCES

Context Diagrams. (2018). https://en.wikipedia.org/wiki/System_context_diagram.

Process Improvements:

5stoday. (2018). What Is 5S? https://www.5stoday.com/what-is-5s/.

6Sixma. (2018). Lean Six Sigma Certification. https://www.6sigma.us/.

American Society for Quality. (2018). *What Is Six Sigma?* http://asq.org/learn-about-quality/six-sigma/overview/overview.html.

iSixSigma. (2018). *What Is Six Sigma?* https://www.isixsigma.com/.

Lean. (2018). *What Is Lean?* https://www.lean.org/WhatsLean/.

Value Stream Mapping. (2018). https://en.wikipedia.org/wiki/Value_stream_mapping.

Process Modeling:

BPMN Specification—Business Process Model and Notation. (2018). http://www.bpmn.org/.

Data Flow Diagrams. (2018). https://www.lucidchart.com/pages/data-flow-diagram.

Helmers, S. (2016). *Microsoft Visio 2016 Step by Step*. Microsoft Press: Redmond WA.

Lucidchart (*great for iOS users!*) http://www.lucidchart.com/.

SIPOC. (2018). https://en.wikipedia.org/wiki/SIPOC.

Unified Modeling Language™ (UML®). (2018). http://www.uml.org/.

Project Management Institute (PMI). (2017). *A Guide to the Project Management Body of Knowledge (PMBOK® Guide)*. PMI: Newtown Square, PA.

Weisberg, Herbert F., Jon A. Krosnick, and Bruce D. Bowen. (1996). *An Introduction to Survey Research, Polling, and Data Analysis*. Third Edition. Sage Publications: Newbury Park, CA.

CHAPTER 5

YOUR FIFTH STEP—KNOW YOUR TECHNICAL ENVIRONMENT

Business analysis is about helping to define valuable solutions for organizations. While rooted in technology, the role of a business analyst (BA) continues to evolve where analysis occurs in all areas of organizations today. However, many solutions still utilize or even rely on technology to enable their success. Technical awareness of the *possible* is one of the values that business stakeholders expect from business analysis professionals. Much like knowing the business environment and what the trends are in the industry, it is important that you stay current on what technology is being used for what purposes. Not everyone needs to be a software developer or programmer, but business stakeholders expect BAs to recommend technology that supports the business requirements and will help the business operate more efficiently and effectively. Information technology (IT) stakeholders expect BAs to communicate requirements in their *language* and not over-promise to the business stakeholders. Often your business stakeholders will hear of a new technology and then ask you if it could be used in their business area. The more that you are aware of technology, the more valuable you will be to your stakeholders. Sometimes the new technology is in its infancy and not yet ready for production use. Sometimes the technology is too expensive for the business area being addressed. Maybe the new technology holds promise for the future and should be included in the business' strategic plan. Even if you are not an IT expert, you should be able to talk intelligently about the possibilities.

And remember your stakeholders—on the business side many of them do not care much about the technology just as long as they are able to get their work done in an easy and efficient manner. You will probably hear more complaints about technology rather than how awesome it is. Your job should be to turn this around. Most complaints come when the technology does not perform in the way that the user expects it to. Were the user's expectations ever clearly captured and articulated in requirements as the system was being implemented? Technical requirements often reflect functionality versus understanding how the user intends to use the system. But even more so, is the user trying to do something with the system that the system was not designed to do—or is even capable of doing? If you do not know the capabilities of the system, then you may start spending a significant amount of time troubleshooting a problem that does not actually exist. While this chapter shares a lot about current technologies, like all of your analysis work, understanding *why* you care about this information will help you gain the most value from your decision making—including solution designs and investment decisions around technology and how you are helping to continuously enable the business.

A BA's background drives the way they approach analysis projects and think about business solutions. When your background is in IT, you may be in the habit of thinking about how to automate and integrate repetitive tasks and provide more sophisticated data for decision making. When your background is business, you may be thinking about new ways of doing business—how better to support customers and how the business can be more successful. These two modes of thinking are both useful in business analysis work. A business analysis professional who combines these two perspectives is the most valuable of all. In developing your skill set, look at your personal background to determine your primary thinking patterns and then work to develop other perspectives. Again, learn as much as you can about technology and its possibilities while constantly working to understand the business needs of the organization and where more value can be achieved.

WHY DOES A BUSINESS ANALYST NEED TO UNDERSTAND THE TECHNICAL ENVIRONMENT?

Since BAs often find themselves on teams or in discussions with both business and IT stakeholders, BAs need to be able to work in both worlds. Technology supports much of the work being performed in organizations today. The more the BA understands the enterprise IT capabilities and assets and how to leverage them, the better they will be able to understand how technology can be used to improve the business. Understanding what technology can and cannot do is critically important when trying to solve complex business problems. There are a few key reasons for a business analysis professional to get familiar with and stay familiar with technology capabilities.

First, learning about the current business requires that the BA understand *how* technology is supporting the work. When a BA begins talking with business stakeholders about their work, the business stakeholder will describe the technology and manual procedures using their familiar business terminology. Descriptions of technological components may not be exactly accurate; non-IT business stakeholders may use words to describe the system that are technically wrong. Many people have picked up technology words and phrases and use them inaccurately. For example: a business person may confuse data with process and say something like, "The database decides if the loan application is complete and gives us a report." The BA must be able to interpret unclear descriptions of current technology and be able to identify the business processes and what functions are being performed by the technology.

When eliciting requirements to learn about a business process, the BA must be able to listen to those descriptions and then determine how accurate they are. This can be challenging. The accusation that *users don't know what they want* could be expanded to be *users do not know what they have*—and that is alright. Business stakeholders should not have to understand *how* their current application software works. But as a BA who is looking to recommend changes or improvements to a business system, *you* need to gain an understanding of both *what* the business is working to accomplish and *how* it is currently done. You need to ask questions, read software documentation, and talk with technologists to understand how the software supports the current work environment before suggesting changes. The BA also needs to determine how effective the current software solution is in meeting current or future business needs.

"BAs must understand technology to allow them to make feasible recommendations."

The second reason that a business analysis professional must understand technology is to allow them to make feasible recommendations. To help formulate recommendations for changes to business systems, the BA must be aware of the possible options. Again, this does not imply that you need to know how to build the software or hardware components, just that you need to know what can be built and what will work in the environment. Each organization operates within many constraints and limitations (i.e., budget, resources, regulation, standards). When considering new technology for a business area, consider the environment into which it would be deployed. The question often is not only, "Can it be done?" but rather, "Can it be done *here*?" Sometimes the answers to these questions are very different. The more a business analysis professional understands the current environment and enterprise technical architecture standards, the quicker they will be able to answer user questions about why certain changes may not be feasible. A question like, "Can't we just add a column to this report with the current market price?" should trigger a whole series of thoughts in the business analyst's head:

- "Where would the system get the current market price to print on the report?"
- "How often does the price change?"
- "What external agent or company would provide the price changes?"
- "Who else would use this?"

The BA should be able to respond to the business user with follow-up questions or offer to investigate the idea. Some business users may expect the BA to have all the technology answers on building solutions. However, the BA should be focused on responding to capabilities and possibilities that need research and validation to confirm the best solution approaches.

The third reason that a business analysis professional must understand technology is that they must be able to see possibilities beyond the solution to the immediate problem. An experienced BA will always be looking at both tactical (short-term) and strategic (long-term) business solutions. The current project may be a small enhancement to an existing system and not require any detailed analysis. An experienced BA will think about this small change within a larger context. Maybe the BA has assisted with several of these small change requests and begins to see a pattern that might be addressed with a larger, more strategic change. Are you constantly fixing bugs in an outdated application versus buying a new one? Maybe a new technology would provide a breakthrough in efficiency, but it is not yet cost effective. Knowing a good enterprise architect from whom you can learn about upcoming changes helps you consider the bigger picture and direction of technology capabilities in the organization. The business analysis professional stays aware of upcoming features and capabilities and works to move the business in a direction where these new capabilities will be feasible in the future.

> "BAs must be able to see possibilities beyond the solution to the immediate problem."

Technology is changing at a rapid pace. Keeping up with the current capabilities and limitations is an important part of the ongoing professional development of a BA. Subscribe to IT newsletters and magazines. Build good relationships with those who work in IT. Attend lectures and webinars. Experience new technologies as often as possible (ask school-aged children how to use the latest technology—you will learn a lot). There are so many sources available in which to learn about what is happening with technology—and the more you know, the more valuable you are to your organization. Focus on understanding how these technologies can impact, disrupt, and drive business and what decision makers need to know. BAs are more successful when they are aware of trends and terminology to have discussions about capabilities and impacts.

Understand Technology but Do Not Talk like a Technologist

The thought behind understanding enough of the technology to support strategic business decision making is the same for technical BAs. BAs that are in a more technical position in the organization still need to be able to communicate the *value* of the technology—not only how it works. This is the reason why the BA role exists today. In the past, technical subject matter experts (SMEs) had a hard time explaining how the organization could get business value from a certain technology choice. As much as having subject matter and industry knowledge is valuable to the BA, you will see the constant emphasis back to the soft skills that a BA must possess and how BAs must articulate and communicate how entire solutions work, not only a single technology.

This is not a problem that is unique to IT or business. Have you ever had a doctor explain an illness to you and end up feeling like you have no idea what is really wrong? How about when your financial planner explains why he is rebalancing your portfolio based on recommended market share penetration and capital ratios? Every profession has their lingo, which is very important and necessary inside the profession. Doctors can talk to each other very efficiently because they have a common vocabulary that is very precise. They do not say that the patient has a pain. They describe the symptom using clinical language that pinpoints the source and cause of the problem because their focus (their value) is on how to solve the problem. Being a BA is all about looking at the total solution. In this medical case, it might include communication and training (education) of the patient, coordinating with other caretakers, or checking with the pharmacy department for in-stock and generic medications that would be suitable for the issue. With a focus on a solution approach, your vocabulary must span all aspects of the solution and the business domains that are required.

At the same time, the experts should be spending their time providing that skill for which they were hired. That means technical people should be designing and building technology. Business experts should concentrate on their business strategies and decisions. But together they need to coordinate on successful solutions that cross multiple areas. The BA is often the role to accomplish this as a facilitator so that everyone has the same vision of success and can bring their respective expertise to the table for the successful delivery of the required solution.

WHAT DOES A BUSINESS ANALYST NEED TO KNOW ABOUT TECHNOLOGY?

There are some fundamentals of technology that every business analysis professional must understand. BAs should have a high level of knowledge as to how things work. The better your understanding of a technology area, the more likely you will make good suggestions for holistic changes and improvements.

Areas/terminology with which you should be familiar include:

- Software development and programming terminology
- Software development methodologies
- Technical architecture

- Operating systems
- Computer networking
- Data management
- Usability and human interface design
- Testing phases, techniques, and strategies

Software Development and Programming Terminology

Does a business analyst need to know how to develop software?

Since the BA role began in IT and grew from there, there continues to be a belief that BAs know how to program. Yet the many analyst roles that are emerging today show that there is less of a need for a BA to have technical knowledge but should focus more on understanding approaches. Regardless of where your analyst role may exist, if you have to work with developers, then understanding their environment, approaches, concerns, and considerations for the work will help you consider options as to how to best approach solutions. Knowing these areas and the industry topics in development aids any BA much more than knowing how to program. So, in short, do BAs need to know how to program or develop software to be successful? No. However, they should know what goes into consideration for various programming languages and why, in addition to understanding the overall business question of why the business should even consider developing software in the first place.

All analysts are going to find that the more they know about a given topic or area of the solution, the more comfortable it is to discuss design and solution options. Rather than knowing the exact syntax for how to program in C# or Java, do you understand the advantages and challenges of each language? Do you know the most common programming language to be used in your organization? Do you understand how code is structured and laid out? Do you know the common troubleshooting situations or major causes of issues with each language used in your organization? While some may feel these questions are too technical for the average BA, knowing these answers is a powerful asset when it comes to understanding how to approach solutions.

Take time to learn whether your developer is working with a procedural language like COBOL or an object-oriented language (OOL) like .NET or JAVA. Learn OOL terms like encapsulation, inheritance, and abstraction. When you hear a term that you do not know, find a high-level definition. Knowing the architectural patterns that are used in programming, such as Model View Controller, helps you understand the logic that a developer uses. Find out if your organization has programming standards, screen design standards, and other governance policies to which your developer must adhere. These standards impact the developer's time to complete work, which should be factored into project time estimates. The most important work of the BA is communication. If you cannot talk with a developer in their language, they may discount your value, thus undermining your creditability. If you worked in the construction industry, you would have some understanding of how things are built. Take the same approach with IT. Utilizing those same elicitation skills that were discussed in Chapter 4, make an effort to understand the areas that you need to work with and how they function.

"The most important work of the BA is communication."

Software Development Methodologies

Methodology and Software Development Life Cycle (SDLC)

Know your developer's process or methodology.

Methodology is a word that was applied to IT software development in the 1970s. Early developers recognized that just sitting down to write code without any preliminary planning or requirements did not result in the best solution and often required a lot of time for rewrites. A methodology, as the name implies, is simply a structured, repeatable process. When it comes to developing software, it may contain very specific instructions. Early methodologies were based on the SDLC, which recognized distinct phases in software development: plan, analyze, design, code, test (see Figure 5.1). This fundamental structure is the foundation of every methodology, development process, and approach that is used in software development. The word *methodology* has lost favor because some of the commercial methodologies sold in the 1980s and 1990s were massive, multi-volume manuals that were difficult to follow. Organizations that purchased these methodologies often felt that the required deliverables took too much time. Teams began to skip steps or take shortcuts.

Over the last 30-plus years there have been many attempts to write a cookbook approach to software development. IT managers yearn for a clear, simple process that their teams can follow to ensure success. Unfortunately, software development cannot be defined that neatly. Understanding business needs and turning them into software solutions is complex, nonlinear, difficult work. It requires expert practitioners (PMs, BAs, architects, developers) and some guidelines about how the work will be done. Since every project is different, every team will work differently.

We can compare an IT development project to the work of making a movie. No two movies are exactly alike, even sequels have significant differences. Each movie has a unique set of people (actors, director, editor, makeup artists, costume designers, set designers, etc.) and a unique plot. They are shot at different locations and not always in sequential order. Movies take months, sometimes years to make and cost millions of dollars. Sometimes they are canceled in the middle of production. Sometimes they are released

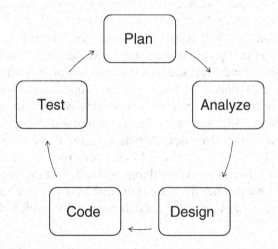

Figure 5.1   Software Development Life Cycle (SDLC)

and then flop. There are very few blockbusters. Although moviemaking sophistication has increased over the years, so has the sophistication of the audience. Expectations are higher, so doing what you did on the last movie will not be good enough. This is very similar to IT development, which faces the same challenges and odds against success. Every project is different with different needs and different stakeholders. The technology available continues to evolve and become more complex. Users continue to increase their sophistication and expectations. Using a software development process or methodology provides guidelines for the team based on best practices both inside and outside of the organization. But no matter how good the process is, having competent, trained team members will always be the key to the success of the project. Blind adherence to a process will not necessarily produce the correct product. This section gives a brief overview and history of software development methodologies.

Waterfall

First structured approach to software development.

Introduced the concepts of phases, tasks, roles, and deliverables.

The waterfall approach to software development is so named because it has distinct phases that are meant to be done in sequential order where high-level project objectives and requirements *fall* through from one phase to the next. The waterfall methodology also introduced the concepts of team roles, deliverables, and sign offs. Team leader, programmer, and user were the first roles that were specified. Deliverables or software design documentation was introduced as a method of getting user agreement on work *before* the work was done. Sign offs were introduced to get user *buy-in* to the work.

All other software development methodologies are based on the waterfall method. Most of the concepts of waterfall are still important and are included in subsequent methodologies. Figure 5.2 shows the classic waterfall approach.

In the waterfall approach each activity or phase is dealt with once and completed for the entire system before the next phase is started (i.e., all analysis activities are completed before the design phase is started). This structured, sequential approach lent itself to being quite successful for certain development projects where teams needed to be up to speed quickly and everyone understood the same concepts. As well, the waterfall approach minimizes risks with schedules and budgets by knowing exactly the work needed to deliver the goals (Kienitz 2017).

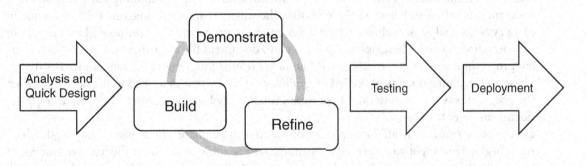

Figure 5.2 Waterfall methodology

However, this same structure also limited the methodology's success. Teams often spent too much time in the early phases of the project and then had to rush through the rest of the process. It is unfortunate that the waterfall approach has suffered from negative publicity because the tasks and deliverables recommended by the approach are necessary and useful. The fundamental idea behind the waterfall approach—analyzing *before* designing and designing *before* implementation—is still the most effective route to success, not just in software development, but in your own business analysis work (Royce 1998). As mentioned, planning before you engage with stakeholders, analyzing resources, and then jumping into your business analysis work can lead to greater success.

Methodologies that were built around the waterfall approach acknowledge the importance of first planning the work, gathering/understanding requirements, and laying out a software design plan before starting to write code. Early developers did all of this work themselves. Prior to the concept of an *SDLC* or *methodology*, developers spoke with SMEs briefly and then began coding. This approach is often still used on maintenance projects. As projects became more complex, software also became more complex. Coding without an overall design plan was problematic—like trying to build a house without blueprints.

- *Planning phase*: the planning phase was intended to help the IT team ask high-level questions of the executive sponsor to determine the true project objectives. This was the first attempt to set customer expectations for the IT work that would be done. It was also intended to help IT people understand business needs and priorities.
- *Analysis phase*: definition of the analysis phase was really the beginning of business analysis work. The waterfall approach recommended that software requirements be written down and reviewed. This was a radical idea in the 1970s when most developers only wrote code. This phase was created because developers had been creating software that did not really perform functions the way that SMEs needed. Initial requirements were very brief and were all functional—they described what the software should do.
- *Design phase*: as software supported more and more business activities, developers created many programs and files to perform different functions. Programs have to know how data is stored in files to be able to share information. Early software systems were much like patchwork quilts with random pieces sewn together. Development was slowed for several reasons: (1) early programs were not documented so developers had to read each other's code to be able to share data, (2) as more and more programmers were working on the same systems, original programmer knowledge was not available, and (3) early programming did not follow any programming standards, so every program was different. For all of these reasons the waterfall approach suggested that someone in IT (a systems analyst or architect) draw a design of the programs and files needed by the system before coding started. These designs also began to document file exchange formats so that different programmers could be working on different yet related programs at the same time. The design phase also included documents called *program specifications* that described to the developer what the program was expected to do. These were initially very brief and evolved into more complete documents over the years.
- *Development phase*: only after completion of the first three phases did actual coding or development begin. This might have seemed a little radical back at the time, due to the massive amount of time and work that occurs before a developer ever actually starts coding. Yet even when you talk

to a number of IT professionals today, most agree that some planning, analysis, and design work should be done before people start creating anything.

- *Testing phase*: the waterfall life cycle helped to really shine a light on a defined testing stage. Prior to this, coding was done directly in *production* environments (there often was not a test environment, development, or *sandbox* area) and the user was given the results. If the results were not correct, the code was changed *live* on production. The waterfall approach recommended that code be tested before being used by business people, leading to many of the testing cycles that organizations often follow today.

Business Analysis Considerations

The concepts introduced in the waterfall approach probably seem obvious, especially given all the project-based work today that follows the same approach of planning before executing and then testing before delivery. Like all the areas of study on any change effort, understanding the methodology that your stakeholders use to create and deliver value to an organization is a key requirement of being a successful BA. Knowing what the waterfall approach is and how it compares to other methodologies is essential.

Know the strengths of the methodology. Waterfall approaches help to minimize risk with schedules and budgets. They build in a lot of time for testing to verify and validate that what was defined as the requirements were actually designed and then delivered as specified. This approach has its strengths in repeatable processes where expectations are known and variances are to be reduced.

Consider a server or other piece of IT equipment that has regular updates or patches. There is a known procedure of the work that must be done. The work can be defined and planned out to ensure that all activities are completed. There is a known list of elements to be tested and verified with each update or patch prior to being pushed to production. The customer (business area) has a clear expectation of what is to be delivered with the update or patch. This scenario works very well with a waterfall approach.

Likewise, BAs should know the challenges of each methodology. Waterfall approaches do not deliver much value until the end of the process. Requirements are gathered up front and the customer is rarely contacted again until testing—and even sometimes delivery! If a requirement changes while the team is in testing, then planning, design, and coding steps must all be repeated—often stopping any further work. The work will not move forward without clearly defined and approved requirements. If the stakeholders have trouble articulating these well and in enough detail to start to deliver, then the entire effort is delayed. Developers had to hope that they had gathered all of the requirements just as the customer envisioned and then had to wait until delivery to find out if it met their expectations. Imagine spending a year or more working to plan, analyze, design, code, and test a great solution only to deliver it and the customer says they no longer want it because needs or priorities have shifted. Talk about a lack of value added to the organization! A BA should know the value that a waterfall methodology can bring—and then identify the scenarios where it makes the most sense to apply. Analyzing and knowing the solution approaches can be just as valuable of an analysis skill as defining the solution itself.

The Evolution of Development Methodologies

The waterfall methodology still has its strengths and that is why it is still around today. While the next sections on other methodologies are more likely to be appropriate to your business analysis work, knowing a little more history on how methodologies such as *iterative* or *agile* came to be is important so that you know the strengths and weaknesses of each methodology to help teams align their approach and achieve the desired outcomes.

As the waterfall methodology gained popularity, it started to bring cross-functional groups of SMEs together to do the planning versus the developers doing all the work. Questions would be asked as more people would need to be brought in to understand the requirements and expectations. As IT systems expanded to support multiple business areas, joint application design emerged. Here, facilitated sessions were conducted to help bring in business owners to get a shared understanding of the requirements with an agreed-upon design. Joint design acknowledged that the IT team members needed to work closely with business SMEs (Wood and Silver 1995). This concept was further expanded on with the desire to speed up the development process. Rapid application development (RAD) centers on including prototyping and involving users in the development/coding work. The idea is to give the business areas and users something to give feedback on sooner in the development process. Features, functionality, and design elements are confirmed and approved for release or changes are given back to the developers to incorporate. RAD also de-emphasized long documentation in place of faster delivery of prototypes (see Figure 5.3). The cross-functional working sessions versus reviewing requirements and designs allowed for greater understanding of users' expectations (McConnell 1996). This approach is the forerunner to the latest group of methodologies known as agile.

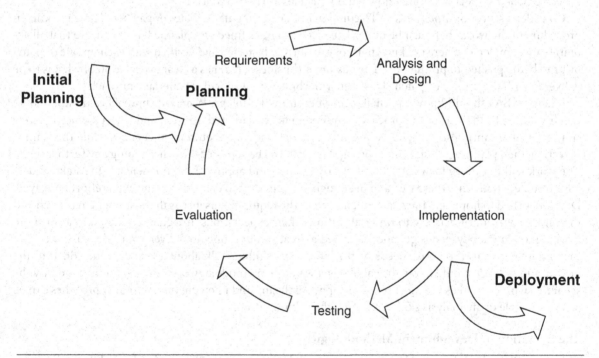

Figure 5.3   RAD methodology

Iterative and Incremental Development Approaches

Recognize the value of revisiting phases to catch missed or new requirements.

Break projects into smaller deliverables that can be implemented faster.

Iterative is so named because to iterate is to repeat and rework based on the work from previous iterations. The phases are still used, but this approach recognizes that one phase of a project may not be completely finished before the next is started. It gives permission for the team to revisit earlier work to pick up missed pieces. Incremental approaches recommend breaking large products into pieces and building each piece to fit with the existing whole. Pieces are integrated as they are completed.

These development approaches have been well received by most IT departments. Iterative approaches recognize that all requirements may not be completely discovered and detailed during the first attempt. As IT architects begin to design solutions to meet business requirements, they will find holes or inconsistencies. The iterative approach allows time for the BA to go back to requirements elicitation to fill in the pieces. The BA can further elaborate on requirements that were unclear or define additional requirements that help clearly articulate the solution that were hard to define earlier in the design process (see Figure 5.4). Incremental work requires that an overall plan is developed and then broken into small, more manageable pieces. This approach allows functionality to be delivered to business people faster and helps the team to prioritize the most important work first.

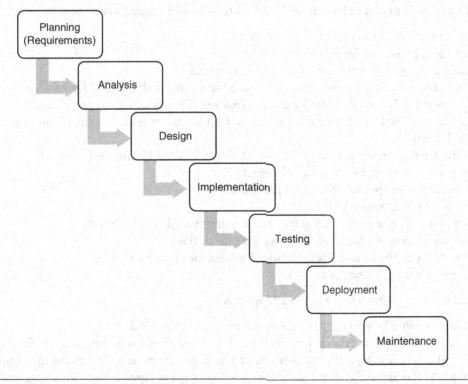

Figure 5.4   Iterative and incremental methodologies

Agile Development Approaches

Focus on small, colocated teams.

Decreased focus on formal requirements.

As the pace of technology continues to advance at exponential speeds, software development approaches continue to evolve to focus on faster development of valuable solutions to business users. The word *agile* means being able to move quickly and easily and is used to describe an approach to solution development that is fast, flexible, and effective. The agile style utilizes both the iterative and incremental characteristics with a goal of delivering working functionality that can add value immediately. Key to this thought of being more agile is some tenets found in the Agile Manifesto (Beck et al. 2001) that help highlight the differences compared to waterfall and more traditional approaches:

- Individuals and interactions *over* processes and tools
- Working software *over* comprehensive documentation
- Customer collaboration *over* contract negotiation
- Responding to change *over* following a plan

Agile development does not mean that processes, tools, documentation, planning, and analysis go out the window, but rather that there is greater emphasis on team collaboration to best determine how to deliver value through working solutions in a short amount of time. Even if only in minor increments, the customer gains value from every phase of work. Characteristics of an agile project include:

- Short iterations (two to four weeks) of work
  - Scope based on highest business value
- Small, dedicated project team working closely together
  - Originally emphasized physically shared space, but today virtual teams are often online using collaboration tools for quick responses, discussion, and ad hoc meetings
- Business stakeholder(s) not only assigned to the team, but expected to participate full time during development
- Daily *stand-up* meetings to keep the project on track (10 to 15 minutes)
- *Design as you go* approach to the solution design
- *Demo as you go* approach to user requirements
- *Test as you go* approach to the solution
- Requirements brainstormed together and communicated very informally
- Documentation of what is useful or needed (adds value)
  - Still prioritized as deliverable work in the scope of each iteration
- Teams become self-managed

There are some real positives to using an agile approach:

1. Business value is delivered to business stakeholders very quickly.
2. Daily *stand-ups* and constant reviews keep all team members' work on track and focused.
3. Because iterations typically run between 14 and 30 days, there is no formal change control process required during an iteration. Once the iteration scope is agreed upon, no changes are allowed

(unless the scope is not feasible). Changes to requirements are considered for a subsequent iteration.

4. No voluminous requirements documents are written. BAs do not have to spend hours fine-tuning every word in the requirements package in long document-review sessions. Requirements are confirmed during demos of the product as it is developed or on whiteboards in the team workroom.

5. Working prototypes evolve from design artifacts to production software so business users can see their requested changes and developers can easily make additional changes to improve usability as the project moves along.

6. Dedicated team involvement including a full-time business stakeholder means everyone stays focused on achieving the objectives within the specified time frame.

These benefits are only achieved by a very high-performing team that understands the agile approach and commits to these characteristics. Including a high-performing business analysis professional on the team increases the likelihood that the resulting product will meet true business needs and fit in well with the current business environment while delivering measurable value. If an experienced BA is not available, at least one team member should have extensive business analysis training and experience (Carkenord 2007). And this is an important consideration for any analyst professional. Even if the roles change based on methodology or other organizational decision, the analysis does not go away. An experienced BA will add significant value to the team. There are still business objectives that need to be achieved. There are still requirements needed to deliver value. Requirements need prioritization. User feedback and alternatives discussions need to happen. And in more agile environments, these happen on a fast-moving timescale. When a business analysis professional is not available, developers are expected to perform analysis and communicate directly with business stakeholders.

Hybrid Methodologies and the Agile Mindset

A BA is focused on helping to enable the delivery of value. As BAs work with developers, they may notice that developers might not always follow methodologies exactly how *the book says* to perform activities. Approaches like *Wagile* (waterfall + agile) and *Scrumified* (elements of Scrum) are used, and even within the agile methodology you will hear that developers are utilizing Kanban boards, doing Scrum, or following SAFe® (Scaled Agile Framework). Whether an "official" methodology defined by a group of practitioners or a modified approach using elements from multiple methodologies (often called *hybrid* methodologies) is used, a BA needs to focus on understanding these methodologies' strengths and challenges and then balancing them with the organization's goals, values, and capabilities. The *right* methodology is what works for the organization to deliver value. What works for one type of change may not be the best approach for another. This analysis of the type of change should be done before diving into the development work. It is often here that the need for business analysis is so apparent.

> "The right methodology is what works for the organization to deliver value."

Additionally, as much as the popularity of agile has increased over the last ten years, some organizations are rejecting agile or are making their own approaches. A discussion of agile methodologies with a capital *A* or agile with a lowercase *a* has occurred. This comes from the initial explanation of agile development as a specific methodology with a *structure* that was defined and followed. If you were not following the methodology then you were not agile. What businesses started to see and are embracing today is the agile mindset, regardless of the approach to the methodology or structure that the organization uses. Are you agile enough to be flexible and reconsider ideas, stop current work to pursue a higher priority, and respond or even drive changes that customer's demand? This is more of a discussion of agility and delivering greater *business agility*. While some organizations leave methodologies to the developers, the BA should be aware of the organization's processes to deliver value and how the development teams fit into the value stream. The BA role, whether titled in position or simply in the analysis work done by multiple team members, continues to evolve as it aims to facilitate innovation through creativity, rapid learning, and experimentation in these more fluid agile environments (IIBA 2017).

An Organization's Formal Methodology

An organization may have adopted one or more formal methodologies that define deliverables. This usually takes the decision about which requirements deliverables to use out of the hands of team members and forces consistency from project to project. Unfortunately, many methodologies do not provide much detail on requirements elicitation and analysis from a business perspective. The business requirements document may be a single deliverable within the methodology. A business requirements document is made up of a set of requirements components and should be viewed as multiple deliverables (see Chapter 6). If you are assigned to a project using a formal methodology, your first task should be to review the methodology for its handling of requirements deliverables and determine if it meets the needs of the stakeholders for your current effort. Part of your planning effort will be to add items to the formal methodology as needed for the project or change effort.

Using a methodology has its advantages and limitations. On the positive side, the BA can read the methodology and know exactly what is expected. The business analysis tasks are easier to develop because milestones are stipulated and defined. The BA knows where the analysis is occurring and can better plan their time and that of the stakeholders that need to participate.

The limitations of this scenario are obvious. Even the best methodologies cannot anticipate the circumstances of every project or the nuances of an individual organization. The prescribed deliverables may not work well for a particular project and you may find yourself forcing round requirements into square holes. Create the required deliverables as best you can, and then use some additional deliverables that make more sense for project needs. Few methodologies forbid you from creating more deliverables than prescribed. Although these additional deliverables may require more time, if they are beneficial in representing project needs, the time will be well spent. If a prescribed deliverable does not make sense for your project, petition the standards board to omit it and capture the information in lessons learned.

An Organization's Informal Standards

Many organizations do not use a formal methodology. Some may have a methodology, and may profess to use it, but if it is frequently ignored, then it may as well not exist. In the absence of a formal methodology, the BA should examine the informal standards and processes that have developed inside the organization and consider them when planning their analysis work. Many informal standards and processes are successful because they have been developed over time by trial and error.

If you take an informal survey of stakeholders about their previous experiences with requirements, you will likely hear things like: "That thing John wrote was unbelievable. It was 100 pages long and he expected us to read every word!" or "We didn't look at anything from Mary's last project, but then the screen didn't really work the way we needed it to. Hmm—maybe we should have looked at it." or "That consultant who was here last year—what was his name—Kevin? He drew a really great flowchart of our whole process and then highlighted in red the areas that were going to change. We all really liked that. I still have it tacked to my office wall!" These types of statements, while ignored by 99% of the corporate population, are like gold to the BA. They hold clues to what the stakeholders liked and what they did not. Success breeds success, so if Kevin was successful, take advantage of his technique and use it. Listen especially to your business stakeholders as to what approaches have worked well for them and then work to integrate these into the overall development approach. The whole point here is to stress excellent communication. BAs need to communicate in the most efficient way possible such that end-user expectations are clear and development is actively aligned to delivering the value-based expectations that best fit the organization's goals.

Technical Architecture

Know your organization's standards and basic architecture.

While it is useful to understand methodologies by considering the systems development process, successful BAs, whether they report to groups within IT or outside IT in the business areas, need to understand the overall structural design of IT—the technical architecture. The software development process is a piece of the overall architecture. Like enterprise architecture (discussed in Chapter 3), knowing the components, capabilities, and structure of an organization's IT is almost more powerful than knowing how each of those components work. The overall enterprise architecture is the top level of technical architecture that helps define principles, standards, and models used by the entire organization. A BA who has to work with any technology should understand the enterprise and technical environment.

There are many components that make up an information system. The foundation of an information system is often referred to as its architecture. This is a great way to describe the design and construction of a system because people can visualize a building's architecture. A BA does not need to understand every possible component or architecture that is available. They need to understand that information systems are made up of a group of objects or components that work together to accomplish a goal. These components may be built by an internal development team or by an outsourced team, purchased or acquired and used as-is, customized, rented or leased, or accessed remotely. The interconnection between these components is much of what makes an information system so complex. Each component interfaces with others and expects the others to perform. Many of the components are very small and on their own do not appear to do anything or have much of a purpose. When combined with other components, however, they provide powerful functionality. The advent of more and more independent, reusable components makes systems development faster. Developers can use pieces of code from various sources and combine them into a new, working product. A simple analogy would be the inventory of a hardware store. Each customer who shops at the store may buy a different combination of parts, lumber, and fasteners, and then go home to build a completely different product. There is an infinite number of products that can be built with the technology components that are available.

One of the important things to understand about the technical architecture is that there is no *one* common design. Each organization's technical architecture has evolved over the organization's history and is unique. Often, there are many different brands and versions of hardware, networking software, operating systems, communication systems, and packages all running simultaneously to support the organization's goals. BAs should consult with IT architects at the beginning and throughout planning of their projects to discuss the feasibility of solution options. BAs who are aware of the complex web of old and new technical components will make more intelligent recommendations and more clearly communicate the possible ramifications of changes to their business stakeholders.

When looking at technical architecture, the elements that are important for a BA to consider include:

- IT governance
- Information architecture
- Data architecture
- IT risk management and security architecture
- Systems architecture
- Application architecture

IT governance includes the rules or oversight of the IT strategy of the organization. It helps align changes to the enterprise architecture and business strategy. It is important for a BA to focus on the rules and decision-making processes that the governance team uses versus the people who help ensure governance is followed, as this plays greatly into the solutions that IT teams can deliver and can even be the deciding factor on funding.

When discussing information architecture, BAs focus on what information is being used and by whom. Information structures are then put in place to enable the use of this information. How is information organized, accessed, reused, and leveraged in the organization? An IT system should be built to enable the use of the organization's information. And this leads even further into data architecture. Here, BAs focus on how the data needs to be structured so it is not only used, but leveraged and reused across the organization. Data silos are very big issues today that can be easily overcome by technical solutions that are built with smart architectural designs and will bring great value to stakeholders who are using the data.

> "BAs focus on what information is being used and by whom."

IT risk and security are growing areas of increasing demands as technology becomes a bigger part of business. A BA must understand how the organization views risk from the IT perspective and its posture for addressing and managing risk. Understanding the risk tolerance levels and how an organization plans to respond to IT risk are key inputs on design solutions and can limit or expand the options available. This applies especially to the security architecture that the organization puts in place. Consider the policies, processes, controls, and security models that are used by the organization. What approach is utilized? What is never allowed and what is always allowed? Like risk, the security structure for an organization exists to protect and enable the organization, not hinder it; so a BA needs to understand what is in place and why in order to support the organization and keep it safe with smart technical solutions.

Knowing how the organization views systems and application architectures is critical for any BA who is working with developing and changing systems and applications. Applications are simpler and provide functionality to the users and the organization. A BA working with application teams needs to understand not only what languages are used, but how the developers reuse elements, create features, compartmentalize their work, and approach testing. Systems architecture looks at how applications and other technologies work together to automate and deliver business value. Applications do not always operate by themselves—they sometimes need services to enable them. Understanding the core operational technologies that enable data processing and automation and support the day-to-day technologies plays into technology designs for successful solutions.

As much as knowing the technology structure is key to solution designs, make sure you do not lose sight of the purpose and value that these technology solutions need to provide. It can help to know the background of solutions, how long ago they were created, and why. So much is changing not only with technical environments but also business goals and perspectives that the original goal may no longer apply—so is the technology still providing a solution? Yet, knowing how all of the technology is related and connected helps to understand why *legacy* technology is often very costly (both in time and resources) to replace or upgrade. You should reconsider outdated technology if there are options and value to update it while delivering needed change. Most IT organizations have an architectural *road map* that describes their long-term strategy for building and maintaining systems. Learn as much as you can about this plan and understand how the current change or project is delivering as part of that overall plan.

Key Technology Terms

Much like understanding the software development process without necessarily knowing how to program, a BA also needs to know key technology components in order to understand the risks and impacts of decisions made around technology solutions.

Operating Systems

An operating system (or OS) manages computer resources and provides applications with an interface to access those resources. A BA needs to be aware of the operating systems used in their organization. Common operating systems are Microsoft Windows®, Linux, Mac OS X®, and Solaris. This knowledge is important on projects where the operating system becomes part of the requirements. For example, when searching for packaged or commercial off-the-shelf (COTS) software applications, the vendor response to a request for proposal (RFP) must specify the operating system(s) on which the package runs.

Operating systems are occasionally changed or upgraded. Operating system changes are usually prompted by the increased functionality available in the new version. These changes are often implemented in a project referred to as an infrastructure project, which implements changes to the underlying IT architecture to improve system characteristics (performance, security, reliability, and expandability). Ideally, the infrastructure changes are transparent to business users, and because of this assumption, business analysis professionals are often not assigned to these projects. This is unfortunate because many times infrastructure changes do impact end users. A simple change, like a new system menu for example, impacts business workers and should be communicated before the change is made. Encourage your management to include business analysis in all infrastructure projects. A BA is the best person to assess the impact of a change on the business community. The BA can communicate changes to the business and prepare users for any possible issues.

Networking

A computer network is an interconnected set of computers. This simple definition belies the complexity of the networking systems used in most organizations. A network of computers is created using a sophisticated combination of hardware, operating systems, networking software, and communication protocols. There are many different types of networks: LAN (local area network), WAN (wide area network), intranet (internal closed network), extranet (internal network with controlled access by outside parties), and internet (an interconnection among or between public, private, commercial, industrial, or governmental networks). There are IT professionals who specialize in setting up and maintaining networks. These professionals should be consulted on any projects that will utilize networking. Business analysis professionals should be aware of potential networking changes and work with the IT professionals to learn about the ramifications for the project and, most important, the business environment.

Data Management

Every successful organization in the world needs information—and a lot of it. Organizations especially need reliable data to make intelligent decisions about launching a new product (e.g., knowing the characteristics of potential customers). They must adhere to government regulations by being able to report financial statistics along with descriptions of where those numbers come from. Organizations that wish to offer useful employee benefits need to know important data about their families. But how do organizations efficiently keep track of all of this information? BAs must understand the importance of data, how it is stored, and more important, how it is accessed.

While a fundamental understanding of the types of databases and how they are constructed is valuable, BAs often need to understand the wider view of data that includes topics such as data governance, business intelligence, data analytics, and artificial intelligence. First, knowing general background information on these topics and why businesses should even care about them is critical to solution designs. However, as you learn the organization, work to understand the organization's approach to data management. Are there centralized data warehouses that are used by the entire enterprise? Are there databases all over the place for every system that was created? Is there a data governance group that meets regularly? Maybe you should ask to join a meeting or two to learn more.

For information that will help to focus on these data management concerns, you should ask questions such as:

- Who owns the data? How is this ownership maintained?
- How is the data used? Why is it maintained?
- What volume of data is expected?
- What is the data's *golden* source? In how many places is this data stored?
- How is data mapped after a merger or acquisition?
- How will data be converted from a legacy system to a new web application?
- How often does data change?
- How often is data in the data warehouse refreshed? Is real-time data needed?

Only when the data is accurate, accessible, and understood can it be leveraged into solutions that drive greater value than simply remaining artifacts of older systems.

> "Only when the data is accurate, accessible, and understood can it be leveraged."

Cloud Technologies

Today's environments—both inside and outside of the business—often leverage cloud technologies. In simple terms, this references the ability to have your data, services, applications, and other technologies hosted by a service provider that are then accessed via the Internet. Again, the BA is not required to know how all of it works or is programmed; however, cloud technologies offer significant advantages over traditional in-house management of technologies that are important to decision makers. BAs must be familiar with the concept of scalability and how this works with cloud services. Cloud services often give organizations the option to *pay for use*. This means you pay for what you need; if you need more then you get more (and are charged for it). If you need less, then you get less (and likewise enjoy a cost savings). The flexibility to scale remains very dynamic and on-demand.

Real World Example: Using Cloud Technologies

An organization hosts their own website. This means there are servers, databases, networking, security, and content all managed by the organization. As the organization improved the content of the website, the website traffic increased. The more the traffic increased, the more the IT team had to respond in order to address any connectivity issues (i.e., ensure no latency) and storage space for all of the new content. After a year of getting set up, marketing decided to streamline the content and really scaled back the amount of content used and leveraged applications and other services that could be linked rather than directly placed on the website. The IT team kept asking marketing if they could delete the old databases of content in order to free up room that could be used for their other applications. If not, they would have to keep buying more servers.

The decision was made to migrate the website hosting to a cloud services provider. The provider would host the website, ensure that there were no latency issues, manage content storage, and provide other services that aligned with the organization's IT governance. Now the marketing team could add, remove, and change content whenever their business needs desired. The service provider was responsible for ensuring there was space allocated for use and then billed the organization based on usage. The IT team preferred this solution because they no longer had to set aside server and database space for marketing just in case they needed more.

There are benefits and challenges to any technology. As you read the example you might wonder why everyone does not choose a cloud service provider to help with their technology needs. Consider an organization that does not want to put their valuable information out on the Internet where it may be more exposed. Hosting providers often maximize space by storing multiple clients' data on the same server. The hosting provider must then ensure no data leakage across clients. The organization has to trust the hosting provider for securing their information and validating no loss of data or inaccurate access. The flexibility gained with cloud solutions is often balanced by many security considerations.

As with the other technologies, understand the pros and cons of solutions and the key features they offer organizations today. This is the best approach to supporting the organization rather than learning specifically how to build and connect the technology yourself. Understand software-as-a-service (SaaS), infrastructure-as-a-service (IaaS), and platform-as-a-service (PaaS) and how organizations are using them today, including if there are requirements around high demand and availability. BAs should also review *edge computing*, which uses a distributed model of cloud computing that brings the information and its use and processing closer to the source. This addresses issues such as latency and other cloud concerns to drive more functionality. These are shifts in IT approaches that are quickly bringing benefits to organizations, but only if they are fully considered and integrated with the organization's technology strategy.

Virtualization

Another trend in technology that BAs need to understand is the concept of virtualization. This has added tremendous capabilities for organizations while providing significant cost savings. In simplest terms, every employee at an organization no longer needs a physical personal computer (PC) individually set up for that user's needs with specific software. A computer is virtualized so that while there is a monitor, keyboard, and other peripherals, the actual terminal is connected to the organization's network. It looks like you are logging into a computer, but you are actually logging into a hosted view of a computer. You are granted access to the software and systems that you need based on your user login. This is beneficial because you can then log into any terminal across the organization and it will seem as though you are sitting at your own desk. All the virtual computers are hosted from a single source that IT manages. There is less hardware to maintain and new computers can be *created* in a matter of minutes, fully configured and ready to go without having to buy any new equipment. Of course, the infrastructure and operations support staff needs to be in place to support this kind of approach. Small organizations may not find it worth the time if every individual has their own desk and does not move around very often. However, understanding the power of what this type of technology can provide to the organization is critical as organizations shift to providing more services rather than providing physical equipment.

Mobile Technologies

Many professionals today work in a mobile environment. They may have an office, but they go to clients' sites. Teams are virtual and work from varied locations, yet all access the same company knowledge and systems. BAs must know and be familiar with the infrastructure and networking that is required in order to allow this seamless access. They must understand how teams can work remotely by utilizing virtual private networks (VPNs) along with the security requirements involved to allow the access while ensuring the integrity of systems and data. It is also important to learn the reason why IT may not allow an application, system, or data to be accessible off the premises of the company. Security serves a purpose that is meant to be balanced with business need and value. Include in your understanding of mobility items such as speech recognition, facial recognition, and other technology features that were often back end, security features only for those most heavily-invested IT customers. These features are now in the hands of the employees and customers as a capability, not a simple support

> "Security serves a purpose that is meant to be balanced with business need and value."

mechanism. This is an area where BAs need to truly understand the implications of both sides of the technology. Consider that almost all of the users whom you work with (business owners, technologists, and end customers) have personal mobile technologies they use daily in their lives already. A challenge for BAs is that business owners and users often expect their work technology to function and operate in the same manner in which they use their personal mobile technology. While this is a great user-centered design perspective, there are risks and costs that must be considered when it comes to how the organization accesses information and what it takes to enable the technology. Obviously, there are a great number of ways that users can approach the technology and gain value. However, understand the architecture that it takes to deliver mobile technologies since this is important for valuable solution designs.

Real World Example: Mobile Application Development

A financial institution wanted a mobile application or *app*. While the requirements for the intended use were easily captured from the business area, an understanding of the organization's infrastructure, technology capabilities, and approaches to mobile development were required to help the team design the best solution approach. The requirements were clearly captured from the business perspective and sent out in an RFP from multiple vendors.

The project team then experienced sticker shock when the proposals came rolling in on how to best approach the application. They could not believe the cost that was being asked for the creation of the app. The funny thing was—the quotes were all very similar because they all approached the development utilizing native apps. This meant a separate app was being built for each mobile device that the app was intended to be used on, so that it would provide the functionality in the manner as described by the business. The business had wanted a very large number of smart devices to be able to access the app, so each designated device required a custom build.

As the BA, I sat down with the developers and shared the concerns on the costs. And, like the business owners who asked me, I asked them why it was so expensive versus how I viewed the apps I used on my smartphones—apps that were simple and seemed available regardless of device. Here is where I learned how the decisions on design and appearance of an app were affected by the device. The developers could not guarantee that the app would look as the business wanted it to because it was not dynamically adjusting content based on the type of device being used. If that is what the business wanted, then the approach to development could be changed. They explained an HTML solution that allowed the app to instantly be available on any device that could get on the Internet. Since they only had to make one app now, the costs were significantly reduced. However, they explained that certain features would not work with this new proposed HTML solution since the app would not be a *native* app that was built to leverage the platform of the device. I had to explain the balance of cost versus functionality/user experience back to the business for them to make their decision. When I did present the options, I had to be comfortable with explaining the different technology approaches and what it meant to the end users and support teams. So, while I was not doing the development or programming work myself, I had to be aware of what the technology options were and how they worked. I could then articulate the infrastructure questions that were greatly impacting the quotes and functionality that the business was receiving.

Technology Usability

The BA plays a key role when considering how to best use technology to create a solution that meets business needs. And the BA needs to ensure these needs are met with the best possible solution regardless of how "exciting" or simple the technology may seem.

Usability is about ease of use. Think about how easily a person can use a tool to achieve a particular goal. The "tool" in this case is technology. It is important for BAs to understand some core principles of technology usability to help design ease of use *into* solutions. These tools help you focus on the end users and how to position solutions that solve their needs while providing business value. User-centered design (UCD) is one approach that helps increase usability. UCD is particularly helpful in technology solutions because it focuses on the user of the technology throughout all stages of development. A lot of work today focuses on user experience (UX) to create value-adding solutions. Understanding how users are going to interact, evolve, and leverage the technology early on in development allows for the creation of better solutions later.

If your organization employs usability professionals, request their involvement on your change efforts as early as you can. If possible, include them in requirements elicitation so that they can learn about the business needs and the business environment as you do. If your organization expects usability design as part of the role of the BA, you will need to learn about the principles and concepts. See *Additional Reading and References* at the end of the chapter for some great resources.

Considering that UX is always key to solution development, the BA needs to understand the impact these usability decisions have on the technology and overall solution. While a business may want something faster or with less issues, the question often comes up as to whether or not it is worth the cost. Continue to present the business case when making decisions where the value for each option is clearly articulated with risks and impacts.

Testing

One reason why you need to understand the technical environment is that you will probably be involved in testing solutions. Even if not directly involved, successful business analysis professionals appreciate the importance of quality assurance practices and are able to step in and help when necessary.

Understanding the testing process helps with requirements elicitation and analysis. The BA must make sure that each requirement is *testable* or *verifiable*. The classic example of a requirement that is hard to test is "the system should be easy to use." There is not a straightforward test that could be designed to validate this requirement. When an analyst thinks about how each requirement will be tested, they write much more detailed, precise requirements. The experienced analyst also considers performance requirements when helping to design a solution. Specific performance requirements must be elicited by the analyst even though they will often be difficult for SMEs and users to articulate. Have questions and examples ready to help users determine their performance tolerance:

- If the query request was returned within 30 seconds, would you be satisfied? Let us sit here quietly for 30 seconds to see what that much time feels like.
- Would 45 seconds be too long?
- Would you accept a system that returned short, simple queries in an average of 15 seconds, while complex queries might take up to 60 seconds?

Understanding what the users and customers are willing to accept is a key link between requirements and the technology solution since it defines the acceptance criteria that is necessary to articulate user expectations.

BAs are often involved in test planning and in designing realistic, useful test cases. When the requirements are written well, it is easier to leverage acceptance criteria, use cases, and scenarios to create descriptive and valuable test cases (see Chapter 6). BAs are also considered key team members in testing as defects are found and corrected. This should feel natural to BAs, who often enjoy problem solving. Since BAs understand the requirements and the solution design, they often are quick to understand whether a test case that "failed" was due to a defect (the system does not perform as designed) or a missed requirement (system performs as designed but the user expectation was not captured as a requirement). BAs help with troubleshooting and root cause identification as well—clarifying the steps that are necessary to address the issue along with the risks and impacts associated with the issue.

There are different schools of thought when it comes to a BA's role in testing. Some organizations will have a testing team where the BA can simply hand off requirements. Others expect the BA to write and then actually execute the testing of each scenario, even with the risks involved when a person performs the testing on their own test cases (missed issues or opportunities due to lack of objectivity). BAs needs to realize the organization's approach to testing prior to implementation. They must know at which stages or phases the solutions are tested *before* they are ever released to the end customer, and then consider how the requirements are driving the test cases and plans. How are test cases created and validated prior to executing? What are the considerations needed for testing, and which types of testing are done? Do not be afraid to ask the organization to bring in help with testing—from the creation to the verification to the execution and validation. Often deciding how much effort, energy, and resources are necessary for testing can be determined by asking the decision makers to answer the question: "Do you want your customers to find the defect first or your own internal team?" And testing is not just about finding issues; it is also about seeing opportunities that could be leveraged as part of implementation or in the near-term future. There might be ways to gain more value from solution designs that were not thought about previously. For example, an end user who is testing time-tracking software may try to filter by certain projects and tasks to report on time spent. While the software originally focused on giving departmental teams the oversight of where their teams were working, the new perspective to think from a project and portfolio viewpoint gives the development team a new angle to consider how their solution can deliver organizational value. Understanding how testing can be of value before, during, *and* after implementation is key to helping a business analyst continue to deliver value.

Software Testing Phases

Most of the software development testing approaches that are used today are based on the standards set by the Institute of Electrical and Electronics Engineers (IEEE). This professional organization dates back to 1884 and has a lot of experience and knowledge from which to draw. What software developers discovered early is that testing software applications is similar to testing electronics products. Each individual component is tested separately (unit testing), then connections between pieces are tested (integration testing), and then an entire product is tested together (system testing). Finally, the product is tested by end users—user acceptance testing, commonly referred to as UAT—to allow them to be confident that the product does what they need. One of the reasons why use case descriptions (see Chapter 6) have become such a popular analysis technique is that a use case leads directly to a test case.

Even if they are not directly responsible for planning and executing tests, every BA should understand common testing phases and practices. When a project's solution is in the testing phase, the BA should be closely involved. As tests are executed and defects found, the BA is a great resource to help determine the cause of the defects and to help with ideas for correcting them. Some of the problems found will require business stakeholders to make decisions, and the BA can help with these. The BA should also be watching for results that were caused by poor requirements. BAs can significantly improve their elicitation and analysis skills by learning from prior mistakes. Look upon these mistakes as lessons learned.

Unit Testing

Unit testing is usually the first level of testing and is performed by the developer. A unit is a small piece of the system that can be tested individually. The objective of unit testing is to find problems in the smallest component of a system before testing the system in its entirety. BAs may assist developers by identifying test cases and reviewing unit test results.

Integration Testing

The next level or phase of testing is referred to as integration testing. Integration testing requires the individually tested units to be integrated and tested as a larger unit or subsystem. The objective of integration testing is to find problems in how components of a system work together. These tests validate the software architecture design. The development team or quality assurance team are often the people who perform integration testing. BAs may assist by identifying test cases and reviewing test results. Inadequate integration testing, often due to waiting too late in the development process, is one of the main causes of project failure.

System Testing

The next level or phase of testing is called system testing. System testing is the last chance for a project team to verify a product before turning it over to users for their review. The objective of system testing is to find problems in how the solution meets the users' needs within the entire system that the solution operates. These tests validate that the solution meets the original requirements. BAs are involved with system testing by making sure that the solution meets business requirements.

Regression Testing

Regression testing is a specific type of testing with which a BA must be familiar. The concept is simple: after any system change, retest the functions of the system that have not been changed to make sure they still work. As simple as the concept is, it is one of the biggest areas of failure in the testing discipline. Why? Because who wants to test something that has already been tested? It is not glamorous or exciting, it often does not expose any defects or quality enhancements, and it can be very tedious and boring. Having acknowledged these issues, regression testing must be done because it is often the easiest way to catch unknown issues with the overall system. Technology solutions can frequently be very complex, and a small change can easily break something that was previously working fine. Regression testing is performed throughout all of the other testing phases when changes are made after the initial testing has been completed. And this is exactly why it is so valuable to build traceability and reusability into all of your requirements. Those requirements, acceptance criteria, test cases, and results that you did the first time the system was rolled out can then be quickly reused on all future change efforts that involve the system. Requirements that drive solutions last well beyond the scope of the project because they represent the scope of the solution.

UAT

Most BAs are involved in UAT—the final phase of testing. Users test real-life scenarios to verify that the system will meet their needs. UAT is an important step in validating that the end solution meets business needs. This conformance testing is named as such because the intention is that the users of the system will run the tests and accept the product. As systems continue to become more complex and less procedural, testing becomes more complex. Testing systems is challenging for even the most experienced quality assurance professionals. If it is difficult for them, think about how overwhelming it may seem to users. This complexity is why many organizations ask BAs to get involved. Typically, when technical solutions are sold outside of the organization, UAT is referred to as beta testing and allows users to try out a new version of the solution before its general release.

Why should users do UAT? Ideally, users are executing tests as they would expect to do with the solution in production. UAT builds the users' confidence that the solution does what they hoped it would do. Unfortunately, assigning a BA to this task often gives users the idea that the end users do not have to participate. They feel that they have told the BA all of their requirements, so the BA should be able to accept the software. Do not allow this to happen. Losing stakeholder engagement at this critical junction in a project may create dissatisfaction with the solution being implemented. This is a dangerous situation and one that every BA should work to avoid. There are several common reasons why this occurs—a few are listed here:

1. Users, like everyone else, are very busy. If they think that the BA can do the work for them, they will be happy to let him or her do it.
2. Testing is hard work, and most users have never been trained in how or why they are doing it. No one likes doing something that they do not really know how to do well.
3. Users often do not realize the likelihood of errors in developed technical solutions. This is not a negative statement about developers; it is a fact that the process of developing systems is difficult and that discovering defects is a normal part of the process. Users may not be aware of the risk if a defect is not found.
4. Finally, users do not realize the significant impending change that the system will have on their work environment and they need to get prepared. When users actually work with the system during UAT, they realize how their corresponding procedures are going to have to change.

As the users interact with the system during UAT, updates to processes and procedures should be captured so that the transition to full use in production is much smoother. Everyone utilizing the system should understand how it will affect their respective work.

Although there are a few obstacles to overcome when trying to get users more involved with UAT, the benefits are enormous. Users who actually participate in UAT are usually more satisfied with the end product than those who do not. They are not shocked by the change after deployment, but rather are gently prodded toward the change during UAT. Users who are committed to the entire software development process are more likely to get the product they need (Kupersmith 2007).

Post-Implementation User Assessment

Post-implementation user assessment is an evaluation of the effectiveness of the system after it has been thoroughly used in the business area. This is an important part of the testing life cycle, but it is often missed. The objective of post-implementation user assessment is to find out how well the solution meets user requirements. BAs, project managers (PMs), and/or quality assurance analysts perform the assessment by observing users at their jobs, asking well-designed questions, and holding other elicitation sessions once the solution is put into production.

The real proof of whether a system fulfills the needs of the business area will only come as it is being used. This is the final validation. After training and a settling-in period, BAs should discuss with users the usefulness of the system. BAs may also take measurements to determine if the system is performing as expected and to determine if the original objectives of the project were met.

If you are doing project-based work, be sure to discuss this type of testing with your PM and the impact to the overall project schedule and resources. Many PMs consider that once the solution is accepted in production by the business, the project is essentially done. Or there may be a pre-determined period of two weeks, for example, for any issues to be addressed after the system *goes live*. The BA may need to emphasize that it is necessary to make time to validate the solution after it has been released to users. Even if there is some time given for post-implementation assessment as part of the project-based work, BAs should always continue to have their enterprise view of solutions and look at the solution well after the project concludes. Understand that any issues or challenges found beyond the project might need business case justification and consideration as to whether to start a new change initiative to take advantage of the opportunity or address the uncovered issue. This is why the analysis work for a BA is never quite done. They are always interested to know how solutions are performing and where more value could be gained.

WORKING WITH IT

BAs in the past have been key for the successful communication of business areas and IT. Many IT professionals appreciate BAs learning the technology so that there are successful and open discussions with the project and business teams. Like any other stakeholder, understanding IT's role, purpose, approaches, and area of expertise, along with building trust and open communication, are vital. The same consideration should go into explaining your role as the BA and how you plan to approach requirements elicitation, documentation, and the hand off to the technology teams for implementation. You want to encourage an idea-generation discussion with these technology experts so that the best possible business solutions can be considered. Clearly articulate what you will and also what you will not deliver. If your role is supporting the business operations more than technology, you may need to be clear regarding the level of detail at which your business requirements will be. For example, business requirements may not have enough information for technology teams to design the solution. It is then important to have a plan to handle this type of situation. Or if your BA role reports to technology in the organization, then you may be expected to deliver very detailed technical requirements from which the developers can instantly start to build the solution.

Work with the developers to encourage them to review requirements by walking through your requirements with them—helping them to see that they are getting useful information. If the developers are not accustomed to using or working from requirements, you may want to give them a small piece of a requirement, schedule a walk-through over the phone or in person, and lead them through the document. You may want to present a use case or a subset of the data model. As you walk through the document, section by section, ask if they have questions or comments, and do not be afraid to ask them what they would want to see that would help them move forward. Too many analysts worry about writing, re-writing, and over-analyzing their requirements rather than simply sharing the requirements they have already or flat out asking the developers what is needed. As the developers begin to develop the system and come back to you with questions, point them back to the document if a question is one that you have already addressed. You want to get them in the habit of looking at the requirements artifacts when they have questions. As they begin to see that you have already thought about things like exceptions and alternate paths, they will become more confident in your documents and more willing to read them (see also *Review Sessions* in Chapter 7).

Most developers are creative and enjoy offering suggestions. Whenever possible, ask developers for ideas within the limitations of the requirements. This is another reason why written requirements are so useful. If you give a developer clear guidelines within which he or she can be creative, you will often get a great design. When not given clear boundaries, a developer may create something that looks great but cannot be used because it does not meet user needs. This can be discouraging for the developer. Be specific about the functionality that is needed and the business rules that must be adhered to but you do not necessarily have to worry about providing every last tiny detail.

Some developers will be interested in understanding why the business needs a particular function, while other developers will be satisfied just to build it. For developers who ask why, share business information. This will help them better understand the reason for their work and often make them more committed team members. For developers who are not interested in understanding the business reasons for a function, do not give them too much information. Many developers are very *black or white*: "Do you want the source data field converted to a data field called Lead Source? Yes or no?" Answer questions directly and concisely. A three-paragraph dissertation on what a source is and how the business people use sources to generate more business is too much information for many developers. Working with the IT teams is no different than any other business partner or stakeholder though. Understand roles and capabilities and work together with team members on how to best deliver solutions that provide lasting value well beyond the immediate change effort.

SUMMARY OF KEY POINTS

Effective BAs understand technology concepts and constraints. They can talk intelligently with technical stakeholders when discussing solution options just as they do with business owners. They appreciate the complexity of the IT environment and properly set user expectations:

- Excellent BAs must be constantly vigilant for new opportunities to use technology so that they can assist with their implementation to better benefit the business. Read about new technology in blogs, vendor white papers, and product reviews. Subscribe to online magazines and communities and review articles frequently.

- Technology is changing every day in new and unpredictable ways. It is very exciting, but it can be very intimidating and overwhelming to try to stay on top of everything. Focus on key topic areas, not the specific software or hardware that is implemented, but rather the type and the purpose—and most important, how it drives value for an organization.
- It is important for BAs to understand the development methodologies and their requirements deliverables that are used in an organization. Knowing what approach the change effort should take to ensure effectiveness and efficiency is a key element of BA planning.
- Business analysis professionals do not necessarily need to understand the underlying details of the technology infrastructure, how it was created, or how it is maintained; however, they must know key terms in order to communicate with IT architects, developers, data managers, and infrastructure support personnel.

BIBLIOGRAPHY

Beck, K. et al. (2001). *The Agile Manifesto*. http://agilemanifesto.org/.

The Business Analyst Job Description. (2018). "Key Skills that Every Business Analyst Must Know." http://thebusinessanalystjobdescription.com/key-skills-that-every-business-analyst-must-know/.

Carkenord, B. (2007). "How Does a BA Add Value to an Agile Project?" *B2T Training*: Fall 2007. www.b2ttraining.com.

Code Academy. (2018). "MVC: Model, View, Controller." https://www.codecademy.com/articles/mvc.

DAMA International. (2017). *DAMA-DMBOK: Data Management Body of Knowledge. 2nd Ed*. Technics Publications: Denville, NJ.

International Institute of Business Analysis (IIBA) and the Agile Alliance. (2017). *Agile Extension to the BABOK® Guide*. IIBA: Toronto, Ontario, Canada.

Kienitz, P. (2017, February 27). "The pros and cons of Waterfall Software Development." DCSL Software. https://www.dcslsoftware.com/pros-cons-waterfall-software-development/.

Leyton, Ryland. (2015). *The Agile Business Analyst: Moving from Waterfall to Agile*. Leyton Publishing.

McConnell, Steve. (1996). *Rapid Development: Taming Wild Software Schedules*. Microsoft Press: Redmond, WA..

Project Management Institute (PMI). (2017). *Agile Practice Guide*. PMI: Newtown Square, PA.

Royce, Walker. (1998). *Software Project Management: A Unified Framework. Addison-Wesley Object Technology Series*. Addison-Wesley Professional: New York, NY.

Spacey, J. (2018, March 13). "12 Types of IT Architecture." *Simplicable*. https://simplicable.com/new/it-architecture.

Wood, Jane and Denise Silver. (1995). *Joint Application Development. 2nd Ed*. John Wiley: Hoboken, NJ.

ADDITIONAL READING AND REFERENCES

Agile Business Consortium. (2018). https://www.agilebusiness.org/business-agility.

Brown, T. (2009). *Change by Design: How Design Thinking Transforms Organizations and Inspires Innovation*. HarperCollins Publishers: New York, NY.

The Business Agility Institute. (2018). https://businessagility.institute/.

DAMA International. (2018). *The Global Data Management Community*. https://dama.org/.

Gartner. (2017, October 4). "Gartner Identifies the Top 10 Strategic Technology Trends for 2018." https://www.gartner.com/en/newsroom/press-releases/2017-10-04-gartner-identifies-the-top-10-strategic-technology-trends-for-2018.

Hasuman, K. and S. Cook. (2010). IT Architecture for Dummies. *For Dummies Publishing*.

IASA. (2018). "What Is Architecture. An Association for All IT Architects." https://iasaglobal.org/itabok/what-is-it-architecture/.

IEEE. (2018). "Advancing Technology for Humanity." www.ieee.org.

Kupersmith, K. (2007). "Putting the User Back in User Acceptance Testing." *The Bridge Magazine*, B2T Training. Fall 2007.

The Scaled Agile. (2018). *Scaled Agile Framework (SAFe®)*. https://www.scaledagileframework.com.

Schwaber, K. and J. Sutherland. (2017). *The Scrum Guide™*. Attribution Share-Alike License of Creative Commons.

Scrum.org. (2018). https://www.scrum.org/.

Unger, R. and C. Chandler. (2017). *A Project Guide to UX Design: For User Experience Designers in the Field or in the Making. 2nd Ed.* New Riders: Indianapolis, IN.

Unified Modeling Language™ (UML®). (2018). www.uml.org.

U.S. Department of Health & Human Services. (2018). *Usability.gov*. https://www.usability.gov/.

User Experience Professionals Association (UXPA). 2018. https://uxpa.org/.

CHAPTER 6

YOUR SIXTH STEP—KNOW YOUR REQUIREMENTS ANALYSIS TECHNIQUES

Business analysis professionals spend the majority of their time working with requirements: eliciting requirements from business stakeholders to understand needs, analyzing requirements for teams to use, presenting requirements to business stakeholders for acceptance criteria and decision making, and reviewing requirements with solution teams for execution. Presenting requirements refers to communicating them to the appropriate stakeholder in the most appropriate format. Business stakeholders must review and confirm business requirements before they are used to design solutions. Depending on the individual business stakeholders, the appropriate presentation may be a formal requirements package or a working simulation of the potential software. Information technology (IT) architect stakeholders and solution designers must review functional requirements to understand the needs of the business and the desired solution functionality. These stakeholders may prefer to see requirements in diagrams or models that mirror system design specifications. Developers must review technical requirements and specifications to build the solution. They often utilize prototypes of screens, report layouts, and use case descriptions that show expected user interaction with the system. Any of these requirements may be presented formally in a traditional requirements package or informally in a slide presentation or handwritten on flip charts or whiteboards in small group discussions. The business analysis professional makes decisions about how to best analyze, understand, and communicate requirements to best support the business goals and values.

Because requirements are so important, every project team should understand and agree upon what a requirement is and how requirements will be expressed and presented. This chapter discusses planning requirements elicitation and analysis, the categorization and management of requirements, useful analysis and presentation techniques, and the criteria for deciding the formality of their presentation. As different techniques are discussed, take special note of the visual communication tools as well. These include diagrams, models, prototypes, simulation, tables, and more. Know your stakeholders and how they respond (or sometimes do not) and consider *showing* your requirements and what they mean as opposed to just *telling* people the requirements. The BA's (business analyst's) role is to work with stakeholders to deliver the business solutions. While the BA may be tasked with doing the work, remember that the ownership is on the stakeholders; thus the BA must ensure they not only understand but also own the resulting requirements and solution designs. To re-emphasize—a requirement is a "usable representation of a need" (IIBA 2015), not a want or demand. Requirements help to break down and deliver how the organization will gain value from the change effort or project. The requirement itself does not deliver the change. The BA works with the requirements in order to move efforts forward, regardless of the approach or where in the change effort they are used.

And while only a subset of the possible techniques and approaches are presented here, know that there is no wrong or right way of truly using any techniques. There are best practices that are best for that time, in that context, with those stakeholders, and with the information that was available to that BA. Does that mean it will work for you? Perhaps. The *right* or *best* technique to use is the one that works. What approach do you need to move the change effort to the next step? What do stakeholders need to do to keep the project moving forward? The purpose of each technique will be highlighted because the common issues that junior BAs face is that they often use a good technique for a different purpose. Planning and prioritizing the analysis that is needed and determining which techniques might be the most successful in order to deliver the need is almost more important than the time spent on the actual requirements analysis. *Best* techniques are the techniques that deliver value while moving changes forward and supporting organizational structure. There is no wrong way to *analyze* or *think*. These techniques are simply tools to help the analyst see a problem or situation from a different perspective. Most change efforts and projects will benefit from the use of several techniques.

> "The right technique to use is the one that works."

BEGINNING YOUR REQUIREMENTS ANALYSIS

Planning Requirements Analysis Work

Before jumping right into eliciting and analyzing requirements, a BA analyzes the work to be completed and what the scope of the requirements work needs to be. What level of requirements is needed for the effort? Are there any requirements that are already gathered? Are there only unconfirmed business requirements that need to be reviewed and validated before even considering getting the technical experts involved? Does the scope of the work involve business areas or solutions that already have captured detailed requirements that could be reused so that the BA only has to define the requirements for the specific elements affected by the changes? What about the project approach? If the project has tight timelines, then a traditional approach to requirements may be best. Is the team working with offshore developers who lay out work by sprints or iterations where a more agile and adaptive approach to requirements should be taken? Even if the BA is doing an informal task on their own, he or she should communicate these questions and decisions with the project or change team. The approach to requirements elicitation and analysis will affect the schedule and budget of the overall effort.

Also, the BA should analyze the stakeholders who would be possible sources of information from whom to elicit requirements. Identify what types of information you hope to get from them. Is it general awareness of how a process works? If so, then you might use some process mapping skills. If it is feedback and input on requirements, then planning document review sessions with the stakeholders might be most appropriate. You should also consider the other elements of the stakeholders during this analysis. If the stakeholders are distributed, do you meet with them one-on-one? And if the team is virtual, what technology can you leverage to still obtain your results? Again, these decisions often not only affect the stakeholders you work with but they also affect timelines and budgets to deliver the expected value to the business.

Planning becomes even more important to consider prior to starting any work because BAs often have to deal with a lot of information when doing requirements. Where are you going to put all this

information? Much of it is given to you verbally, but additionally you will receive e-mail messages, documents, forms, example reports, files, old requirements documents, and much more. One of your critical skills as a BA is the
ability to organize all of this information, consider its importance to your project, and maintain it in a retrievable, usable form. You are effectively considered
the repository for the project or change efforts' requirements. You will want to
expand your repository beyond documented words. Consider process maps, a
prototype of a screen layout, scenarios described, and user stories. Your requirements packages or deliverables consist of whatever artifacts you can create to
help the organization define the needs in such a way that teams can implement valuable solutions. Planning how to manage, organize, and continually leverage your hard work well beyond the current change
effort constantly promotes the true value of the BA.

> "A requirement is anything that can be used to deliver the solution and, ultimately, business value."

The other key consideration in how you organize requirements is traceability. The idea behind traceability is critical to quality analysis. Traceability ensures that every requirement is addressed and everything addressed is actually a requirement. Every requirement should be supporting the achievement of
the change goals and providing business value. Otherwise, it is not a requirement. Regardless of the methodology being used to implement the requirements, consider how you will show that the requirement has
not only been delivered as expected but also that the desired business value outcome will be achieved. If
you are working with other BAs or team members who will be providing input while the requirements are
broken down in further detail, how are you tracing each of their details back to the original request? Risk-
averse change efforts and projects will need to have this traceability from start to finish. Prior to starting,
it is important to set up how you plan to capture the requirements with their origins, approvals, changes,
acceptance criteria, and other factors.

Some organizations have sophisticated requirements management tools or systems. These allow requirements to be captured, categorized, and retained for ease of reuse, governance adherence, and overall
management. Some organizations are lucky if any requirements are captured during a change effort or
project. Hopefully, this is not the case, but realizing that you might have to start from scratch is important
during planning so that you set yourself up for success. You want to consider reuse of all your business
analysis work, particularly the requirements, as much as possible and at every step.

Now not only should you plan to reuse your own requirements artifacts, but you should also consider
what requirements you are able to reuse. Are there requirements documents or artifacts from a similar
project that had been created for the same system or business function that would give you a good starting
point? Iterative work will have you building on the requirements of the prior iteration.

Business Analysis Governance

Requirements have a storied history of being the reason why projects fail or why they are delivered on
time and within budget, but fail to provide business value (PMI 2018). With that said, decision makers
will want to have input on requirements prior to committing resources or further investments. You need
to understand the organization's requirements governance processes so that you can build these into how
you elicit, track, and utilize requirements.

This is often why traceability, as explained in further detail later in the chapter, can be very helpful. Does each requirement need to be reviewed and signed off on? Will the entire requirements list be

approved after a structured walk-through session with the project team? What about verification or validation of each requirement?

Knowing your governance needs before you start is important in order to drive the decisions on how you plan to support the governance. A long list of requirements in an easy-to-read format is not necessary if your stakeholders are helping you write them and approve them on the spot. However, if a technical team will not move forward with technical requirements until the business has signed off on their completed business requirements, then you need to structure your approach to clearly show the sign-off.

Real World Example: Getting Requirements Approved

On a project, the project manager (PM) wanted to know when requirements sign-off would be complete. I asked her what she meant by this and she said, "When will the requirements be approved by the project sponsor?" She told me that development on the project should not move forward until the project sponsor approved all of the requirements.

I considered that there were a number of technical requirements that would need to be defined to address the initial business requirements we had elicited that the project sponsor may not understand (or even care about). Since we were just beginning the project and planning our approach, I recommended that we do two structured walk-throughs of the requirements with different groups of the project team. The core project team (which included representatives from all business areas involved in the project) would walk through the business requirements to verify that they were correct and validate any assumptions. They would also verify the acceptance criteria needed to help build test plans. Then, upon verification and validation of the business requirements, solution and technical requirements could be defined. I would then walk through the solution and technical requirements with the technical team members to verify the requirements and validate the solution approach. After both sessions, the project team confirmed that they had no more questions or changes to any of the requirements. The confirmed requirements could then be provided to the sponsor with a recommendation for approval; at which time the sponsor could approve or deny the requirements to quickly move to development. Once the project sponsor approved the requirements, any changes to requirements would need a formal change-control process and this is where I asked the PM to set up the structure for the change requests. I would capture only approved changes and the updated verification and validation in the requirements documentation. The PM would get the official approval on changes and record that the approval had been made to change a requirement.

I utilized a requirements traceability matrix (RTM—discussed later in this chapter) with columns for verification and validation included that were checked complete during the structured walk-throughs. With each requirement traced through its appropriate hierarchy, it was easy to show the completeness of the review. As the team discussed requirements and agreed in person at these structured walkthroughs, changes were made live without an official change management process; however, any changes made after the sponsor's approval would go through the formal change process.

Technique: Estimation

One of the common techniques that a BA will utilize in planning is *estimation*. Before starting, you will need to analyze the current situation and create an estimation of not only what work the BA role should be performing, but how long it will take and with whom the BA will need to work. Regardless of the project approach that is being used, there is basic information that will need to be addressed.

Estimation is a powerful technique that aims to forecast the effort and cost of a particular course of action (IIBA 2015) by providing quantitative assessments (PMI 2018). Estimation is used to support decision making because it can help give insight into items such as expected benefits, potential value, and potential risk impacts.

> "Estimation is used to support decision making."

When estimating anything from the time it will take to complete requirements elicitation to the completion of user acceptance testing, consider the following:

- What you are estimating (*Clearly defined scope!*)
- Due date of estimate
- Type of estimate requested
- What you have access to
- Your experience with estimating
- Resources to support your efforts
- Dependencies on the estimate
- Consequences of the estimate
- Risk adversity of owner, team, and organization
- Measurement of success and improvement plan

Estimation is a skill that BAs continue to hone throughout their careers and is needed for many analysis positions. While challenging at first, remember that your estimate will only be as accurate as the time you put into it. Acknowledge that you will not be able to come up with a valuable estimate on the spot as to how long it takes to define all the requirements for a large project without first taking some time to research and define an approach. Always consider the complexity of what you are estimating and clearly articulate what is known versus unknown. Call out what the risks are as you consider the organization's risk tolerance level. And not only aim to put the quantitative numbers in your assessment but also highlight the qualitative measures and the expected value of the estimate efforts.

> "Your estimate will only be as accurate as the time you put into it."

We will talk further about the presentation of business analysis information later in this chapter—and the same concepts also apply to estimation. Too often BAs will either give a number with no context or provide too much information when all the stakeholder needs to know is the date you can deliver the task assigned to you. When presenting estimates to others, again, like all of your other business analysis deliverables, think about *why* the person needs the information and what they are going to do with it. This shapes what information you present. To keep estimates simple and effective, consider presenting information in the following format:

- *Goal*: what goal needs this estimate?
- *Estimate work*: potential value, cost, benefits
- *Given*: background, assumptions, current environment, timeline
- *Identified risks*: identify what would change or affect your estimate from being correct
- *Recommendations*: what to do to ensure or maximize the accuracy of your estimate

To see the power of this short and concise approach, consider the situation where a PM is asking when the requirements will be *done*:

- *The goal is to deliver business requirements so that the technical design can be completed accurately and as scheduled on December 1.*
- *I estimate business requirements will be identified, documented, verified, and validated in 10 business days to include use cases to facilitate test planning.*
- *Given that our stakeholders are available and we complete the requirements walk-through as planned by day 8.*
- *There are minor risks with some of the stakeholders' availability to review and validate requirements that would delay delivering work to the technical team. This will be mitigated with the creation of acceptance criteria and scenarios by the team during the requirements walk-through session.*
- *I recommend that all requirements meetings are scheduled and attendees confirmed prior to moving forward with an estimate of requirements to be completed in 10 days.*

This is a great approach to any estimate request, whether for business analysis work or not. You re-emphasize the goal and why you are doing the work up front; then you give the details of why the work is important, i.e., what areas are affected by the work you do; and then you reconfirm the action you want taken to support the positive delivery of value.

CATEGORIZING REQUIREMENTS

Typically, requirements need to be categorized. Categories are needed because when requirements are correct and complete, they are usually detailed. Most projects include a large number of these detailed requirements. When there are a large number of *things* to keep track of, organizing these things into logical categories allows them to be found easily and used quickly.

Requirements are the same. Separating them into categories and uniquely identifying them helps keep requirements organized and easy to reuse. To build consistency into the analysis process, the same categories should be used on every project within an organization. Any team member on any project will know the categories and be able to organize and review requirements quickly.

The second and maybe most important reason for categorizing requirements is to separate them by audience. Remember that the only reason why requirements are formally documented and presented is to communicate and confirm understanding (and to decrease reliance on people's memories). Different types of requirements will be reviewed and approved by different stakeholders. Business stakeholders review business requirements to make sure that the true business needs are understood and that nothing has been missed. Developers review detailed solution and technical requirements. This points to the practicality of categorizing and presenting like requirements together. Using the same logic, technical requirements are rarely reviewed by business stakeholders and as such should be categorized separately and presented specifically to the technical team.

A third reason for categorizing requirements is reusability. True business requirements will outlive any systems, technology, or procedures. This is why business requirements are so focused on *what* the business hopes to accomplish and not *how* it would be accomplished. This way the technology can always be changed to support the business need. Reusing requirements saves time and encourages enterprise-wide consistency. These are excellent results of the business analysis discipline. Functional requirements may be reused when enhancements are requested to existing systems. The original functional design can then be used to show the change. Technical requirements become important documentation for developers, support people, and the maintenance team. In addition, a successful technical design may be copied and reused for another application. Reusability goes well beyond your *own* ability to reuse your prior requirements work. Consider as you approach requirements if *any* person in the organization could pick up your requirements and easily reuse them?

Finally, a reason to categorize requirements is to facilitate impact analysis for managing change requests. Impact analysis refers to the assessment made to determine the ramifications (impact) of a proposed change. Impact analysis relies on requirements traceability. After a solution has been deployed, changes are often requested. Maybe the business has decided to offer a new type of product or service. Business leaders will ask: "What is the impact of this change? How much will it cost to change our systems?" Impact analysis requires the analyst to review existing systems to determine what changes need to be made. Having requirements clearly categorized and organized provides the analyst with the material needed to quickly assess the task at hand.

Deciding on categories is time consuming and challenging, so it is inefficient to develop a new set of categories every time you start a project. An organization will be most efficient if it decides on one general categorization scheme and uses it consistently. Review the system periodically to make adjustments. The following are some suggestions for setting up your own system.

Developing a System for Organizing Requirements

There are many factors to consider when designing a requirements categorization system. You must balance these factors to create the best system for your organization. Understanding why you are documenting requirements will help you decide how to best categorize them. Consider the questions in the upcoming paragraphs.

Should requirements be separated by type—business versus solution? This is a great question and one that initially seems very obvious. The business requirements (business needs that are independent of the solution) may be listed separately from solution requirements (features and performance expectations), but for some requirements components, this results in repeated information (i.e., description of a piece of business data listed in the data model and with screens where it is used).

In what order will the requirements be gathered? This is the least useful approach to organizing requirements—even though it may initially appear to be the easiest. Unfortunately, requirements are often not elicited or gathered in a logical order. Business stakeholders do not always talk about their needs in a straightforward, linear fashion. In addition, the iterative nature of requirements development means that the BA will often be presented with unrelated requirements and then have to figure out where to *put* them. Imagine if a publisher delivered a large box of books to your bookstore that were not in any particular order. Simply placing them on the shelf as they come in will not be useful when a customer is looking for a particular book.

Who will review each requirement? A BA's most important job is to clearly communicate with stakeholders. Often, several stakeholders will be reviewing and even collaborating on the requirements documentation. It would be most efficient for the BA to present the requirements in an order that will make reviewing as easy as possible. Is a stakeholder from accounts payable who only needs to review a few key financial requirements required to read the entire package and search only for the items in which he or she is interested? On the other hand, do many of the requirements that affect accounts payable also affect other stakeholders?

How is each requirement used? Which different group of stakeholders needs to utilize certain requirements? Most developers are not anxious to read volumes of business requirements. They want to know exactly what you want the system to do. They also prefer the requirements to be separated by the technology needed. For example: put all data elements together to assist the database designer, or list all users together to make the security access design easier. Is it easy for the marketing and training staff to review the transition requirements that they need in order to ensure successful rollout of the solution? And also, consider the team composition. Are all team members on site or are you working in virtual teams? Do you have external stakeholders such as consultants or developers who will need to access the requirements? These factors will also play into your decision (and why your stakeholder analysis is so important).

How are the requirements related to each other? Tracing requirements to each other is a very important technique in order to ensure completeness and decrease change management time. These relationships between requirements make their presentation more complex. This aspect of requirements argues for a unique name or number for every requirement. These unique identifiers are invaluable for tracing (see the section on traceability matrices later in this chapter). This is one of the many areas where a requirements management tool is very beneficial.

> *"A BA's most important job is to clearly communicate with stakeholders."*

Should the same requirement be presented in different ways for different stakeholders? Ideally, the answer to this question is no. It is not efficient to re-package the same information in multiple ways. However, a BA's most important job is to clearly communicate with stakeholders. If a requirement is clear to one stakeholder in a graphical format and clear to another stakeholder in a sentence, then it may have to be presented in multiple versions. If this is necessary (make sure that it is absolutely necessary), then both versions must be kept up-to-date when there are changes.

Which requirements are reusable? Many requirements are reusable on future projects, and it may be helpful to document them together. Business requirements that are technology independent can be reused on future projects and as such should be kept together in a format that allows other analysts to access them. Data requirements are reusable and most easily referenced when they are documented in the same format in the same place. This is another area where a requirements management tool is very helpful.

If your organization does not have a consistent categorization schema—implement one. Create one, try it, revise as you learn, and incorporate changes as part of your business analysis improvements (see Chapter 7). Any system is better than none. Most projects have a large enough number of requirements to justify categorizing them into groups. These groupings make the requirements easier to document, double check, and review.

As often mentioned throughout the discussion of business analysis, four very common categories emerge when discussing requirements: business, solution, technical, and transition. These categories are fairly common and are used in many industries. Organizations are most successful when they initially implement a simple system with a small number of categories to get the people in the organization familiar with the categorization idea. Categorization can also help ensure that areas are not missed as analysts dive into gathering detailed requirements. They help articulate the entire picture regardless of the methodology or approach. Of course, many organizations utilize additional categories as well, so as part of your business analysis planning and research of the business, ensure that you find out what categorization schemas may already be in place before you create another one. Remember—reuse is a BA's middle name.

Business Requirements

Business requirements are the detailed descriptions of information, business activities, business rules, and external interactions that are needed to accomplish the business mission. They are described using business terminology and presented in formats that are easy for business people to review.

Business requirements address business problems, needs, and goals independent of how they might be solved and accomplished. Business requirements include the project initiation components (statement of purpose, objectives, risks, etc., discussed in Chapter 3) and the core components of data, processes, and business rules. These components together comprise a picture of the business, which may also be referred to as the business model. Business requirements should be understood in detail. A common misconception is that business requirements are high level only. This view causes analysts to miss critical business needs. These requirements are elicited and analyzed to gain a complete understanding of the business in order to recommend effective solutions. If the business is not understood in detail, solution recommendations may be inappropriate and not solve the business problem. You may also hear business requirements defined as stakeholder requirements.

Some classifications utilize this additional category of stakeholder requirements to break the requirements apart in order to separate the business goals and objectives from the specific stakeholder needs that are to be addressed. As long as you can show that the requirement delivers the business value of the intended change, then it is fine to lump them together. However, occasionally the business requirement focuses on a high-level goal, such as to increase revenue, while the stakeholder need is more specific to their process or product that generates the revenue. In this case, as long as you show the traceability, then the subcategory can be helpful.

Business requirements do not describe how work is done but rather what work is accomplished. Business requirements are elicited, analyzed, and documented by business analysis professionals. BAs must be able to differentiate between a business need (what) and a procedural or system function (how). To understand the difference between a *what* and a *how*, look at a business process such as selling a product. This process is a business requirement because it is a core business need (see the section in Chapter 4, *What Is a Business Process*) and is named to describe the business goal without indicating how the goal is accomplished. There could be many ways that this business process can be performed. Once a product is sold in a store with a customer and salesclerk talking face-to-face, the customer could pay for the product with cash, a check, or a credit card. The clerk could record the sale in a ledger book, on a cash register, or with a scanning machine. The customer could carry the product out of the store or request that it be delivered. Another way the business process could be accomplished is that the product could be sold via the

Internet. A customer in a remote location could select the product from an online catalog, pay through an online service, and request shipping. The salesclerk in this case may be a fulfillment worker who boxes the product and gives it to the shipper. If the product can be transferred electronically, another possible sale could be a download to the customer.

All of these possible procedures support the core business process of selling the product. Business requirements are those core, fundamental components of a business that change only when strategy changes. They are aligned to the organization's strategy and therefore support the mission and vision of the organization. They are the most important requirements because all procedures, solutions, and even business decisions should support the core business requirements. Identifying the true fundamental business needs allows many possibilities for delivery or distribution. These possibilities are the solution requirements.

Solution Requirements

Solution requirements describe how work will be done. How does the solution function? How will data be collected and stored? How will business rules be enforced? How will communication with people, organizations, and systems take place? For each business requirement, there may be several solution requirements that support it.

These solution requirements are often further broken down into subcategories of functional and nonfunctional requirements. Functional requirements focus on the capabilities of the solution. These are the features and how it works. Nonfunctional requirements, which include quality-of-service requirements, describe the conditions that the functional requirements must operate within (IIBA 2015). Keep in mind as we talk through these types of requirements that your stakeholders may often not need to know (or even care) about the categorization you are using because it could confuse them. Focus on categorization for what helps you stay organized and is easily reusable by any analyst. No matter what analysis activity you are doing, never forget the *why* or the value that you should be producing with all of your efforts.

Functional Requirements

Functional requirements describe observable behaviors the system should exhibit. They are a view from the user's perspective of how the system or process will work. Functional requirements typically include a design area scope description that shows the boundaries of the solution. This scope may be shown in a use case diagram, with a list of processes or features, or in a narrative. Once the scope of the solution is defined, functional requirements are developed to describe the functionality. Functional requirements include descriptions and diagrams showing how the user will interact with the solution. This could include screen designs, report layouts, and warning messages based on business rules. To design these components, analysts and solution architects will often develop a list of potential users, indicating each user's needs and goals (called a use case). In addition to describing how the solution will interact with users, functional requirements also include detailed data definitions. These definitions are developed directly from the business data requirements and describe how the business data will look, be entered, be validated, and be reported.

Functional requirements are typically documented by BAs. Deciding how a solution will be designed is a collaborative effort between the business people and all staff designing the solution. The BA facilitates discussions with individuals from various stakeholder groups to come to a consensus on a design that meets business needs and is technologically feasible.

Nonfunctional Requirements

Once the features are defined through the functional requirements, great consideration should be given to what is needed to ensure that these features deliver the intended value. The qualities that a solution needs to have and the conditions where it will operate and provide the intended value emerge in nonfunctional requirements. The list below of considerations helps to drive a meaningful dialogue when the BA is facilitating a discussion around the solution so as to not end up with any missed requirements. As you can see, nonfunctional requirements are often referred to as the *-ility* requirements.

- Accessibility
- Auditability and controllability
- Availability
- Certification
- Compatibility
- Compliance
- Effectiveness (resulting performance in relation to effort)
- Efficiency (resource consumption for a given load)
- Extensibility (adding features and carry-forward of customizations at next major version upgrade)
- Legal and licensing issues
- Maintainability
- Performance/response time
- Portability
- Quality (e.g., faults discovered, faults delivered)
- Reliability
- Resource constraints (processor speed, memory, disk space, network bandwidth, etc.)
- Safety
- Scalability (horizontal, vertical)
- Security
- Stability
- System availability
- Usability and learnability

These nonfunctional requirements may be elicited and documented by the BA in conjunction with subject matter expert (SME) resources. While not every term on the previous list will apply to every solution, the importance of recognizing these types of requirements and ensuring that they are captured helps to create solutions that add value well beyond the initial implementation or rollout (a key BA concern).

Technical Requirements

While not every solution has to have technical requirements, the subject matter expertise that is required to break down solution requirements to a level that can be used to start delivering change often calls for technical or other subcategories of requirements. While technical requirements are discussed here, the same concept applies to any functional area. Remember the goal of requirements is to provide a "usable representation of needs" (IIBA 2015). You can break down solution requirements into subcategories as long as you can trace the requirements and manage/track them so that every subcategory requirement is traced to a solution requirement. Later in this chapter, traceability will highlight the fact that decomposing into further detail is always a great approach when it comes to ensuring clarity on requirements as long as they are needed. The traceability will prevent SMEs from adding requirements simply because they want to add them. Tracing the requirements helps to prevent scope creep and ensures each requirement achieves the intended value.

Technical requirements include detailed descriptions of the technical architecture framework, database definitions, business rule engines, program logic, development objects, application interfaces, network architecture, security components, and many other of the technical specifications of a solution. These technical requirements (also referred to as *specifications*) specify how the solution should be built and integrated into existing systems in the organization. The technical requirements are developed based on the functional and nonfunctional requirements that were agreed upon by the business stakeholders and sponsor. They include hardware descriptions, database designs, programming standards, and guidelines. They may include specific product names of software development tools that will be used. In addition, the technical requirements will include a description of how interfaces to outside systems will be accomplished. These descriptions include data sent to, or received from, other applications and any required conversion algorithms. BA roles may or may not write technical requirements based on the role expectations and responsibilities, but they are almost always involved with reviewing the resulting requirements. This review process allows the BA to confirm that the technical plans support the true business needs (via traceability to the functional and nonfunctional requirements).

Stepping through the categories of requirements and their relationship to each other shows the importance of identifying complete requirements from the beginning. When business requirements are used as the basis for solution design discussions (as they should be), they must be complete. A missed business requirement will result in several missed functional requirements and may drive the technical architecture design in a way that prevents the business need from being easily added later. However, this does not mean that requirements are only categorized and broken down on traditional or waterfall projects.

Transition Requirements

One core area that is often missed, but is key to solution success, is the transition requirements area. These are the requirements to get the solution from the current state to the future state successfully, but often are no longer applicable once the new solution is in place. Think about the training, communication, marketing, and other activities that often are involved with launching new products, changes to existing products, or complete removal. The focus is on ensuring the successful solution, not just the product, so there needs to be consideration to things such as: Who is going to support the solution? Do they know how to support the solution? Do we need to update existing users about the changes? Sometimes PMs may suggest that these requirements are outside of project scope; the project implements the change. However, a BA should stay focused on whether or not the solution is providing organizational value. Share with the PM that the project effort to implement a new product or system is not successful if no one knows how to use the final product or even knows that new features or capabilities now exist. Be sure that these requirements are part of the solution scope that is clearly articulated to the stakeholders so that the requirements are fully addressed and enable the change effort to provide the most value.

Categorization of Requirements on Iterative or Incremental Projects

As Chapter 3 highlighted, there can be multiple approaches to projects. If you are on a change effort that is iterative or incremental, a need to organize requirements is even more important as the value of reuse and extending the requirement comes into play more often. These approaches work to understand the high-level business requirements first before moving forward. Each subsequent iteration will build on the prior, taking only the next subset of requirements that achieve a certain value or goal. Those selected business requirements are further broken down and refined to deliver the business value of that phase. The next phase will take additional business requirements and break them down into solution requirements based on the scope of implementation. When the team works the second phase they also want to ensure all the prior changes are still applicable and working. The requirements you completed for the first phase are still applicable and can be reused for validation and testing. As changes and additional ideas are brought into play on each subsequent phase, prior requirements are re-validated and confirmed, and can still be broken down into further detail as needed by the implementation teams.

The categorization mentioned before can still be used for managing requirements in iterative and incremental projects. In managing the requirements, you might add in status or version metadata to more easily track the requirement and where it is in the development or delivery process of the organization. Think about what information would make it easy for another BA to simply pick up your work and start using it. As long as the categorization remains consistent throughout all the phases of the project or change effort, the same approach for categorization of requirements on traditional project-based work can generally still apply to iterative or incremental projects.

Categorization of Requirements on Agile or Adaptive Projects

As much as agile approaches can help deliver business value in faster, smaller iterations, this does not mean that you throw out the requirements work. Even if there is not a BA role, remember that the analysis does not disappear. There are still requirements that are identified and need to be implemented to deliver the value as defined by the product owner. In many more formal agile environments, teams will refer to user stories rather than requirements.

User stories are simple and concise ways to articulate the functionality required to deliver value for a defined user. They are often written from the perspective of the end user. They have a simple format that helps emphasize the desired value without having to articulate how to implement the requirement—an excellent approach that all *good* requirements should utilize (see more later in this chapter on *good* requirements). They are then shared with the development teams to discuss ways to implement and what level of effort it may take to deliver the needed functionality.

As requirements are identified in agile development, when they are found to be *necessary and sufficient* to help achieve the goal of the project, they are often added to a backlog (Agile Alliance 2018). This is a running list of the requirements the team maintains and uses to decide which element of work to tackle next (in an iteration or sprint). Some of the identified requirements may be too large to be left in user story format and are then considered an epic. Epics are larger elements of work that are then broken down into detailed user stories as the work is prioritized. Some agile teams even use the format of *initiatives* to group collections of epics together that achieve a common goal. Initiatives may then be identified to support certain themes or areas of focus that can apply across the organization (see Figure 6.1).

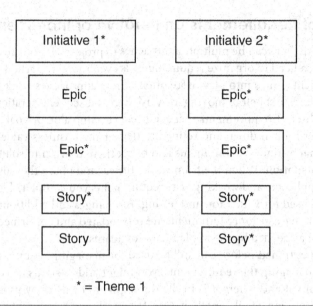

* = Theme 1

Figure 6.1   Hierarchy of agile and adaptive requirements

Backlogs may have their own categorization to help organize the requirements. Product backlogs define the list of everything needed for a product. This is owned and maintained by the product owner. A sprint backlog is defined by the development team that articulates what requirements from the product backlog are selected to be worked on in the next iteration as well as the plan to achieve the goals of that iteration. And then increments identify what work has been delivered (is *done*) during the increment and the value of all previous increments. Additional backlogs used in some agile methodologies might also include program backlogs or solution backlogs. See *Additional Reading and References* at the end of this chapter for more sources on how to categorize your backlogs.

As work is prioritized, the product owner will help to lay out how the requirements are addressed for implementation. With the product vision in mind, the product owner may prepare a product roadmap that will help the team with release planning. This articulates what functionality is being delivered by breaking down into iterations that define the features (user stories) that will be implemented (PMI Agile 2017). See Figure 6.2 for how this breakdown delivers value.

Regardless of how detailed the categorization gets, remember that the categorization itself is simply meant to help the teams have meaningful and productive conversations in an efficient manner. Do not overcomplicate it if you do not need to and only categorize if it adds value. The categorization style and names may appear to be different in agile and adaptive methods then when done in a traditional setting. But, the need to continue to capture and organize needs in ways that teams can utilize them in order to provide meaningful changes does not disappear. Enabling others to use your valuable analysis outputs should remain at the heart of your requirements work.

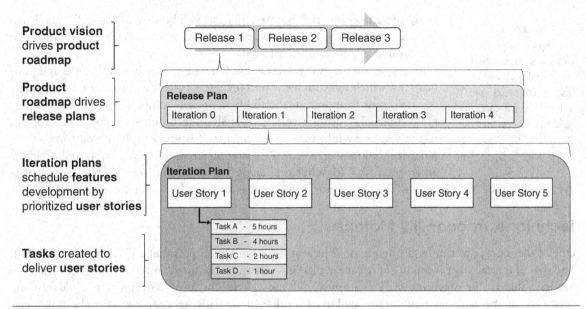

Product vision drives **product roadmap**

Product roadmap drives **release plans**

Iteration plans schedule **features** development by prioritized **user stories**

Tasks created to deliver **user stories**

Figure 6.2 Agile and adaptive implementation planning hierarchy

ANALYSIS TECHNIQUES AND PRESENTATION FORMATS

There are many techniques for analyzing and presenting requirements. Each technique has a purpose and approach to delivering a particular aspect of value for the requirements. However, not every technique has a prescribed way or format of doing things. The techniques available are guidelines to support your analysis work, not a cookbook of step-by-step instructions. As mentioned before, there is no wrong way to *analyze* or *think*. These techniques are simply tools to help the analyst see a problem or situation from a different perspective. Most projects and change efforts will benefit from the use of several techniques. The hardest part for a BA is determining which technique to use when. While there are some guidelines, know that a *best practice* was best at that time, in that context, with that given stakeholder set, and given challenges. So, which technique do you use? Whichever one works. The technique that delivers the results you were looking for is the correct one. This is why it can be helpful when starting out to know the purpose and rationale of the technique before you immediately jump in and start trying it. This helps you remain focused on achieving the outcomes, not about how "right" you perform the technique. If the results do not help your change effort, then it was not the technique to use.

It is important for a successful business analysis professional to be familiar with many analysis techniques. The more tools you know how to use, the more flexible you will be. Imagine a plumber with only a wrench in his or her toolbox. Although the wrench is an important tool, it may not always be able to solve the problem. Over time, a plumber adds more tools (and skills) as he or she confronts new problems and situations.

It is often easiest to learn each technique as it was originally developed before trying to change it. Each technique has a specific intent. It is important that you understand and can apply a technique thoroughly before trying to modify it. You will be tempted to make up your own techniques, and as an experienced analyst you may succeed. But new analysts will be wise to use well-established techniques as they were intended until they have gained enough experience to feel comfortable making adjustments.

Every technique in this section has been described in other books and publications, which I encourage you to review. As you learn to use each technique, you will come to appreciate the ability to present complex requirements in simple formats. Try using a variety of analysis techniques on the same problem to see what new information is exposed. It is amazing how well some of the older techniques work. Presenting complex requirements simply and clearly is an essential skill for a business analysis professional. This section gives a brief overview of some techniques and the reasons for using them as you dive into your analysis work.

Technique: Traceability Matrices

One of the most powerful (and often quite simple at the start) techniques that a BA can use is an RTM. The goal of traceability (or linking of requirements) is to identify how the requirements are delivering the needed value for the organization. This is one of the most useful forms of item tracking. By identifying which requirements components are related to each other, along with any characteristics about the relationship, the analyst will find missing or inconsistent pieces. Almost any two requirements components can be linked. Deciding which links will be useful for each project or change effort depends on the project type and risks.

The general approach utilizes the functional breakdown (see the section on functional decomposition analysis later in this chapter) of project and change goals into the deliverables that are required in order to achieve those goals. From there, the deliverables are broken down into the business requirements that, when completed, produce the deliverables. Business requirements can be further broken down into solution requirements that deliver the value defined by the business requirements. Solution requirements can be broken down into technical requirements that deliver the solution. These are examples where you would want to trace the requirement from one level to another. The idea would be that if all the solution requirements are delivered that trace to a business requirement, then delivery of the business requirement can be validated. See Table 6.1 for an example of a simple traceability matrix.

Traceability is an important concept for BAs to understand because recognizing that requirements are related to other requirements is critical for complete understanding. Thinking about traceability helps develop complete requirements. When you identify a new requirement, ask questions about possible related components. Traceability is extremely useful in validating that the deliverables have been completely delivered. However, traceability also helps to ensure that only the necessary requirements are included in the scope of the effort. If a business area such as IT or marketing states that something is required, the BA would trace the requirement to which deliverable is helping to achieve the need. If the BA cannot find a related deliverable, then it could be raised to the business if the requirement is part of the solution scope of the effort. Now, traceability helps to keep the team on scope of the solution.

Part of the business analysis planning work with traceability is to determine what you will need to trace for your current project or change effort. Verification and validation tracking of requirements is often

Table 6.1 Requirements traceability matrix

Goal	Deliverables	Business Requirements	Solution Requirements	Technical Requirements
Increase revenue	Updated sales platform	Customer Service able to sell new product from sales platform	Product visible in product listing in sales platform	Product name needs to be in "product" table
				Product name needs to be in "bundle" table
			Product pricing in sales platform	Product pricing needs to be in "pricing" table
				Bundle pricing table needs updated values for new product
	Training	Sales staff able to communicate benefits of new product	Updated sales platform training with new product information	

helpful because you do not want to waste your time breaking down and analyzing business requirements that have not been verified and validated in case they are not applicable. A key element that is encouraged on most traceability matrices is the acceptance criteria. Walking through the requirements with the stakeholders to define what they are willing to accept as delivered for each requirement is extremely valuable. First, you clarify the expectations as the stakeholders and get a better understanding of what they are picturing in their minds of the end solution. Second, the established acceptance criteria lends itself to more easily creating test cases. You have a sense of the expected use and behavior that the solution should provide, which is valued by all who use the requirements.

This increases the value of the traceability matrices. Each requirement should be validated that it is delivered, which is done with testing and thorough test plans. For each requirement, there should be the corresponding test case(s) that validates that the solution does provide the required functionality as defined. Now each requirement may have more than one test case since there may be many ways to validate the solution; however, once all test cases have successfully passed, by using traceability you can then validate that the requirement has been delivered. Table 6.2 shows some test cases for the previous requirements examples. These are great for helping to make the BA's work even easier, especially if he or she is responsible for creating the test plans. While it may take some significant time to trace all of the requirements to the detailed level that the team needs in order to successfully implement the solution, a thorough RTM provides a foundation to quickly produce quality test plans that stay in scope.

Traceability matrices are most often valuable on traditional project approaches especially where there is a low risk tolerance, such as in highly regulated or risk-averse industries. Traceability helps to verify that no aspect is missed and complete solutions will be delivered. However, traceability can also be utilized on more adaptive projects. In fact, backlogs are great ways to trace the requirements to delivering the goals of the efforts, such as discussed earlier with product and solution backlogs. Further, product roadmaps and iteration planning are used for this same approach since the traceability aspect of these adaptive techniques helps to validate that the resulting solution provides the intended value.

Table 6.2   RTM with test cases

Goal	Deliverables	Business Requirements	Solution Requirements	Technical Requirements	Test Case	Expected Result
Increased revenue	Updated sales platform	Customer Service able to sell new product from sales platform	Product visible in product listing in sales platform	Product name needs to be in "product" table	Customer Service agent selects product in service platform	Product added to customer's online shopping cart
				Product name needs to be in "bundle" table	Customer Service agent selects bundle A that includes product	Bundle added to customer's online shopping cart that includes product
			Product pricing in sales platform	Product pricing needs to be in "pricing" table	Customer Service agent selects product in service platform	Correct pricing for product shows in customer's online shopping cart
				Bundle pricing table needs updated values for new product	Customer Service agent selects bundle A that includes product	Correct (updated) pricing for bundle shows in customer's online shopping cart

Technique: Process Modeling and Analysis

Process modeling is one of the most common visual techniques that BAs use to effectively show the business processes of the organization (see Chapter 4). With a clear model—the analysis of what opportunities are possible—it is easier for the analyst to see where the process is not providing maximum value, thus making it easier to understand the scope and impact of changes.

Process models show how work is accomplished, including the sequence in which things are done. They can also show how information flows through the processes and how business people and other external agents are involved with the process. They show the triggers that start the process and help articulate the results of it. They may be used to visually represent a current process (*as-is*) or to represent a recommended future process (*to-be*). Including both a current and future state is helpful to ensure requirements understanding. Figure 6.3 shows how a sales process changes dramatically with the introduction of online ordering. The visual model makes it easy to quickly see how many process changes are occurring and helps articulate the scope of the change effort.

Process models are also a great tool to use for note taking during requirements elicitation. Business stakeholders frequently describe their work as a series of tasks, interjecting notes about worker involvement and current system support. The analyst draws a picture of the business process to help the team

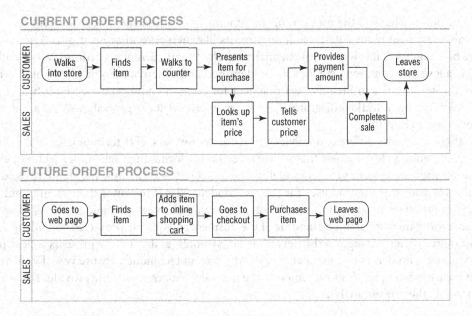

Figure 6.3   Current and future state process models

understand the process and confirm that understanding with the SMEs. Using a process model as a conversation tool does not imply that it must become a formal deliverable; however, if it helps other team members understand the challenge at hand or envision the solution, then be sure to share the resulting diagram and continue to reuse it whenever the process is brought up. Process models are especially helpful as part of a requirements package when the requirements are going to external or third parties.

Process models are such powerful tools that BAs should become quite comfortable creating and working with them. A junior BA may elicit information about processes and then go back to create the models for the next meeting with stakeholders. However, mid- to senior-level BAs should become quite comfortable creating these models immediately with their stakeholders. Regardless of whether you create the process using sticky notes on a whiteboard or utilizing technology such as Microsoft Visio®, creating the process flow visual model *live* enables the collaboration with your stakeholders that good solutions require. When you have a diverse team present to see what others are doing throughout a process, you are encouraging understanding. Decisions on which elements are changing and what the downstream effects are can be quickly and easily discussed as a team so that your stakeholders have a better understanding of the change effort or project. Getting everyone on the same page is one of the most valuable facilitation activities a BA can do. Ensure that whatever is produced—whether it's working materials or a final approved model—is shared with your stakeholders for immediate feedback. Then continue to bring the model to every discussion and meeting so that if there are questions or new information arises, you can quickly reference and update the model for continued use.

Because workflow diagrams are so flexible and can be created using many different standards and notations, they are useful on many types of projects. Business process improvement projects rely heavily on as-is and to-be diagrams. Software development projects benefit from their use at either the business requirements level (what will the user do) or the functional requirements level (how will the user do it). They are also very helpful for enterprise-level projects like mergers and acquisitions. When two departments are being merged, it is worthwhile to analyze each of their current procedures (as-is) and compare them. This allows the common activities to be identified and differences to be highlighted. The project team can also use metrics to identify best practices for recommending the merged future (to-be) procedures. Additionally, workflow diagrams have become critical for organizations that are developing a service-oriented architecture.

While there are many different nomenclatures, model formats, and technologies, a BA should stay focused on presenting clear models that utilize a consistent formatting. Like other techniques, the best format to use with the present process models is the *one that works*. Review the standards and common techniques that your organization uses for process models. Also, find out if there is any kind of tool or repository for processes that are captured. An organization that categorizes and tracks all of its processes helps to ensure organizational understanding of the business and quickly promotes not only reuse but also faster and more efficient changes. Whichever format, symbols, and structure presents a clear picture for you and your stakeholders is the one that is best. And like all techniques, ensure you always think about what you hope to accomplish *before* diving into the diagram. Process modeling provides the visual so that you can then do the process analysis.

Technique: Functional Decomposition

Functional decomposition is a proven approach for breaking a complex system into manageable pieces. The objective for utilizing this technique includes being able to measure and quantify an item such as an estimation (see earlier in the chapter), analysis of optimization or substitution, and analysis of design. Visual models are often used to show the breakdown of the large, more complex item into subsequent smaller parts. Figure 6.4 shows a simple example that takes a business object of an order and breaks it down into some of the example components. This is a great way to show the same model to multiple stakeholders. The business stakeholders understand the high-level deliverables and objects (an order in this case), while the detailed SMEs and implementers can see the discrete components, such as that an address has different fields.

Because the diagram itself follows the same general rules as an organizational chart, many business people are comfortable reviewing requirements using this presentation. The strength of this technique is in the separation of process from sequence. To truly understand business processes, it is useful to look at each process step as an independent task. By isolating each task, you see the core building blocks upon which all of the complex business procedures and systems are built. Looking at each task as an independent unit facilitates creative brainstorming around how it might be structured or be built to be done differently in the future.

As with all techniques, make sure that you understand the purpose. With functional decomposition you are trying to understand a process or component and need to analyze it independently of its relationships and other factors. However, many BAs struggle when analyzing business elements using functional decomposition as they either do not go far enough in the breakdown or, more likely, go too far down into granular details that are truly not needed. Begin with the objective in mind. Functional decomposition might be used when trying to measure, estimate, or forecast a cost, resource, or

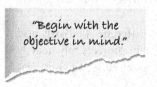
"Begin with the objective in mind."

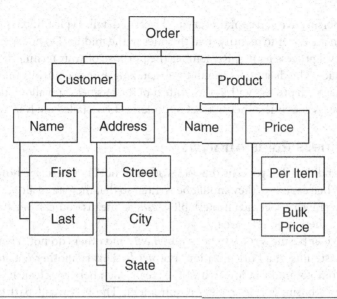

Figure 6.4   Functional decomposition

element of a solution. Trying to find substitutions or optimizing bottlenecks and identifying areas of reuse are other common goals. Knowing the objective of your element helps you know how far to *break down* the topic at hand.

As with many diagrams, the decomposition diagram is easy to review. This clarity deceives readers into believing that the development of the diagram is just as easy. In reality, this is one of the most difficult diagrams to create. There are few rules for its development, which leaves the analyst room for subjective representations. SMEs may get frustrated if presented with an empty whiteboard and asked to describe their organization's processes using a top-down approach. When using this technique, draft a diagram of your functional breakdown on some of the key elements you already know and even some of the assumptions present. Then show your draft to the SMEs for feedback. SMEs will be able to more easily correct a partially drafted diagram than build one from scratch.

There are a few key rules for building a decomposition diagram that enforce consistency and rigor. Having guidelines for requirements helps all BAs use them consistently and helps stakeholders who are reviewing them to expect predictable patterns. Rules for building a decomposition diagram are:

- Only one type of relationship between components is shown on the diagram—parent to child (shown with a line between boxes)
- Only one type of requirement is shown on a diagram (i.e., if you are decomposing processes, do not show any business rules—show only processes)
- Every parent has more than one child
- No sequence is shown (no arrows)
- A child must be at a lower level than its parent (more detailed, finer distinctions)

Although there are specific rules for developing a decomposition diagram, no two BAs would create an identical diagram, even when given the same set of requirements. Each decomposition diagram can represent a different perspective and contain varying levels of detail. Typically, the processes at the top and bottom of the diagram are easier to identify than the ones in the middle. Do not spend too much time discussing the middle-level process names. Remember the purpose of your technique and why you decided to use it in the first place. The diagram is useful for organizing and structuring analysis work. It gives the team a visual way to see each process within the context of the business and allows the group to then focus on one particular process at a time. It helps to set boundaries for detailed analysis work.

Technique: Business Rules Analysis

A business rule is a condition that governs the way work is done. They describe how operational business decisions are made. When captured, they should be written so that they stand alone. They should not need interpretation as they are very specific and testable. *Testable* means you can verify whether the rule has been followed or not—there is no gray area.

Some analysts consider business rules to be *requirements* and others do not. There is an argument that business rules are constraints of an organization, not *needs*. This is another debate that is important to be aware of so that your communications with other team members are clear. It does not really matter whether you consider a business rule to be a requirement. The important part of business analysis is that business rules must be elicited, captured, and confirmed. They may be included in the requirements package or in a separate document. Be sure to find out if your organization uses any tools or repositories to store these. Always check before you start so you can reuse as much as possible, as well as prepare your content to be reused by others.

It is important for the analyst to write business rules carefully. References to data (nouns) must use the exact same nouns as defined in the data requirements. Similarly, verbs must be used consistently within process and in use case names. There are some commercially available syntax systems for documenting business rules, such as Rule Speak (Ross 2003). In addition, there are software systems called business rule engines that store and execute rules. Rules can be very complex, and each organization should have some standards around documenting them. Rules are often reused in an organization by different departments. This argues for a rules administrator and shared repository. Rules are frequently changed in many organizations, so it is important to clearly define and maintain them separately from business processes, use cases, and data structures. While some rules will be represented logically in a data model, most must be described with more detail than can be shown in a diagram.

Finding Business Rules

Because business rules define constraints or rules about a business, they can be thought of as decision points. Each rule helps a business stakeholder make a decision. The rule has been articulated to ensure consistency in making these decisions. Imagine a business area where each employee makes decisions based on his or her own opinion. Customers would get a different response depending on with whom they spoke ("But the woman I spoke with yesterday told me that I could return this item . . .").

Identifying, capturing, and confirming business rules improves the consistency of a business area even if the rules are never codified into software. Often during a requirements workshop that is focused on business rules, two different business stakeholders will realize that they had a different understanding of a rule. Exposing these unknown discrepancies is the value of analysis. Business areas realize improved communication and increased consistency immediately.

Often, business rules are exposed during requirement elicitation around processes and data. As business SMEs discuss their work, you should listen for decision words like *verify, validate, check, determine,* and *assess*. When a person or system makes a decision, they are enforcing a business rule. That rule needs to be articulated, reviewed, and documented. Business rules are an important requirements component that should be managed and maintained after the implementation of a solution. Once implemented and "designed" into systems, procedures, or processes, these rules drive the work of the business and should be easy to review and change.

Technique: Decision Modeling and Analysis

Knowing the business rules often leads to some analysis on how these decisions are made and if they are driving value through the organization. Decision modeling is a great way to visually show how repeated decisions are made. These models lay out how information comes into the process to drive decision making based on the business rules in place. Many business owners are unaware of how decisions are made daily. Visually showing what information is considered, the business rules that are applied, and the resulting choices that are reached based on the logic in place is extremely powerful in order to have meaningful discussions with stakeholders. The idea behind this technique is to show how *repeatable* decisions are made. First, as you will often find out, if it is up to an end user (i.e., not an automated system), these decisions are not always made the same way. Laying out decision-making processes so that stakeholders agree on the decision in the first place is a great way to get your stakeholders engaged to really dive into the analysis of deciding if the decision is even appropriate. Decision tables, decisions trees, and decision requirements diagrams are all easy ways to show how these decisions are being made. A simple decision tree model is shown in Figure 6.5.

This is extremely important when analyzing how operations are run today. Many process improvement and solution evaluation efforts draw out the processes and analyze how decisions are made throughout to see if there are opportunities to maximize their value. For example, when an airline is

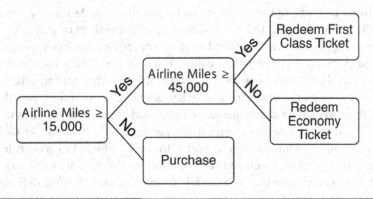

Figure 6.5   Decision modeling

considering how you earn free flights or other perks with your airlines miles, the business owners would want to consider if these awards were appropriate. If they are too low, that might scare off customers and affect the revenue the airline receives. If they are too high, that might see costs rising more than expected. Until all the options are laid out, it is hard to decide if the current setup is driving the most value. Having the visual before you start a deep discussion and analyze options can save BAs a lot of time and avoid rework with stakeholders.

Technique: Glossary

An important component of strong communication is the consistent use of terms and phrases. It is easy to forget how dependent human beings are on language. Every conversation involves a common understanding of terms. When someone uses a term that you have never heard before, or uses a known term in a different way, the message is incomplete. Your brain may even get distracted thinking about the unknown term and miss the rest of the communication. Understanding the importance of terms is critical to successful analysis. Analysts must be precise when discussing and presenting requirements. The accurate use of terms, especially terms that are unique to a business domain, will ensure successful communication of requirements.

This points out another important lesson for the business analysis professional. You must be able to use the terms that are used by each business even when they are foreign or unfamiliar to you. This is where a glossary can help. The analyst should begin jotting down important terms from the very first meetings with stakeholders. Terms that seem common and well-known should be confirmed. Each term should be defined and the definition should be agreed upon by all project stakeholders. Undefined terms create ambiguous requirements.

An SME may describe a process as: "A customer purchases products by logging into the website and placing items in the shopping cart. When the buyer is ready to check out, the screen should display the total shipping charges and the total order amount."

Is the customer the same person as the buyer? Is an item always a product? What is the difference between the shopping cart and the order? Using inconsistent terminology in requirements often leads to mistakes in solution development.

Analysts must listen carefully to the use of terms by stakeholders. As inconsistencies are found, they must be exposed. Be aware, though, that simply exposing an inconsistency will not correct it. If one department has been using the term *customer* and another department has been using the term *client*, you will not be able to quickly change either of their habits. You must first determine if they are using the terms in exactly the same way. If not, there may be two different words that are important and relevant here. Your job as the analyst is to point out the inconsistency, get agreement on the term's definition, and work to bring the group to consensus on shared language to be used in procedures and systems.

The glossary itself can be a simple list of terms that, in general, only you may use. Or the glossary can be a full appendix to your requirements package as part of the deliverables. As a good rule, include a glossary of terms in all your documentation when you start out. Find out if there are any knowledge management systems in use at your organization where you can add terms with their clarified definition so that it is easy to reuse on future analysis work. However, if your requirements are going to any external entities, such as a vendor or consultant, ensure that you include the glossary in your deliverables to help the parties clearly understand what is meant in all documentation.

Technique: Data Requirements and Analysis

Data is everywhere. Whether working on a technical solution or not, there is data that is used, interacting, and produced in solutions. Since data has features and formats called metadata, the data is often captured in more detail than simply being included in functional or technical requirements. Calling out the data separately helps to clarify meanings and communication among stakeholders. It also allows for a detailed level of specification of the solution for implementation teams. This clarity helps solutions not only be implemented faster, but ensures that the solution is successful by correctly addressing the specific needs.

Data Modeling

Data models help visually show data attributes, characteristics, and relationships between the data. The models allow data to be better managed as a resource. Like other modeling, the visuals allow for easier analysis and design as well as helping to support solution evaluations and continuous improvements. These can begin as conceptual models that are independent of technology or implementation that artic-ulate how the business perceives its information. Then the conceptual models can evolve into logical data models that include normalization rules that are used with the design of the solution. As is often the case with a technical solution, these models can be further defined into physical data models that implementa-tion experts use to build the solution.

Data model diagrams—often referred to as entity relationship diagrams (ERDs)—are often used along with class diagrams. Both help the analyst develop questions about information needs. The popularity and long life of data modeling is attributed to its rigor and simplicity. The diagram can show a complex business domain in a straightforward, concise manner, making communications much clearer. The model shows not only information needs but also many business rules as they relate to data. The rules are the *relationships* in the ERD. When using an ERD to document business requirements, the diagram and related details combined make up a logical data model. Object-oriented programming leverages the use of class diagrams to help define data requirements. Figure 6.6 shows the example formatting used for an ERD that helps with these models. Figure 6.7 then shows an example ERD with the data structure for school data.

The most important reason to build a data model is to confirm the user's and the analyst's understand-ing of the business data requirements and ensure that the solution that was developed satisfies the business need. Data modeling provides the analyst with a structured tool and technique to conduct analysis. Most

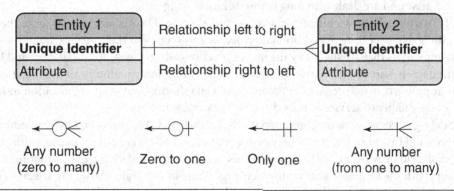

Figure 6.6   ERD explanation

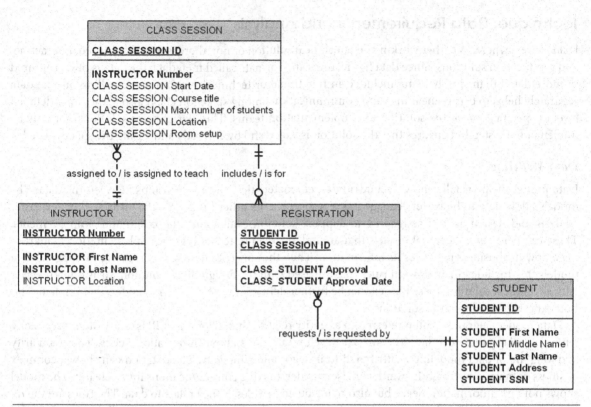

Figure 6.7 ERD example

SMEs can articulate problems and possible solutions; unfortunately, their problems and solutions are often based on current system constraints, not true business needs. Asking business people to detail every piece of data (attribute) requires them to understand and articulate every aspect of their business. This approach allows the business to drive the system design, not the other way around. It also stimulates more detailed discussion and thoughts. By identifying and detailing data in a model, further requirements and problem areas arise and are dealt with long before solution design.

A logical data model also facilitates data reuse and sharing. Data is stable over time; therefore, the model remains stable over time. As additional project teams scope out their project areas, they can reuse the model components that are shared by the business. This leads to physical data sharing and less storage of redundant data. It also helps the organization recognize that information is an organization-wide resource, not the property of one department or another. Data sharing makes an organization more cohesive and increases the quality of service to outside customers and suppliers.

Data modeling is very useful on commercial off-the-shelf (COTS) projects. Understanding the business data needs and including them in a request for proposal (RFP) is crucial for package selection. Reputable vendors should provide an ERD that represents their system's underlying data structure. Comparing the COTS data with the business data requirements, attribute by attribute, allows the selection committee to make an accurate assessment of how well each package would support the business. If a package cannot accommodate business data requirements along with their associated business rules, then it should be rejected. Missing data cannot always be rectified by custom programming.

There are data modeling tools that support the creation of an ERD and its associated details. Many of these tools are capable of using the ERD requirements to build a database design. These tools are used by data analysts, administrators, and database administrators to create, update, and maintain data structures used by application software. Even if you do not have access to these tools, the absence of a tool does not mean that one should ignore this technique. Many process modeling software programs include stencils for articulating the models that developers can then use. Again, BAs should seek to understand how best to present information to the developers and others who need to know about data requirements and their structure so as to help facilitate the efficient development of the solution. Data models are great additions and compliments to other models, diagrams, prototypes, and visuals that help articulate the overall solution.

Data Flow Diagrams

Data flow diagramming is an approach to show the transformation of data—where data comes from, what tasks process the data, and where the data is stored or consumed. They are extremely useful when trying to lay out the boundaries of systems by showing what happens to the data and the external agencies they interact with. These diagrams are meant to be simple and focused solely on the data. A *bubble* or circle on the diagram represents a process. Arrows show data flowing into and out of each process. The basic assumption is that a process must have at least one input and one output flow. This assumption serves as the foundation for all other process analysis techniques (see Figure 6.8 for structure). These are great diagrams to quickly get teams agreeing on the scope of the data work.

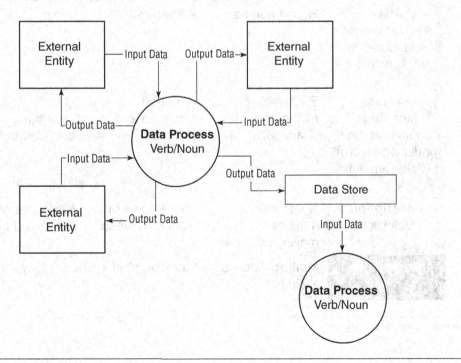

Figure 6.8   Data flow diagram

Data Dictionary

Just as the glossary helps provide a standard vocabulary, a data dictionary can provide a standard definition of the data elements you are working with. Data dictionaries aim to provide a common explanation of each data element, what it is used for, or where it is applicable, along with the values the data may have. They define the metadata for the specific data element and also show the composite values the data may possess. See Figure 6.9 for an example section of a data dictionary.

For maximum value, the metadata for the data elements needs to be leveraged for the enterprise. Organizations often have data warehouses and data governance teams that work to organize and catalog the data. Always try to leverage existing data before creating anew. If you have to create a data dictionary of new data elements, then work to incorporate it into organizational standards so that it can be easily reused.

Primitive Data Elements	Data Element 1	Data Element 2	Data Element 3
Name Name referenced by data elements	Street number	Street	City
Alias Alternate name referenced by stakeholders	House number	Address street	Town
Values/ Meanings Enumerated list or descriptions of data element	Required minimum 1 character	Required minimum 2 characters	Required minimum 2 characters
Description Definition	Numerical number of mailing address	Street name of mailing address	City name of mailing address
Composite	**Mailing Address** = Street number + Street + City + State + Zip code		

Figure 6.9   Data dictionary

Technique: Use Cases and Scenarios

Use cases and scenarios are great ways to show the interactions that people or systems have with the solution to accomplish specific goals. They articulate both the primary and alternative outcomes for these actors when attempting to accomplish these goals. These are written from the actor's point of view. They do not consider how the solution works.

Scenarios are great for articulating the details of an interaction. Think of a story that tells the tale of a single action, incident, or response at a very precise and detailed level. This exactness, though, can be quite time consuming since all of the possible alternatives and options will create a significant number of scenarios. Yet, this can help risk-averse projects. The scenarios not only define the requirements, but then become a great foundation for the test plans—articulating the steps to be taken and the desired outcomes.

Use case diagrams are ways to model the relationships between actors and the use cases. A use case diagram shows the main use cases along with the actors who are involved with them. The use case diagramming technique was developed to show functional requirements—or how a software system interacts with its users (actors). It is typically used to present a future view of a system. Scenarios show very specific actions for clarity on the use of the solution whereas a use case explains several scenarios. Figure 6.10 shows a simple example of a use case diagram. Use cases are depicted as ovals and actors are shown as stick people. Actors are people, organizations, or systems with which the solution interfaces. Associations (depicted by the arrows) show what functionality the actor has access to in the use case. Associations to actors often represent user interfaces like screens and reports. Associations to system or organization actors represent automated or electronic interfaces. The relationships between use cases show where they include functionality that is in another use case or extend the functionality of a use case.

The use case diagram is done in the standard notation of Unified Modeling Language™ (UML®) (see Chapter 5). It is a simple diagram for stakeholders to review and can help the communication between

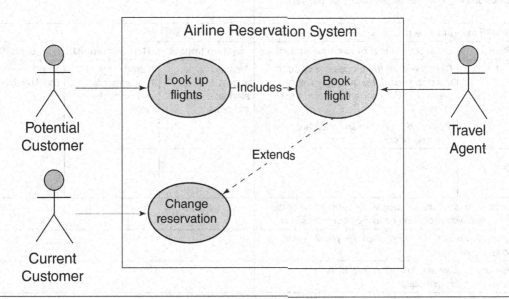

Figure 6.10   Use case diagram example

business and technical stakeholders. The resulting diagram is not as important as the discussions and decisions that are made during its development. This is a great technique to use with business stakeholders, specifically decision makers, because it requires decisions about how people (actors) will work with the solution. A simple line on this diagram between an actor and a use case could completely change a business person's job. It may necessitate job description and responsibility changes and new procedures.

When defining a use case, begin with a clear name. Utilize a noun-verb association to clearly depict the action that is being taken. Then, articulate the goal to identify the outcome of the use case, keeping the perspective of the actor in mind. Identify all the actors from the perspective of any person or system who interacts with the solution. Preconditions are defined along with the trigger that initiates the steps of the use case. Then, identify the steps to execute the use case, often called the flow of events. Once finished, find any post-conditions that must be true at completion of the use case. Table 6.3 shows the structure you can use to clearly articulate a use case.

One of the major weaknesses of the use case approach is that a use case description may contain several requirements components (data, process, business rules, external agents) instead of documenting them separately. Documenting components together makes it easy to miss requirements and makes reusability of components difficult. To make your use case descriptions more concise and consistent, define the individual requirements components separately (with unique names) and simply refer to them in the use case descriptions. This alleviates the need to change every use case description when a data or business rule requirement is changed.

Table 6.3   Use case template

Actors—list of external entities and data stores involved in the use case				
Assumptions—identify any assumptions for this process				
Preconditions—must be met prior to the process starting				
Step #	Normal Flow of Events—Action	System Impact	Requirement ID	Data ID
1.	Describe what the process must do. If the step is complex, you may want to break out into a separate process use case. Include in each step any alternate flow(s) that may occur.	Identify any impact to the step as a result of the project	Identify any requirements related to this step	Identify any data used by this step
Post-conditions—indicate successful completion of the process, including exception handling post-conditions				
Frequency Information—how often this process occurs (i.e., daily, weekly, etc.)				
Notes—any additional information helpful in understanding this use case				

Use case descriptions—especially the primary and alternate paths—are great for brainstorming with users of the solution on design options. Working through the specific interactions between the user and the solution helps design a system that more accurately mirrors the natural workflow of the user. Even when the team thinks it has a consistent vision of the solution, writing down these specific steps/interactions highlights different views and allows decisions to be made before coding begins.

Technique: Interface Analysis

Interface analysis is great for articulating where information is shared across boundaries of solutions or solution components. Interfaces can refer to users (both internal and external to the organization), business processes, and data, as well as technology components and systems. They are very good at defining the requirements regarding who interacts with the solution, what information is exchanged (including how often and where), why this interface is being created, and what is required to create it.

Very few business systems operate in a vacuum. Interface analysis is a technique for identifying interfaces that may impact or be impacted by the current project or change effort and for planning the changes that are necessary to smoothly integrate the new solution into the existing environment. Identifying existing interfaces also helps to identify stakeholders who use and support those interfaces. They will be important SMEs as you work to design the changes. Interface analysis can be done using system documentation and procedural manuals (especially for technical solutions if these documents are up-to-date) and traditional requirements elicitation and analysis.

Technique: Prototypes

Prototypes are great approaches to product design that can truly consider the end user perspective. It allows the stakeholders to interact and engage with an early model of the final solution, the prototype. These can be non-working mock-ups, representations with partial functionality, or digital solutions including simulations. Simple sketches on paper of each screen the user may encounter in a system, for example, can validate the user's expectations in a quick (and inexpensive) manner while forming the basis of the design. Alternative process flows with exceptions are identified and alternate behavior of the user that was not planned for can now be addressed in solution requirements as you watch the user and verify their expectations.

Anything that allows the user to *experience* the solution is a successful prototype. Think in iterations rather than trying to deliver the final solution in one try. You present the prototype and get feedback to incorporate. You incorporate and present the revised prototype back to the user and get additional feedback. New ideas can surface and build on prior ones. Places where you thought you addressed the user needs are no longer missed because the requirement will come up in the next iteration. Do not get married to the first iteration. Feel free to use throw-away prototypes, where you literally scratch the design and create a whole other prototype for the next one. This is why scratch paper and using arts and crafts supplies can be beneficial. The BA is looking for what the *stakeholder* is willing to accept, not the BA. You have presented the correct solution if the stakeholders are all willing to accept it.

> "You have presented the correct solution if the stakeholders are all willing to accept it."

Solution evaluations produce opportunities and corrections through the experience that end users can share with the analyst. Prototypes are valuable for the BA and should be considered as part of your planning work when the success of the solution is based on the end users' use of the solution. Finding out how the users intend to use a solution and whether they are willing to support the continued development is important to do early on in development where changes are less costly and easier to implement. However, do not get frustrated if after multiple iterations, you feel that you have to scrap the design and start all over. You at least have feedback of what the solution is *not*. This is important as you move forward since a two-cent piece of paper with pencil drawings is easier to throw away and repeat than having the organization invest millions of dollars only to find out the user has no intent to interact in the manner the organization had assumed.

On the opposite end of the spectrum, be careful with doing prototypes too early on projects where stakeholders do not fully understand the purpose of the prototype. A risk with prototyping is that it can set some unrealistic expectations. Stakeholders may see a design idea and then hold the team to deliver that design. You do not want to show a design the organization is not capable of implementing or supporting. Also, stakeholders often notice the aesthetics and worry more about the look and feel than the core functionality. Ensure the expected use is addressed in your reviews, not just the presentation. This is why active collaboration with your stakeholders is so important. Utilize multiple iterations of the prototype so that stakeholders see how their feedback is incorporated into the design and continues to evolve the requirements. Keep communication open and continuous so that stakeholders remain active and involved.

Technique: User Stories and Backlogs

User stories are a way to start conversations with the team on defining elements of value. These elements are the requirements. The discussions focus around the potential value that these requirements could bring to the product and ultimately the end user. They may feel less formal at first, but that is okay. You want to generate feedback and ideas from the team, including product owners and decisions makers, on what this value could look like. You then capture the requirements in user stories. User stories are often written down on small notecards (or virtual index cards) to keep the focus on the required features. The format is often something like this: "As a [user], I need to [functionality] so that I can [purpose, context]." Defined acceptance criteria are then added to the back of the card. An example for a finance project might be: "As a financial analyst, I need to be able to access month end reports, so that I can prepare financial status reports for executive presentations." The acceptance criteria might be stated that: "On the first day of the month, the prior month's profit and loss statements are accessible and downloadable to financial analysts." Acceptance criteria should be defined by collaborating with your stakeholders to discuss what they are willing to accept. This helps to clarify the definition of *done* so that you will be able to determine when you are finished with the work. Getting very clear acceptance criteria agreed to early on will save a great deal of time and rework as you deliver solutions (see discussion earlier in this chapter on traceability). This is even more important in traditional approaches that do not have iterative feedback loops. Again, user stories are short and specific descriptions of the functionality that is required to support the overall project. This way the development team can take each card individually and discuss what the approach may be to develop the functionality and estimate the level of effort.

As user stories are defined, they are added to the backlog. On agile or more adaptive project teams, the authoritative source for the requirements is the backlog. However, the backlog is not to be mistaken for a *requirements document.* It is instead the collection of user stories that the team prioritizes and reviews to pull the prioritized pieces of work from. In colocated teams, this could be the physical notecards or even sticky notes that user stories are written on and posted to the wall. Virtual teams use the same approach with online collaboration tools. Like most tools, the backlog is only as good as those teams that use the tool. Successful agile teams spend time doing plenty of backlog grooming. The analysis of what has been added to the backlog is done to ensure there is clarity of details so that implementation teams can quickly deliver the intended functionality without questions. This is where feedback and improvement opportunities from retrospectives (see Chapter 7) are incorporated. Collaboration with the stakeholders is key to clarifying the user stories down to the detail that the implementation members are comfortable assessing and quantifying the effort. Decomposition (see earlier in the chapter) is commonly used to break down the stories into manageable work efforts, and this is also a great time to elicit acceptance criteria if not previously identified. Having a prioritized backlog helps teams determine which stories are further defined in greater detail first since lower prioritized items often have less detail. This process continues with a team through each iteration of the solution so that teams can not only plan the next piece of work but can also look forward to future iterations by knowing what may be involved. This analysis work is what drives value in these agile artifacts.

Technique: Storyboarding

As you work to collaborate *with* your stakeholders on solutions, storyboarding can be a valuable technique to add to your requirements toolbox, especially if you work in more adaptive environments. This technique asks you to describe the requirement from the perspective of how stakeholders interact with the solution. This allows the requirements to be presented both visually and textually by articulating the user's interactions with the solution by the sequence of activities that occur. Think of comic strips; simple sketches depict what is happening at each step with added notes or clarification (see Figure 6.11).

Storyboarding is a cheap and easy way to do prototyping as again you are focused on the customer experience. It facilitates the validation of requirements with your stakeholders when they can visually see what the expected user behavior is. Storyboarding is also valuable to technical teams because it provides expected outcomes and acceptance criteria within which developers can work. This clarification then helps facilitate testing and validation work. Start by looking at the scenarios for the solution. It is best to pull out the most complex scenarios with which to develop a storyboard. The visuals help to eliminate the complexity by looking at each step (see functional decomposition earlier in this chapter). Draw out

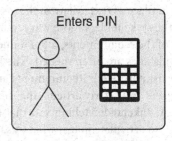

Figure 6.11   Storyboarding example

the sequence of steps for that scenario, sketching an image for each step. As needed, add clarifying details in notes. You want to make it so that each segment of your storyboard is able to stand alone for analysis with the team. Review the storyboard with the team members one scene at a time. Then walk through the entire storyboard and confirm the flow of events and expectations. Try to stay away from how each step will be done and drive the team to focus on ensuring that the steps add value and help achieve the goals. Couple this technique with business rules (see earlier in this chapter) to help ensure that no constraints were missed.

Choosing the Appropriate Techniques

A BA may choose one technique for their elicitation of information, another for their analysis and under-standing, and yet another technique for the presentation to business stakeholders. Most projects and change efforts will be supported by several requirements techniques and deliverables. This section pro-vides some suggestions for considering these selections.

There are three primary approaches to consider for documenting or presenting requirements: text, visuals, or a combination of both. The main purpose is to provide requirements in the format(s) that best communicates your goal to the intended audience while encouraging collaboration and stakeholder buy-in. Be sure that your stakeholders understand not only *what* is going on but *why*. As you mature in your career, senior BAs develop the skills to be able to present the same information to different audiences with consistent understanding by all. A secondary goal is to always present the requirements in a format that allows for fast, efficient reviews. Knowing your audience and what they need to do with the require-ments information is important to establish up front. This is one of the reasons why graphics (diagrams, tables, etc.) are so popular. And finally, always think about how best to capture requirements for reuse. Consider here that you might not be the one reusing the information and that you may not be around to answer questions. How can you capture, collaborate, retain, and manage requirements that the organiza-tion will continue to leverage business value from them for years to come?

Using Text to Present Requirements

Text has been the traditional approach to documenting requirements. It has the main advantage of being easy to produce (no special software is needed) and can be written and reviewed by anyone (e.g., SME, BA, PM, developer). Unfortunately, textual requirements have many limitations. As requirements get more and more detailed, textual requirements get longer and longer. Since detailed requirements typically describe how solutions should work and look, there are many stronger analysis techniques that should be used in place of text. Many of the visual techniques discussed in this chapter are so valuable because they give the stakeholders more ways to help express the details of how, where, when, and why versus just the *what* of the requirements, often found in text. Long textual descriptions of solutions are difficult to review and mistakes are often missed. The English language can be ambiguous; requirements are often unclear and misinterpreted. Requirements are a representation of a need. Picturing what is in the minds of the end users and clearly articulating their expectations can be challenging in text format, especially for new BAs. A stakeholder telling you that the solution needs to be "pretty" can be interpreted in many ways. Trying to articulate in text what this requirement means and should be expected to deliver may not be the best use of the BA's time. A simple image might capture all the requirements in one try versus rounds and rounds of interviews with stakeholders trying to capture all the elements to describe this one requirement.

Remember that a BA needs to value the time they spend on all activities and ensure that they are delivering the value of the intended activity. Do not write requirements for the sake of writing requirements. If you use a text format for your requirements, it should be to help others be able to use them. Write only enough to move the change effort forward. If text is not working, then try a different format.

Using Visuals to Present Requirements

Depending on the particular type of requirement, a visual or graphical representation of a requirement may be easier to review and approve than a textual description—as the saying goes, "a picture is worth a thousand words." Diagrams, models, screen layouts, mock-ups, sketches, storyboards, and designs are all effective approaches to presenting and communicating requirements. They allow for the articulation of ideas so that everyone is seeing and reacting to the same image. Further collaboration comes from presenting more interactive forms of requirements such as prototypes, simulations, and even role playing where the users get to experience the solution. Experiencing a solution gives valuable feedback and validation on the requirements while clarifying context from the user's perspective.

Creating visual models is a great approach when you need to really draw the stakeholders into the solution. BAs should work to be the facilitator as much as possible, having the stakeholders do the work of designing and creating. Like the text-based formats, stakeholders can easily approve requirements someone else created. Yet those same stakeholders will then take issue with the solution because they did not fully understand the requirements that were presented. When you have stakeholders walk through your designs, or even better, create the designs themselves, they have a much better grasp of what is happening. In fact, this should always be the goal where stakeholders take ownership (and you can step back and let them do much of the presenting work). However, preparing to create these visual models often takes more time for planning in order to ensure that the right stakeholders are participating; that you have the right tools, technology, and supplies to create the visuals; and that the stakeholders know how to leverage the products beyond the current change effort. The BA also has to be comfortable in his or her facilitation skills so that they drive not only the activity, but also the ownership by stakeholders throughout the requirements analysis (see Chapter 7). Working sessions need to stay on track to the intended goal of producing valuable deliverables. It can become easy for stakeholders to continuously talk through ideas versus acting on helping deliver them.

Using a Combination of Text and Visuals

Most BAs use a combination of text and visuals to present their requirements. Diagrams and process models are supported by labels and annotations on the diagram and attached textual descriptions. Textual descriptions are structured as much as possible to describe components of the prototypes and designs. In an excellent requirements development tool, a digital model would link directly to these supporting textual descriptions and related requirements components, providing a complete model of the requirements. This goes back to understanding your stakeholders and really paying attention to who needs what information. While business stakeholders tend to quickly understand the visuals presented, technical teams may request more detailed information clearly outlined in a tracking list. Your business analysis planning work should consider your audiences before selecting the deliverables and the formats utilized.

Many new BAs start with a text format for their requirements. Capturing requirements in tables such as an RTM (see earlier in the chapter) is a useful way to start to track and manage the requirements that you begin to collect. As you get more comfortable with these techniques, try more visual formats. See what kind of feedback you get. Many mid- to senior-level BAs, once they get comfortable with the techniques, find that creating visual models of requirements actually takes them less time than capturing all of the requirements details in a text format.

Real World Example: Using Multiple Techniques

In replacing a critical piece of software, multiple departments needed to be consulted because the software supported numerous processes in the organization. Since the software replacement effort was to be bid on via an RFP process, there was the need to have very detailed and specific requirements developed for the potential vendors. However, there was concern that the stakeholders who managed these processes today would not be able to articulate to this detail. This was where the need for a BA was identified.

Stakeholders were invited to a one-hour meeting to discuss what processes they performed that (possibly) utilized the software (assumed to be true, but asked to validate). The PM literally identified a different group every hour that would walk in and for 60 minutes explain to the BA (me!!) everything that they did and how it worked. To capture the processes, we used process modeling where I would map out the processes as they talked. Doing the models *live* in front of the stakeholders allowed them to quickly correct me and then verify that the models were reflecting what they were articulating. This worked well because often there were cross-functional teams present for different process discussions, allowing them to each better understand the entire process by hearing and seeing what the others did to complete a task. They often asked clarifying questions of each other while I acted as the facilitator who kept us on track and on time, as well as the scribe. It also allowed us to get through numerous processes over the course of a week since all the stakeholders did was talk while I captured information. Models were then printed and all stakeholders were given copies to review and validate. This made review sessions go quickly as people came in ready with their changes and validated follow-up information.

After 161 process models were completed, the text-based requirements were then captured. Process analysis clarified business rules, data requirements, and information flows in a text-based format that accompanied each process model. These made the details specific and clear to the vendors included in the RFP discussion. In addition, the PM appreciated the approach since she was comfortable with text-based requirements from prior project experience and utilized these for her vendor selection process. She then reused the process models when testing came into play to help validate the outcomes of test scenarios back to the deliverables that were produced through the process models. As a bonus, the business areas actually leveraged the process models to help with turnover and new-hire training to articulate how processes worked at the organization.

Choosing an Approach

As part of the business analysis planning work (see Chapter 7), the BA needs to consider what approaches and techniques will best move the change effort forward. Requirements are not captured solely for the purpose of capturing requirements. Requirements have a purpose. While it might be easiest for you to track all requirements in text format in a long spreadsheet, this may not be easiest for the person who has to use the requirements. Consider who will be using the requirements and what they intend to do with them. Feel free to combine multiple approaches to the requirements so that there is no ambiguity as to what is expected, and remember to only capture as much as adds value to the change effort. Short, iterative development cycles need only enough information to create the prototype or solution component that stakeholders can comment on. Highly regulated environments will need to see all the details laid out that address each regulatory requirement and can benefit from detailed, traceable text formats. Always consider who is using your requirements and what they are doing to best detail the requirements for *their* use. You may produce the requirements but, remember, you do not own the requirements.

Consider everything that you know about one of your key stakeholders. Does the person like to talk about what he or she does? Does the stakeholder sometimes draw diagrams to explain his or her processes to you? Does he or she write long textual descriptions? Being aware of how the SME presents information will give you a clue as to how the person would like to see information presented back to him or her. If you are working with an SME who is a financial, accounting, or numbers person, you may be successful using Microsoft Excel® spreadsheets (or something similar) to present requirements. Accountants see the world as rows and columns, so if you can present your requirements in a similar format, an accountant will be more likely to review them to help you spot errors and holes. An SME who is a marketing person may like to see colorful graphs, pie charts with percentages, or high-level slogans. This SME is more likely to review a requirements document that is pictorial—maybe colorful with clever icons. Remember that the whole point of requirements documentation is to communicate. If you cannot get an SME to look at a requirements document, you have wasted time creating it and you are going to lose valuable feedback at a critical point in the project.

Another approach to consider is giving an SME small chunks of requirements to review, one chunk at a time. This helps the SME feel less overwhelmed and allows him or her to focus on a particular area. Eventually you can put all of the pieces together and remind the SME that he or she has already reviewed this document piece by piece. One advantage of this approach is that as you are preparing and reviewing each section, you can ask follow-up questions and get clarification as you go. The SME will also see value in your documentation because it helps you both find missing pieces. It also helps the SME see progress on the project and become aware of how much work the project really entails.

Some SMEs may prefer to write down their requirements instead of spending time talking with you. This is a tricky situation to manage because often the requirements that an SME documents do not meet the criteria for *excellent* requirements. The good news is that these documents give you a lot of information about the SME. The level of detail in the document tells you how much complexity the SME sees in the processes. Many SMEs do not realize the complexity in their business area because they are doing the work every day and it is simple to them. It also shows you their priorities because the most important issues are likely to be mentioned numerous times. If an SME says he or she will write the requirements, always take it and tailor your tasks to help verify and validate them. Think about working *with* the SME to deliver the requirements. Requirements should be as much of a collaboration activity as they are a communication tool. The entire team should help collaborate on getting the requirements captured well enough to deliver the changes requested while providing the information necessary to ensure solution success.

Your planning work should consider not only the deliverables needed and the organization's approach to requirements, but also the approach to the change effort. RTMs work great for very traditional (waterfall) projects, but what if you are working with an offshore vendor whose team members utilize agile methodologies? Or, what if you are working with a finance technology whose product owner wants to roll out one feature or piece of functionality at a time, waiting to validate after each month's end closing? Customer-centric approaches where the user or end product owner is heavily involved (i.e., agile) will often use much more visual approaches and keep documentation to a minimum (note: not ignoring information, but only writing down the minimum to help move the effort forward). Highly regulated industries and risk-averse efforts will insist that the details are clearly spelled out to very specific levels that might require a lot of written documentation. Consider the change effort as well as your own skill set. Do not be afraid to try another technique and/or combine it with your tried-and-true approach (see Chapter 7 regarding your skills). Using more than one technique is often valuable because additional techniques can increase clarity, but you will need to balance the time that you are given to create and facilitate the delivery of these deliverables as well as the stakeholders' availability to share, collaborate, confirm, and validate the requirements.

Standards

Setting standards for analysis techniques and deliverables is difficult. Projects and change efforts vary greatly, and the necessary analysis differs in quantity, perspective, and level of detail. Organizations should be careful when setting business analysis standards. Requiring a particular requirement deliverable for every project seems like a good way to introduce consistency into requirements, but may result in wasted work for projects for which the technique is not appropriate. New BAs need guidance when choosing techniques. Ideally, this guidance is provided by a mentor rather than a set of standards. The approach to the change effort, stakeholders, environment, and many other factors often weigh on the decisions made about how requirements are captured.

There is a benefit in trying to use the same set of presentation formats on most projects, though, because stakeholders will become accustomed to them and become efficient at reviews. Some organizations might introduce requirements templates rather than standards. These templates give the structure or starting point for organizing requirements but do not detail exactly *how* the requirements are captured, let alone the elicitation and collaboration activities to achieve the details. Like all business analysis work, the approach, technique, or documentation style that is best is the one that works.

Real World Example: Modifying Templates

In developing a mobile solution for an organization, there were numerous communication requirements of the project team to work with an offshore development team. Many of the organization's stakeholders were accustomed to waterfall-based approaches due to their low risk-tolerance levels. The offshore team worked in a very agile environment and was quite comfortable with doing small increments of development for constant feedback. In working to capture the requirements from the project stakeholders and deliver them in a format that the development team could use, I found myself spending considerable time between meetings trying to take the business requirements and shape them into the details that the developers could use to write their user stories. In addition, every time project stakeholders met with the development team directly, there were more questions than answers, which seemed to stall the project. I began to add diagrams to the requirements packages that would be created during working sessions with the project stakeholders while the developers listened in. I then inserted these diagrams

continued

into the requirements package template that the organization used for all project work. Now I had the powerful combination of images along with the text requirements in each section of the business requirement documentation template. The resulting business requirements were then easily used by the operational support teams to develop their support documentation (which was the purpose of the requirement template). Lessons learned were shared on the usage of the template and it was communicated to other BAs that the template was the format in which to capture requirements, but there was freedom as to what information the BAs would enter in each section that best helped move the change effort forward and support the resulting solution.

"AS-IS" VERSUS "TO-BE" ANALYSIS

When eliciting, analyzing, and capturing requirements, BAs must always be aware of the state of the business environment they are capturing. There are two states: the current state of the business, commonly referred to as the *as-is*, and a potential future state of the business, commonly referred to as the *to-be*. It is easy to forget about this difference and allow requirements to include both in a confusing mix of a single diagram. This is an easy mistake because when business stakeholders talk about their work, they will often tell you (1) what they currently do, (2) why they see a need for a change, and (3) their recommendation for a change. An experienced BA listens carefully for these three very different pieces of information and dissects them into their components. For example:

> *"I log in to our accounts receivable (AR) system to enter the customer purchase information and make sure that the information is correct. Then I have to log in to our customer relationship management (CRM) system to enter the customer profile. This is a waste of time because I have already entered the address into AR and yet I have to type it again. The AR system should send this information to the CRM system to save me time."*

The BA must be careful to listen for the facts versus opinions or ideas in this discussion. The current process (as-is) was described briefly, but the speaker got distracted by describing his or her problem and a recommendation. Did the BA get a clear, complete description of the current state? No. The BA needs to ask more detailed follow-up questions:

- What specific data items are entered in AR to process the payment?
- How is the information validated?
- What if the payment information is not correct or is incomplete?
- Is the CRM system still updated?
- What specific information is entered into the CRM system?
- How many fields are entered into both systems?
- Are the fields names the same?
- Why does the procedure require this double entry?
- What if this customer is already in the CRM system?
- Is the profile updated?

Business analysis professionals must be careful not to jump to conclusions or recommendations without understanding the as-is state. If solutions to business problems were obvious, they probably would have already been implemented. An analyst would not be needed in such situations. Rarely are good-quality solutions that obvious or simple. There is a whole complex set of parameters that impact the problem and situation, and all must be considered before a solution is proposed.

Do you need to document every detail of the current state when you know that it is going to change? This is a judgment call that the BA and team must make. The current state needs to be understood and considered carefully, but it does not always benefit the team to create detailed, presentation-quality documents that describe the current situation (see the discussion in Chapter 4 on learning the current system). If there is confusion as to what is changing, then you would be more likely to capture the current state so that it is easier to articulate the change elements. If the effort is to add a new capability that does not exist today, then there may be no current state to capture because the business does not perform the process today. Like all business analysis work, value your time spent on these efforts so that you are only performing activities of value to the organization that move change forward.

Every change effort, project, and situation within the effort must be evaluated individually. Depending on the reason for a project, the BA will determine the type of documentation that is appropriate. Returning to the AR example, why are you learning about the *as-is* procedure? Is the goal to document the current procedure because new employees will be hired and must learn this job? Has the BA been asked to look for possible process improvements or to streamline the efficiency of this task with measurable results of the change? Is a new AR software package being installed that will change this procedure? Is the organization considering building an interface from AR to CRM? From CRM to AR? This reinforces the importance of understanding why a project was initiated (see the section on project initiation in Chapter 3).

If a process improvement project was initiated, understanding the current system is very important when making recommendations for changes. If you will be proposing a change, you will probably be asked to present your reasons for the recommendation. Showing the current process next to the proposed process is a great way to articulate the improvements that you anticipate. In addition, when planning for the change itself, it is important to know where you are starting from in order to build a detailed change plan. In other words, if moving from A to B, you need to know where A is before you can make the move. This also allows for the impact of the change to be measured. BAs need to present solid business cases, thus, any change effort should have a forecasted value to justify the expenditure and time commitment to the organization. Comparing the current state to the future state allows for a measurement of the effort.

If a project was initiated with a solution already selected (e.g., a new AR package), recommendations will be limited to how to best utilize the new functionality. In this case, it may not be necessary to formally present the current state because the organization has already decided that it is inefficient or not appropriate. In this situation, the BA needs to understand the current state to ensure important tasks are covered by the new system. The BA needs to be able to write conversion requirements, but may decide not to create any documentation about the old procedures or processes.

PACKAGING REQUIREMENTS

How Formally Should Requirements Be Documented?

One of the skills of an experienced business analysis professional is the ability to decide how to formally document each requirement. The main reason why many organizations do not spend as much time as necessary on requirements is because there have been many past projects where analysts have created large volumes of documentation where most of it was never read. The agile development approaches represent a contrast against this formal documentation approach because the focus is on delivering value as fast as possible. Consider this in your business analysis planning activities when you are deciding on your approach to requirements and documentation. As you determine what you are going to document for the requirements, consider the value of what you are producing. Are you documenting requirements that are only needed during the development or implementation of the change but that might not be applicable after iterations with the customer? If so, these requirements should be as short and fast as necessary to move the project forward (very agile approach). Or, are you capturing designs that show how the solution works that will be needed and used by support staff after the change is implemented? These requirements should be detailed, verified, and validated so that your resulting documentation becomes a living artifact used by the organization. Remember that the definition of requirement is a *usable representation*—so always keep in mind who will be using your requirements; how, when, where, and why; and then utilize that analysis to determine your approach to requirements documentation.

You also need to think about how you plan to get the requirements. Some of the traditional approaches to requirements focus on the BA eliciting and analyzing requirements from not only stakeholders, but also from operational artifacts, documentation, and research. The BA is expected to pull the information together and *deliver* the requirements. This approach may require more formal documentation. Especially in customer-centric solutions, there is often the need to be much more collaborative with the stakeholders, including end users, to develop and analyze requirements *with* the stakeholders rather than *for* the stakeholders. Throwaway prototypes of design ideas, whiteboard sketches, and brainstorming activities might be the approach required to elicit the requirements that are then constantly iterated for additional feedback. This approach may require less formal requirements documentation, especially up front. Consider whether your initial requirements documentation will evolve into a user guide, training tool, or other solution support, or whether it is a more permanent artifact. This changes the requirements from being a completed document to a value-adding component of the solution. Planning your business analysis work early will save you from spending a lot of time documenting information that is never valued.

What Is a Requirements Package?

In traditional methodologies, the concept of a requirements package was developed as a way of organizing and presenting all of the requirements information. The package was presented to the sponsor and SMEs for approval before being handed over to the development team to start building the proposed solution. It is called a package because analysts recognize that requirements may be contained in various documents, diagrams, forms, etc. A requirements package may include a table of contents, executive summary, and reviewer instructions. It may also contain links or references to electronic requirements, such as simulations. Putting all of this important information together into a package organizes the information and allows it to be reviewed by others. The same concept is used in many financial organizations: a loan package includes the application for the loan, income verification documents, collateral documents, underwriting notes, etc., and allows everything about a loan to be presented together. In the medical profession, a patient's file contains lab results, medical history, prescription information, etc. When a *package* contains a lot of different documents from different sources in different media, automation is difficult. This is why requirements management tools may not be used. Some requirements management tools support one format (mostly text) for requirements but have a difficult time storing, retrieving, and organizing different types of deliverables.

As organizations move to a more iterative and incremental style of development, the use of a complete requirements package is giving way to smaller, more incremental presentations of requirements. Specific requirements deliverables are presented to SMEs to review and revise in each iteration. Packages may still be created for ease of presentation and delivery, but a package may include just a portion of the requirements and/or rough drafts of some deliverables. In agile teams, the requirements hardcopy package notion completely disappears with the focus on the dynamic backlog of solution functionality. Requirements are still managed and presented, but it is rather the presentation of prioritized work (user stories) from the backlog identified per iteration or sprint. However, some teams may view the collection of epics and user stories that results from the development as the requirements package.

This leads us into the idea of waiting until requirements are finished before they are packaged and presented. This is an unrealistic and often detrimental approach. The sooner requirements are reviewed, even in a rough draft form, the more likely it is that major flaws will be found and corrected. Requirements, whether formal or informal, will go through iterations regardless of the methodology. In traditional project approaches, the requirements are often verified when collected. Then the requirements are validated that they help deliver the solution. Yet only after validation are acceptance criteria and test cases created (as analysts do not want to waste time on requirements that are not required). And even agile projects go through many iterations before a user story is defined, broken down, clarified, and then prioritized to be worked on. This is why collaborating with stakeholders on developing the requirements is not only important but streamlines the effort. A process of working to get feedback, analyzing, and then returning for more feedback can take a significant amount of time. Doing requirements elicitation and analysis live with stakeholders often gives you the fastest and most accurate results. The more you can collaborate *with* stakeholders, the earlier on the design impacts and changes will be discussed and confirmed—which will save time.

Regardless of the type of requirements deliverable you produce, it should be tailored to its intended audience and reviewed carefully before being distributed. All diagrams should be clearly labeled. Long textual requirements should be organized under major and minor headings. The package should be as clear and easy to review as possible. It should use terminology consistently and, if need be, contain a glossary. A customized cover page can be added to each package indicating the pages or sections on which an individual stakeholder should focus. Make the deliverable as usable as possible since your role is to enable faster, more efficient delivery of the planned change. You should never be adding more work to the effort, but rather making the work easier and perhaps even helping make less work for the project or initiative team. Generating large requirements packages that are difficult to review and use does not work.

A circumstance when a BA may find the need to write a more formal requirements package comes when dealing with external vendors and organizations. An important use of packaging is in the creation of a request for information (RFI), request for quotes (RFQs), RFPs, or other formal external requests. These packages are formal documents because they are sent outside an organization and are used to make decisions that lead to legal agreements with vendors. When the package is going outside of the company, information is typically presented more formally, and confidential information is only included if absolutely necessary (along with a confidentiality agreement). As the goal is to clearly articulate the needs of the organization, significant time is often spent to ensure clarity on the requirements and designs, to not only ensure that the solution is appropriate for the organization, but to also minimize the back-and-forth time with vendors to clarify the details. These can turn into very large packages because in addition to the written text-based requirements, diagrams, use cases and scenarios, and current and future states work flows and data, other organizational requirements and artifacts are often included to give the vendor as much context to the request as possible. Again, an RFP or other formal external requirements vehicle should be developed *with* your stakeholders to ensure that they are not only clear on what the request is, but to validate that only the required information is shared and no more until all contracts and agreements have been finalized.

Remember that the business analysis work is to understand, collaborate, and communicate requirements to help enable solution teams. Find the communication approach that works best for your stakeholders and the given approach to the change or project. Presenting requirements in sections, conducting requirements walk-throughs, and offering to sit down and discuss the detailed deliverables are just a few of the approaches to consider in order to guarantee effective requirements communication. Requirements are meant to be *usable representations* of what the organization needs to be successful and successful BAs are always focused on those who will be using the requirements, including how to maximize reuse and efficiency.

Characteristics of Excellent Requirements

Many BAs often ask what *good* requirements look like. And how do you know when they are done? The characteristics of excellent requirements have actually been understood for a long time (Wiegers 1999). Wiegers made a list of the characteristics of excellent requirements that many analysts use as a foundation for approaching requirements. According to the list, requirements must be:

- Complete
- Correct
- Unambiguous
- Verifiable
- Necessary
- Feasible
- Prioritized

The first characteristic points out a real challenge. Can an individual requirement ever be complete? When you break requirements down into components and show their relationships to other requirements, completeness is difficult to assess. Requirements are complete at a specific time in a specific context with a specific set of stakeholder groups. Requirements then are changed or elaborated as more of the solution is explored—so when is a requirement actually complete?

The same can be said for all of these characteristics. This is why it is so important to keep coming back to the definition of a requirement as "a usable representation of a need" (IIBA 2015). To adequately evaluate excellent requirements, you must look at the entire requirements package. Within the defined scope of the project or change effort, the package should be complete, correct, unambiguous, verifiable, feasible, and prioritized. Are stakeholders able to envision the entire solution (complete)? Is the solution being designed free from errors (correct)? Can the stakeholders work with the requirements package without any questions (unambiguous)? Has every requirement or component been verified by a stakeholder or stakeholders? Does each requirement trace to the deliverables and objectives of the project or change effort (necessary)? Are solutions able to be built from the requirements and design (feasible)? And finally, has there been an analysis of the value of each of the requirements (prioritized)?

Getting Sign-Off

Getting official approval of your requirements work is always an important consideration for any analyst. This should be considered in your business analysis planning effort as you consider the formality, level of detail, and risk adversity of your stakeholders and change effort. On project-based work it is best to discuss this concept with the PM when first starting out and are discussing the approach, deliverables, and overall project details.

If the approach is to be formal, detailed, written down in text formats, or captured in software tools with tracking, then there is often an official approval or sign-off of the requirements prior to development. Like all business analysis work, considering the value of each effort is critical. If the change effort is high risk, then formal requirements reviews are important for team understanding. Upon completion of the plan, an official signature by the project sponsor is normally captured because that is the signal for the development and implementation teams to begin their work. This approach is fine if you have both a solid change management process in place for the requirements as well as stakeholder understanding that there is no work developed until formal approval has been received. Having the stakeholders' review and sign-off on requirements in a single session is usually the most successful option. Often, if you e-mail a lengthy document to a stakeholder and expect them to read through and approve the whole thing, you find yourself spending more time sending follow-up e-mails trying to explain segments or trying to get the stakeholder to approve something they have not read and do not fully understand. Getting sign-off should be about validating the stakeholders' understanding of how they will be achieving the desired value and less about you checking off a box on your checklist.

Sign-off does not have to be a formal signature on the last page of a requirements package though. It can be approval at a meeting or even a review with the implementation teams that they have the details necessary to move forward with creating the solution. This is why planning up front on your approach to the requirements is important. Know your stakeholders and the type of requirements you will be gathering first and then decide the best approach. In an agile setting, the team reviews the requirements together and comes to an agreement with key input from the product owner as to what requirements are going to be developed next. The creation of iterations and sprints filled with requirements is the *sign-off* that the requirements generate. If the requirements are not at a level of detail and clarity for the development team to properly assess the work and develop it, then typically the requirement remains in the backlog for further analysis. The approval from the product owner and team on the prioritized work is the sign-off approval equivalent. Should something be missed, it will be included in the next review iteration. So like all good business analysis work, the official sign-off on requirements deliverables should be tailored to the change work and the environment in which the change is occurring.

Requirements Tools, Repositories, and Management

As emphasized throughout, requirements should be developed with the maximum return of value to the organization as possible. To achieve this, especially the concept of reuse, emphasis is put on managing the requirement from its inception to its retirement. Consideration for how to categorize your requirements is important. Are they categorized by system, type of project, business area, or functionality? How would someone be able to find the requirement again? It is easiest, as part of your business analysis planning, to learn how the organization manages requirements before starting. Mature organizations utilize requirements management tools that provide the categorization, traceability, and easy search features that allow analysts to quickly find, add, and reuse requirements. These are especially valuable for whenever changes to existing solutions are being considered so analysts can quickly understand what functionality exists today and consider the scope of the impact. The software available today also helps track changes easily and often includes the approval that workflows in highly regulated environments demand. As costly as they are, the requirements management solutions often save analysts serious time and are a great business case to consider. But even if the organization does not have an official requirements management solution, there is often a repository where requirements artifacts are saved. Identifying where this is located, the business rules for use, accessibility, maintenance, and utilizing for reference before you start your own requirements are all keys to successfully planning your requirements work. Knowing this before you start allows you to pick the best approaches for capturing requirements information. You want to save yourself time and avoid creating new templates or standards if they already exist. Do not recreate the wheel, but rather leverage the prior requirements work already created by the organization.

SUMMARY OF KEY POINTS

Every change effort requires the use of analysis techniques. An analysis technique provides a structured, thinking approach to help the BA understand a business problem, opportunity, or other change effort and their resulting requirements from different perspectives and angles. BAs should be able to use many techniques and tailor their approach for maximum effectiveness while promoting reuse.

- BAs are most effective when they plan their analysis work and choice of techniques prior to starting, including understanding the approach that the change effort is taking and what level of governance and formality needs to be considered
- BAs must be aware of the differences between types of requirements and understand the value of categorizing business requirements, solution requirements (functional and nonfunctional), and technical requirements or specifications for traditional project-based approaches
- While many of the techniques appear structured toward eliciting requirements in traditional (waterfall) settings, understanding how the same approach can work in more adaptive approaches can enable valuable requirements work and is critical to analysis work today
- BAs should approach requirements work as a collaboration opportunity for the stakeholders to clearly articulate how the solution will deliver value to the organization
- BAs use analysis techniques not only to understand the business needs and communicate requirements, but to also build buy-in and ownership from stakeholders
- There are numerous techniques available to analysts—well beyond the scope of this work—but understanding their purpose, strengths, and weaknesses is important to a BA's success

- Delivery of any requirements' artifacts should be planned, considering the organization's approach and reuse of requirements, what change processes are in place, and who needs to use the requirements—both today and in the future
- The *best* technique for any situation is the one that works—where requirements are elicited, understood, and validated by a vested group of stakeholders who are excited to help move the change effort forward

BIBLIOGRAPHY

The Agile Alliance. (2018). *Glossary.* https://www.agilealliance.org/glossary/.

International Institute of Business Analysis (IIBA). (2015). *Business Analysis Body of Knowledge® (BABOK® Guide).* IIBA: Toronto, Ontario, Canada.

IIBA. (2017). *Agile Extension to the BABOK® Guide.* IIBA: Toronto, Ontario, Canada.

Project Management Institute (PMI). (2017). *Agile Practice Guide.* PMI: Newtown Square, PA.

PMI. (2017). *The PMI Guide to Business Analysis.* PMI: Newton Square, PA.

PMI. (2018). "Success in Disruptive Times." *PMI's Pulse of the Profession®.* PMI: Newtown Square, PA. www.pmi.org.

ScrumGuides.org. (2018). "Scrum Guides." https://www.scrumguides.org.

Wiegers, Karl. (1999). *Software Requirements.* Microsoft Press: Redmond, WA.

ADDITIONAL READING AND REFERENCES

The Agile Alliance. (2018). https://www.agilealliance.org.

Project Management Institute (PMI). (2015). *Business Analysis for Practitioners: A Practice Guide.* PMI: Newtown Square, PA.

Ross, R. (2003). *Principles of the Business Rule Approach.* Addison-Wesley: Boston, MA.

Ross, R. (2018). *Ronald G. Ross "The Father of Business Rules."* http://www.ronross.info/.

Ross, R. and G. Lam. (2015). *Building Business Solutions—Business Analysis with Business Rules, 2nd ed.* Business Rules Solutions, Inc.: Houston, TX.

The Scaled Agile. (2018). *Scaled Agile Framework (SAFe®).* https://www.scaledagileframework.com.

Schwaber, K. and J. Sutherland. (2017, November). *The Scrum Guide™.* https://www.scrumguides.org.

CHAPTER 7

YOUR SEVENTH STEP—INCREASE YOUR VALUE

One of the best things about business analysis is that you can increase your value to an organization by learning new techniques and continuously improving your skills. A business analyst (BA) initially learns the foundational skills of requirements analysis and communication techniques and then builds on that foundation, maturing as they gain more experience. The skills used in business analysis work are highly valued and offer BAs the opportunity to move both vertically and horizontally in an organization as well as across industries. Analysis work is always valued regardless of the job title.

There are numerous ways to improve your skills: read books and articles, practice new techniques and skills, and learn from other BAs. You also improve your skills when you teach other people. Join a business analysis community, such as your local International Institute of Business Analysis (IIBA) chapter or your company's business analysis community of practice, and help the group schedule meetings and find speakers, volunteer to mentor new BAs, and give presentations to share your knowledge. Join other industry groups focused on information technology (IT), process improvement, change management, or your specific industry. Sharing your experiences helps other BAs and improves the profession as a whole.

The skills and techniques presented in this chapter are not acquired in any particular order. They are grouped into the following general sections:

- Build Your Foundation
- Value Your Time
- Build Your Relationships and Communication Skills
- Sharpen Your Analysis Skills
- Start Adding Value

BUILD YOUR FOUNDATION

Skill: Planning Your Start

One of the hardest skills for a new BA is getting started. When first assigned to a project, a new BA can easily become overwhelmed by the complexity of the business and the sheer volume of information that is not yet understood. If you are a new BA, try to find an experienced BA who can act as a mentor and help you through some of these roadblocks. Every BA gets overwhelmed occasionally but, with experience, you can learn to structure your work and manage the volume.

BA planning, as highlighted throughout these chapters, is a key success factor for professional analysts. This is not *project* planning, but rather taking some time, even if only a few minutes, to consider what the change effort is and exactly what role you are going to play. Knowing your role and how you are planning to add value is key to your success in an organization. Most projects do not add additional people just to add them, but rather, they serve a purpose. Know your purpose. Know the approach that the organization is wishing to take to achieve the desired outcomes. Or at least know if there is no approach decided upon. If possible, identify the people with whom you will work. Know what rules or governance you will have on your analysis activities. Will you require formal sign-off and change management of requirements or will these be constantly reviewed and refined with your stakeholders? Where are you going to put all of this information as you collect and analyze it? Do you already have a system for taking notes? Is there a central requirements repository at your organization? BA planning focuses on being able to answer all of these questions. A seasoned BA who has facilitated numerous change efforts in an organization will still consider all these points. Junior BAs who are just starting out should work to capture all of these questions and answers right from the start. Always do it on your first effort because then you can reuse your own template for the next change effort. Capturing these questions and comparing them to what you actually did or how you modified your approach as you worked with the organization then leads to the final BA planning element—how will you improve yourself? It is one thing to say you will do better next time, but it is an entirely other approach to identify gaps, plan steps to improve, and then apply and re-measure to *show* the improvement.

When starting out, regardless of whether it is a formal or informal project; a traditional, adaptive, or agile project; a solution assessment; or enterprise strategy planning; the following paragraphs contain some guidance to consider before diving into the analysis work.

BA Approach

- Do I know what the goal of the effort is?
- Is the goal well-articulated?
- Does the organization have an approach in mind? That is, does it already plan to purchase a third-party tool or is it simply research and analysis of opportunities to consider?
- How does the organization approach change work? Do they follow certain methodologies?
- What is the organization's risk tolerance?
- How have they approached this kind of change in the past? Did it work well?
- Where do they most need business analysis support?

BA Stakeholders

- What is my role in the change effort?
- Who might I need to work with to perform the business analysis work?
- Are there other stakeholders who may perform the business analysis work?
- Are there pre-conceived ideas on what a BA does in this organization?
- Who might I reach out to for help on the BA work and deliverables?
- How will I need to work with the stakeholders? What techniques and approaches would suit the stakeholders with whom I will be working?
- Are there specific approaches I want to try with these stakeholders?

BA Governance

- How formal will the analysis work need to be?
- Is there a structure already in place on how business analysis is to be performed at the organization?
- What approvals are required?
- What change process is in place for when (*not if!*) requirements or deliverables change?

BA Information Management

- What information might I have to work with?
- What BA artifacts can I reuse?
- Where will I put the information that I gather?
- How much detail is required?
- Which deliverables will I need to create?
- How formal are the deliverables?
- Where will I put the deliverables I create?
- How will I go about sharing the information?
- How will I encourage collaboration on the information?
- Are there tools I have never used but want to try on this effort?

BA Performance Improvement

- What are my skill sets and capabilities walking into this effort?
- Where do I want my competencies to be at the end of this effort?
- How will I measure my success?
- How will I create a plan to meet or exceed my desired level of success? How will it be applied to the next effort I work on?
- Are there any resources I *need* in order to be successful?

Notice these questions are directed at you as the BA and the analysis work to be performed. They have nothing to do with the change effort or project work from the perspective of what tasks, schedules, and budgets are required to deliver the solution. Too many BAs dive right into the work only to find themselves spending time organizing and rewriting all their notes and identifying additional stakeholders late in the game who are frustrated at not being included in the beginning. Some BAs repeat the same mistakes on future projects—having never learned from their prior experience (or put in a plan to change the behavior).

These questions are worth the time it takes to go through them. As you work, you may modify these questions so that you have a reusable template in which to push yourself to grow in your analysis work.

These questions are great regardless of the change effort or type of project. They give you a great foundation on which to begin your BA work. The more you put into thinking about these questions on your first BA assignments, the more comfortable you can be with doing the analysis work regardless of how junior you may feel on an effort. A plan gives you greater confidence to start to be a valuable member of the team, even if you feel inexperienced.

Technique: BA Assessments, Lessons Learned, and Retrospectives

A good practice for a BA to get into the habit of doing is assessments. An assessment is a measurable way to rate your business analysis skill sets. The key word here is measurable. It is one thing for a BA to say that he or she will do a better job with the requirements on the next project. But what is *better*? Do you know how well you were able to complete requirements prior to your last project? How well did you manage requirements during this project? What was the feedback from your stakeholders at the end of the change effort? If you measure before *and* after the project, you will have a measurable value to address in your learning and growth plan.

Assessments can be simple or much more formal. With a simple assessment, you can quickly assess your analysis skill set. As a project gets underway, pick an aspect or task that you know you will have to perform and assess how well you think you will do. The rating can be simple such as "comfortable doing on own" or "needs assistance to complete." Then, assess yourself again after the effort and see how you did. Rather than focus on an assessment measurement, focus on what you do with your assessment since this gives you a starting point to improve. For example, I might want to consider my skills in facilitation. Prior to facilitating a workshop, I assess myself on a scale of 1 to 10, with 10 being able to teach others, and I estimate that I'm at a 7. After facilitating a requirements workshop, I re-assess and think I'm more at a 5 and that I need more practice keeping the group on track and focused. More important than the value of your assessment; however, is what you do with it. You can request to facilitate additional workshops and/ or shadow senior BAs and watch their next facilitated workshop. This is the important part of defining the action or task you will perform to bring your skills to where you want them to be. Incorporate your BA assessments and action plans into your BA planning work and see what opportunities you have with every assignment to address and improve your skills.

What you assess can be basic business analysis techniques, competencies, or even project activities. Many organizations have job competencies and performance expectations for formal (and informal) analyst positions. Do not wait until the end-of-year performance evaluation to look at these. Take these as your own personal BA assessments right from the start. Then with every effort, re-evaluate yourself and define actionable and measurable steps to improve. See Figures 7.1 and 7.2 for examples of BA assessments.

On project-based work, lessons learned (for more traditional work) and retrospective (for more adaptive) sessions are common. Both are aimed at improving the team and organization. These sessions try to identify what worked well, what did not, and then how to improve so that the next change effort goes even better. These are not blaming sessions since they are meant to encourage positive items as well. If something worked really well, then not only would you want to repeat it but also share it with others. Often teams spend time identifying opportunities and challenges—even capturing them—but then never do anything with them. And then during the next project, the same issue happens again. Why? Because you only identified lessons, you did not *learn* the lesson. This same type of review is what you should be using on yourself and how you perform your business analysis assessment. Before you start, assess yourself. If you already have, then review your assessment and what action items you identified. Look to see if your next change effort can address any of these action items or can leverage those successes you have had in the past. Throughout the effort, continue to review what is on your business analysis assessment so you do not lose sight of it. Then, at completion simply walk through your assessment again and see what measures have or have not changed. Create or modify your action steps for the next effort once gaps have been identified. Figure 7.3 shows an example of lessons identified and the steps that are necessary in order to

BA Task	Proficiency Ranking	Explanation
Prepare for elicitation		
Conduct elicitation		
Confirm elicitation results		
Communicate business analysis information		

Proficiency Ranking

1. Never performed this task
2. Awareness of activity, but never used it on a real project
3. Inconsistent use of activity
4. Consistently performed this activity successfully
5. Can teach others

Figure 7.1   BA skills assessment

BA Job Function	Proficiency Ranking	Explanation
Deliver Requirements		
Develop Business Cases		
Identify Operational Support Models		
Conduct Requirements Workshops		

Proficiency Ranking

1. Does not perform function
2. Completes task with help from senior analyst
3. Completes task individually, but requires rework
4. Able to successfully complete task individually on first attempt
5. Able to teach others how to complete task

Figure 7.2   BA job assessment

BA Task	Actual Results	Current Ranking	Expected/ Desired Ranking	Steps to Achieve Desired Proficiency	Date Review/ Re-assess
Prepare for elicitation	Was not prepared for additional attendees at stakeholder session	3	4	Create checklist for elicitation sessions to use	2/15
Conduct elicitation	Elicited requirements successfully within scheduled time	4	5	Pair up with junior BA on next project	4/30
Confirm elicitation results	Had to follow-up individually with participants to confirm results	3	4	Structure elicitation session to include time for confirmation; add to elicitation checklist	2/28

Proficiency Ranking

1. Never performed this task
2. Awareness of activity, but never used it on a real project
3. Inconsistent use of activity
4. Consistently performed this activity successfully
5. Can teach others

Figure 7.3   BA lessons learned in an action plan

learn and improve. Take the same approach with yourself as you do with your teams when doing lessons learned and retrospectives.

Skill: Think Analytically

Some people do it more naturally than others, but training yourself to think analytically requires practice. In order to learn to analyze, train your mind to break down problems and complex systems into small, manageable pieces. Breaking down complex systems is not easy. The analyst must learn to look for business patterns and significant facts (some of the information an analyst will hear and read is insignificant) and to discern the relevant from the irrelevant.

> "Train your mind to break down problems and complex systems into small, manageable pieces."

Take the opportunity to practice whenever possible. There are problems and complex systems everywhere in the world. As you order breakfast at your local coffee shop, think about the steps necessary to get a cup of coffee to you. What questions would you ask if you were learning about the business? Which facts would be important? Is the flavor of the coffee relevant to the process? What is the country of origin of the bean? Does the price of the coffee affect the process? Try to always keep your analysis brain turned on—consider what requirements there are, what processes are working, who are the stakeholders involved or, even better, affected. The more you practice daily, the more natural it will be in your work efforts.

Skill: Try New Techniques

Try using a variety of analysis techniques on the same problem to see what new information is exposed. Do not ignore tried-and-true techniques (e.g., item tracking) just because they have been around for years. Many analysts still use the same time-tested techniques successfully on their projects. Every technique you learn provides another opportunity for you to expand your analysis skills. Newer techniques are often developed from older ones, so understanding an old technique makes it easier to learn a new one.

You can always try older techniques in new fashions and scenarios. If you are really comfortable with reviews, workshops, and focus group sessions, then try using them when you work with a virtual team. You will need to utilize the foundational goals and approaches of these techniques, but also leverage technology and facilitation approaches that you may not have tried before. You can also use a technique for other than its traditional purpose. Try, for example, utilizing a process model for elicitation of requirements. Did you get a different outcome? Put these same items into your BA assessment and plan to try different and novel approaches to techniques so that you are always growing. Remember that the *right* technique for a situation or effort is the one that works. This gives you freedom and creativity, but also requires you to plan your approach on how best to accomplish the task at hand.

Technique: Brainstorming

Brainstorming is used as a tool to generate creative ideas in a group session. The technique has become popular because it helps participants think outside of their current procedures and generate new innovative ideas. Brainstorming is often used when trying to streamline an existing process, resolve a complex problem, or develop a new business opportunity.

Brainstorming encourages group members to contribute all of the ideas that come into their minds without filtering them. Ground rules should be set for the session: no idea is a bad idea, one person speaks at a time, do not evaluate any ideas during brainstorming, and do not eliminate or organize ideas during the session. Remember, there is no analysis during brainstorming—the analysis comes after you have completed the brainstorming effort. For shy groups, try the round-robin approach of asking for an idea from one person at a time.

"There is no analysis during brainstorming."

When a team is experiencing groupthink, brainstorming can help the BA break through. Groupthink occurs when a group works well together and members have affection for each other. Sometimes the team members value the team more than the development of a quality solution. They are hesitant to disagree with each other or point out flaws in recommended solutions. To break groupthink, conduct a formal brainstorming session to generate as many different ideas as possible. You may offer a small reward to the person or team that comes up with the largest number of new ideas.

Brainstorming can also be used by a BA working alone on a project. Allow yourself to imagine possible solutions to a problem that initially seem outside the realm of possibility. You probably did some brainstorming of ideas on your BA assessment. You thought about what is possible and what should be considered. This is a valuable skill that should be exercised often to consider new approaches, market opportunities, and ways to expand the capabilities of all areas of the business.

Skill: Systems Thinking

Systems thinking presents the idea that there are behaviors, properties, and components that emerge from different items working together than would be present when analyzing each element individually. This is an important concept for BAs today as the world grows more and more complex. When you understand how things work together, you gain a more holistic view of the enterprise. Look at how a change to one element of a process affects the entire system as a whole.

Real World Example: A Simple Upgrade

An easy example to consider in the context of systems thinking is upgrading the operating system on your smart device. You are prompted to upgrade because there is an upgrade available—seems simple enough, so you upgrade. Are there applications (apps) on your device that are not compatible with the upgraded operating system? Do the apps need to be upgraded? What about your behavior? A feature was moved, so you have to change your process concerning how you access that feature. A function is now turned on by default, so do you change your usage of different applications? Did you get new functionality with the upgrade that was not present before that might have made some of your applications obsolete? Are you able to communicate with other devices, and therefore people, that you could not before? Are you able to connect via video where before you could only use chat? Does that change how you communicate with your friends? Your grandma? Considering all the aspects of how the components interact, what external forces are present, and which people might be involved is the perspective you need to consider regarding the entire system and what value it is providing the enterprise and its customers.

VALUE YOUR TIME

Every activity the BA plans should be adding value by helping deliver quality business analysis artifacts, collaborating with stakeholders for buy-in, and helping ensure that solutions are maximized. To help attain these goals, the BA needs to closely consider where they are spending their time.

Skill: Prioritization

Take a look at how typical BAs work each day. They start by reviewing all of the tasks that have been assigned to them. Often, they are assigned to more than one project or change effort, so the tasks vary. They must use the information provided by management and key stakeholders about priorities and dependencies in order to decide which of these tasks should be attacked first. Many of these assigned tasks are large; one task may actually represent 80 hours or 2 weeks of work to complete. There will also be tasks that have been started but are on hold because more information is needed and has not been delivered.

Having to prioritize work and make decisions about how to spend one's time is very different from a first-in, first-out task list that is common in other business areas. So where do you spend your time? The simple answer would be to ask what action delivers the most value to the organization. Of course, being on projects and large change efforts, the BA is but one person working together with others to deliver the solution. The BA does not single-handedly deliver game-changing solutions each day. They actually help the different teams move efforts forward. With this in mind, the BA needs to consider who is waiting on artifacts that the BA can help deliver. What items need researching or analysis to help the team make a decision and move forward? What information is the BA waiting on?

Just like prioritization that is done in backlog grooming work and strategic planning, prioritization of your own BA work starts with defining the criteria to use. Prioritization is about understanding relative value. And this is extremely important to remember. What your manager may value, and therefore prioritize, is probably different than what your project manager (PM) will prioritize, which is probably different than what the different business areas' managers will prioritize. Defining the criteria first helps you to keep an objective view. The value to the organization or measures of risk or opportunity are those big picture considerations that make great prioritization criteria. Even if you do not work on project work and are more of an operational support role, you will find prioritization of your day-to-day tasks exists. The criteria have often been pre-defined (e.g., an outage for all computer users is a major issue versus one user not being able to remember his/her password is a minor issue). Resources are then prioritized to help support troubleshooting the major computer issues rather than an issue that only affects a single user.

Real World Example: Prioritization Challenges

Imagine you have been assigned to two projects. One is to add a new field to an existing screen so that marketing can track an additional characteristic of each customer. This is important for marketing and sales of future products to specific customers. The second project is an enterprise-wide initiative to restructure customer service and streamline order processing activities. This project requires that you collaborate with stakeholders from several departments to understand the business functions and needs, and then develop current and future workflows to design new processes.

To which project would you allocate most of your time during the day? Since the first project is small and fairly straightforward, your tendency will be to just get it done. You already know how to update a prototype, define a data element, and communicate a change to IT. The second project is less straightforward. It requires planning, scheduling, and collaborating with a large group of stakeholders. Simply getting the needed people in a room to define the current processes without jumping to conclusions on the future state seems like an arduous amount of work. You feel tired before you even begin and an easier move would be to put off starting this major effort.

If you spend the majority of your day on the first project, the strategic project waits. In addition, the next morning there will probably be another small, easy task on your desk that will get in the way of the bigger project. The natural tendency is to put off the more complex tasks. However, BAs should focus on the greatest value to the greatest population. While something may be easy for you, often you will need to learn to prioritize those greater, more challenging tasks as they deliver the most value to your organization. Keeping your eye on the delivery of value is key to being a successful BA.

Defining value can mean defining *importance*. Getting good at identifying your measurable criteria will not only help you in your own work, but will help you collaborate with stakeholders to define priorities of work elements and change efforts. This criterion should be defined while being impartial toward any stakeholder or area of expertise. Avoid vague criteria such as *easy* or *hard*. What may be *easy* to the finance department may be *hard* to IT. Include measurements or other tangibles as much as possible. An example for your own BA work might be *time to complete*. A junior and more experienced BA could both estimate their work using this criterion, which their manager could use to prioritize activities.

Technique: Time Boxing and Grouping

With criteria defined, you can then prioritize the work based on a number of factors. You might do some ranking based on the criteria selected—from small to largest. Or you might need to use a technique called *time boxing*. Time boxing aims to prioritize as much work as possible within a predetermined time frame—meaning you will not have time to do everything; but with the time you are given, you determine how much you can accomplish. Time boxing is good for not only time frames, but it is also very useful if you have been given a predetermined budget. How much work can be accomplished given the budget that was approved? This is often what the agile approach entails—putting value on elements of work and then prioritizing working on those elements that will give the most value. Then as long as you have time left (and money) you pick the next most valuable item and include that one.

When estimating the value of items, another popular approach to grouping includes thinking of items as *t-shirt* sizes, which is basically looking at criteria as being small, medium, or large (i.e., the sizes of t-shirts). This is why criteria are so important. What makes an effort *small* versus *large*? Could the IT team estimate sizing as *large* because they have to do major coding changes while the marketing department estimates the work as being *small* because they only have to update one field on their form? By grouping, it then can be easier to prioritize which types of efforts to work on first, such as having everyone work together to complete one large effort at a time. Or the team may focus on getting as many small items completed as fast as they can.

Like estimation, there are risks that can emerge from your prioritization work. Be sure that you articulate and communicate these risks as you work with the stakeholders and let them know the impacts or tradeoffs that emerge from different prioritization rankings.

Prioritizing one's time and the organization's resources is one of the most important benefits a BA contributes to the bottom line. How many times have you been in a meeting or working on a task and you realized there is no value being added to the organization? Or that you are not adding any value to the meeting? Those *aha* moments are when you need to stop and rethink your priorities and better focus on your work. Doing this for both yourself as well as the teams you work with can start as easily as asking a series of questions, beginning with the *why*:

- Why are we doing this activity?
- What is this activity doing for the project or change effort? The organization?
- When do we expect a payoff from this activity?
- Is the payoff bigger than the effort that we are expending?

Prioritizing work is a skill that requires practice and diligence. One habit to embrace daily is looking at your to-do list (which is usually longer than you will accomplish) and identifying the most important tasks. Some of these tasks will be quick and easy to complete, and these are often the most attractive. You might think: "I can get that out of the way this morning and be done with it!" But do not leave the larger, more difficult tasks until last or they will never get done. Often, those more difficult tasks are related to long-term strategic projects that are important to the organization. Also, do not forget to break things down into simpler parts (see Functional Decomposition in Chapter 6). Smaller chunks of work can be easier to prioritize when you can clearly articulate the work and level of effort it will take. Choosing the appropriate task on which to work each day is critical. And when you consider what you could do to move those larger efforts forward, those larger pieces of work are often much more valuable to the organization. This value to the organization is the key prioritization perspective that a BA should always keep in mind.

> "Choosing the appropriate task on which to work each day is critical."

Skill: Understand the 80/20 Rule

It is well-established that BAs spend 20% of their time eliciting 80% of the requirements. The other 80% of analysis time is spent collaborating on the other 20% of the requirements. This occurs because the majority of requirements (roughly 80%) are fairly straightforward and can be elicited fairly quickly. An experienced BA can interview business stakeholders briefly and immediately begin to understand the high-level requirements. An analyst can quickly get the big picture and then fill in all of the details. Some of these details will also be straightforward and fairly easy to capture. Then there are the rest of the requirements. Every business area has at least a few processes, business rules, or data needs that are complex and difficult to understand. These may be the 20% that take the most time to find and are the most important because they are complex. Try to determine whether the most important requirements are in the 80% (straightforward) or the 20% (complex). The difficulty and complexity may be related to industry specifics or they may result from a business area where policies and procedures have never been clearly articulated.

BUILD YOUR RELATIONSHIPS AND COMMUNICATION SKILLS

Skill: Build Strong Relationships

Building relationships is an important skill of a successful BA. Every day that you interact with other BAs and with your current and potential stakeholders, you can be practicing this skill. It is important for people in the business analysis role to build strong, solid relationships—both in and out of the office. There are two key reasons why you should always be working on building relationships to improve yourself both personally and professionally:

1. *Knowledge and experience*: "No one lives long enough to learn everything they need to learn starting from scratch. To be successful, we absolutely, positively have to find people who have already paid the price to learn the things that we need to learn to achieve our goals"—best-selling author

Brian Tracy. You cannot know and experience everything. What you can do is to be connected with people who have the knowledge and experience you need for any challenge.

2. *Access and openness*: Your project is the number one priority for you, but it may not be for the subject matter experts (SMEs) and other stakeholders from whom you need time. Having strong relationships with those stakeholders prior to and during a project will help open the necessary doors and encourage them to talk to you. As previously discussed, trust is a big part of a good relationship. SMEs will be more open and honest with you during a project if they trust you.

Skill: Ask the Right Questions

An important analysis skill is that of developing good questions. Questions are used to elicit information. The focus on this skill set is working to develop good questions, not worrying about correct answers. If you knew the answer already, then why would you be asking the question? A business analysis professional should always be thinking of more questions to which an answer is needed. For initial meetings and interviews with stakeholders, use broad questions and elicit answers that describe an overall view. Subsequent elicitation sessions will require more detailed, clarifying questions. After asking a question, repeat the answer back in your own words to confirm that you understand it correctly. This is a great way to verify that you have captured the response accurately. Asking additional clarifying questions can then help you validate the information. When stakeholders tell you how they perform a task such as accepting a customer order, follow-up questions may include things like:

- What if the customer's payment is not approved?
- What type of payments do you accept?
- What are the typical dollar amounts of these payments?

An experienced BA will ask detailed questions regarding each process, piece of data, and business rule. Some of the questions may be slightly out of scope, but it is important to make sure nothing is missed. Asking these additional questions provides context. BAs need to understand context to ensure that their solution, not just the product of the change, will be successful. Strong questions are open-ended and encourage the stakeholder to talk at length about the requirement or topic. Often, a stakeholder provides information over and above the required answer. This additional information may prove relevant.

Junior BAs who are just starting out should use their planning time to develop and organize their questions prior to meeting with stakeholders. When you are having trouble getting started, write down all of the questions that you can think of. Use open-ended questions to evoke a response that is more than just yes or no. Even if the plan is not followed, having a good list of questions to reference helps ensure the elicitation session is valuable.

Use the journalist model to think through the who, what, where, when, why, and how. Each of these question starters will generate many specific questions for a particular project or business area. Formulating a list of questions is something that any BA can do at any point in a project either working alone or in a group. Creating and reviewing this list exposes the analysis work that needs to be done. Sample questions could include:

- Who performs the process?
- Who manages or approves the process?
- Who provides the input to the process? Who receives the output?
- What data, materials, forms, or systems are used?
- What constraints, policies, or procedures guide the process?
- What problems occur with the process?
- Where is the process performed?
- When is the process performed? On a regular basis? After a triggering event?
- Why is the process performed?
- How is the process performed?

Once you have a list of questions, look at each question and think about:

- How could you best elicit this information?
- How will you best record it when you receive it?
- How critical will the answer be?
- What type of requirement component will be found in the answer?
- Who would have the answer?
- Who is going to use this information?

As you are formulating questions, you should think about who would be able to best answer them. Most change efforts and projects involve many stakeholders, each one able to provide unique information or pieces to the puzzle that you are putting together. It is important to think about which questions you will ask each stakeholder before your scheduled interviews. Stakeholders from different departments and at different levels of an organization will be able to provide different information. It is important to ask the right questions to the right people.

Typically, the *why* questions are best asked to high-level stakeholders. Executives and managers often see the bigger picture and know the reasons for the organization's decisions. Middle-level managers and supervisors can answer questions about who does what, where activities are performed, and what the goals of each activity are. Business workers will be able to answer specific, detailed questions about how work is accomplished and what specific activities are related to others.

Planning your questions is part of your overall BA planning. Always start with the goal—what do you hope to accomplish or learn by asking the question? For what purpose will the information be provided? Be clear about your goal(s), as this will not only keep you focused but this information is often also desired by your stakeholders so they know why you need their help and more important, their valuable time. Then take a moment and think of all the questions that would help you get this information. With these questions in mind, you can then consider which stakeholders will best provide the desired information. Following these steps means you have just developed a simple communication plan. Do this exercise even if you do not know all of the information. This will reveal any gaps as to what you do not know and should clarify before moving forward, regardless of what technique you might be using.

Real World Example: Asking Good Questions for the Clarification of Requirements

Imagine you have been assigned to create a new financial report for your chief financial officer (CFO). He wants to see consolidated profit and loss numbers for all of the company's product lines. Even though you have only been given a two-sentence description of this project, you should be able to generate a long list of questions (both obvious and more complex). For example:

- What is the name of the CFO? What is his phone number and e-mail address?
- What type of communication does he prefer? What are the best times to contact him? What is his availability?
- Where is the CFO located? In what time zone?
- When is the report needed/expected?
- What do existing profit and loss reports look like?
- How are these reports created?
- What are the product lines? How many are there?
- What should the format of this new report be? Should it be the same as existing ones?
- Are the product line financials all managed by the same software?
- If not, how do accounts map from one product to another?

No matter how little you know about your assignment, you can always develop questions.

Skill: Listen Actively

Listening well is an important skill for all people, especially for people performing business analysis. Eliciting requirements often involves asking excellent questions and listening carefully for responses. Listening is difficult and is very different from simply hearing someone. Most individuals have never been formally taught how to listen. Listening is an active, conscious decision that is made during a conversation. The BA must decide to listen and be actively involved in the listening process.

"Listening is an active, conscious decision."

Becoming an excellent listener brings the BA many benefits. People enjoy talking to good listeners and really appreciate the attention given. Good listeners are able to help resolve disagreements and conflicts by finding common ground and clearly articulating opposing viewpoints. Listening allows you to carefully make decisions based on solid facts.

When you listen actively you are engaged. Studies show that as much as 55% of a message is received non-verbally. Consciously watch body language and facial expressions. When a business stakeholder is telling you about a task, watch for signs that will indicate how they feel about the task. Is it enjoyable? Is it tedious? Do they see value in it or is it just busy work? Are they interested in helping to improve the process? You can gather valuable information about a business area by listening with your eyes and your ears.

Communicate your own interest and curiosity through your tone of voice and body language. Be aware of the non-verbal messages that you are sending. When you are engaged physically with a stakeholder, by actively leaning toward the person, concentrating on their answers, taking notes, and being honestly interested in what they are saying, you encourage the individual to give much more detail and elaborate on unclear points. If you are disinterested, sarcastic, condescending, demeaning, or negative in any way, the stakeholder may shut down and not be willing to provide important requirements.

A great way to be truly present and thoroughly engaged in the conversation is to get someone to help you out by being the scribe. Introduce the scribe and let your stakeholder know that the scribe's role in the conversation is to simply capture the information that is being shared. The scribe does not speak during the conversation, but rather focuses on the note taking. This allows you to be able to look directly at your stakeholder and focus on all their thoughts, actions, and emotions. After the session, you can then go through the notes with the scribe, adding what emphasis you saw during the session. If you can, find someone to help you who is *not* familiar with the content. Do this because the scribe will have no bias toward the topic (which can occur when you take notes) and will only be interested in getting the information down in writing—capturing almost everything. They are not sure what is important and what is not, so they try to get all of the statements. This gives you a wealth of information and word choices that you might not have caught during the conversation. Using a scribe is also a great way to mentor junior BAs. They get to be present and see a more experienced BA in action. Of course, you could always record the session either in an audio or video format. However, be mindful that many people are uncomfortable with sharing thoughts in these recorded formats, especially if they are talking about challenges or problems in the organization. Remember that regardless of how you ask the questions, letting your stakeholders know exactly what you do with the information that you gather will help to build and maintain trust. When the stakeholders see that the information they share is taken objectively and is used to better the organization, they will build more trust with you and become much more willing to continue to share and support your change efforts. A simple e-mail after the session including a summary of your notes can buy you a great amount of trust and support moving forward.

Barriers to Listening

There are many barriers to listening. These barriers prevent the listener from accurately interpreting the intended message. Identify your barriers and work to eliminate them. One barrier is filters. An individual's brain processes each new piece of information through filters that have developed since childhood. You may not be aware of the filters that influence your ability to hear an intended message. Filters are based on prejudices, beliefs, values, attitudes, past experiences, interests, and fears. Become aware of your filters. Try to determine how they were developed and how they influence your thinking. Improve your communication skills by recognizing your filters and their effect on your ability to listen. A BA should always be as unbiased as possible and focus on the best solution for all stakeholders involved. In addition, be aware that other people also have filters. Listen for these and be aware of their impact on your intended messages.

> "The BA focuses on the best solution for all stakeholders."

Another barrier to listening is lack of interest. When a BA is not curious or interested in learning about an SME's business area, their body language and behavior will reveal that lack of interest and this can be interpreted by the speaker as a lack of interest in him or her as a person. Determine why you are not interested. Are you feeling tired? Are you distracted by unrelated problems? Do you think that you already know what the speaker is telling you? Once you determine why you are not interested, you can correct the problem. Listening is committing—decide prior to starting that you want to get value out of the conversation.

Preconceived ideas can also be a barrier to listening. Preconceived ideas and thoughts are almost always present when dealing with a familiar topic or person. The tendency is to selectively listen for what you expect or want to hear. You may screen out information that does not meet your expectations. If you have worked in the business area being analyzed, you risk missing important information because of your preconceived ideas. Although having some previous knowledge of the business is helpful, it can also be a hindrance. You may not reconfirm specific information because you think that you already understand it. You may also fail to probe for differences between what you already know and what the SME is telling you. Keeping an open mind rather than relying on preconceived notions is critical to eliciting requirements that are clear and complete.

Be careful not to formulate responses or follow-up questions while an SME is still talking. When you allow your mind to jump ahead to your next comment or question, you may be missing valuable information. Try to stay open and actively listen until you hear the entire thought. Paraphrase the message back to the SME to be sure you heard it all. Actively take notes on the information being provided. Once the SME has finished, take a few moments to compose your response and follow-up questions. The SME will appreciate the fact that you were focused on listening while they were talking.

Another barrier to listening is finishing other people's sentences. This will diminish an SME's desire to continue to communicate with you. Finishing other people's sentences is a habit that can be broken. If you become aware that you are exhibiting this habit, work to break it by listening for periods and question marks from the SME. The SME will pause when they finish a thought, and this is the opportunity for you to respond. If you have a hard time keeping silent, drink water while the SME is talking. Try to count to three once the SME has paused to ensure that they have finished and allow yourself to gather your thoughts before responding. Use body language like nodding and eye contact to help the SME finish his or her thought. Dispersed teams may amplify these communication barriers. Refer to Chapter 2 for suggestions on working with dispersed teams.

Listening for Requirements

There are common phrases an analyst can listen for to find requirements. Table 7.1 lists words and phrases to listen for and the possible requirements components that could be discovered from that information.

Table 7.1   Phrases to requirements components

Words or phrases	Possible requirements component
Has, performs, does	Functional requirement
If . . .	Business rule
Sometimes . . .	Conditional business rule
Of course . . .	Assumption
It would be nice . . .	Unnecessary or low priority requirement
Hopefully, envision, imagine, would like	TO-BE solution possibilities/ideas
Existing, current	AS-IS procedures and processes
Only when . . .	Business rule, possibly a security issue
Quickly	Performance requirements
Not	Business rule
Always, never	Mandatory business rules
When . . .	Business rule
Save, store, capture, write down	Data
Access . . .	Nonfunctional requirements

Skill: Write Effectively

Business analysis professionals communicate and present information to stakeholders verbally and through the written word. The ability to write clear, concise, unambiguous sentences is highly valued. BAs should be purposeful with all of their written communication: e-mail, memos, meeting agendas, meeting minutes, and most important, business analysis and requirements deliverables. Clearly communicating requirements in text is very difficult. Experienced analysts use diagrams and models as much as possible, but this does not eliminate the need for textual descriptions. Models, diagrams, and tables are all supported by definitions and detailed descriptions that can only be documented with text.

New BAs should focus on using consistent terminology and developing strong definitions. Have others review your writing as often as possible to find areas for improvement. A good approach is to write your content, then go back and remove a third. People often write more than is required to get the message across. Work to be very clear on your message. Text that supports requirements should be as specific as possible with as few words as possible. Do not include assumptions or further considerations when defining work elements because this can create confusion. Put assumptions and recommendations in a different section. When presenting information for decision making, use a structured approach to help keep your writing in focus (see Figure 7.4 for an example). If you are asking for a stakeholder to make a decision, be very clear as to what you are asking. Then provide the information needed to help your stakeholder make the decision. When writing, think about all of the questions that someone may ask about what you are writing. If you can anticipate these questions, putting the information in your presentation speeds the actions by those using your information.

NEED: Decision to expand scope to include mobile access.

IMPACT: Mobile access development will require additional 10 weeks of development resulting in increase of $10K in budget.

Estimated annual profits from sales increase from $30K to $45K by adding the additional mobile capabilities.

BACKGROUND: Marketing surveys shows that most customers interact with services via their mobile devices. This new product, while designed to be sold in stores, could easily be used on a mobile platform.

ALTERNATIVE: Continue project as planned without mobile capabilities. Marketing will conduct customer surveys to gather product feedback once product is launched.

Development of mobile access post production will take an estimated 16 weeks and cost $30K.

RECOMMENDATION: Include mobile access as part of scope of initial project.

Figure 7.4   Structured writing approach

Skill: Design Excellent Presentations

One of the communication skills used frequently in business analysis is presenting information. BAs are constantly presenting information, formally and informally, to stakeholders. Some of the information that BAs present includes:

- Business cases with cost/benefit analysis to executives to get approval for recommendations
- Work plans and time estimates to PMs and sponsors
- Business requirements to business stakeholders for verification and validation
- Business requirements to the solution team stakeholders to jump-start design meetings
- Functional requirements and design ideas to various stakeholders to get feedback

These presentations vary in formality and audience size but are always important opportunities for the BA to increase the success of the project or change effort.

Formal presentations must be carefully planned and practiced. Like all of your BA work, be sure you have a clear goal for why you are presenting the information and why a formal presentation is the best format. For some, delivering a formal presentation is one of the most frightening human experiences. Confidence in speaking comes from knowing your topic well and practicing your presentation. Focus on your goal and what information you need in order to complete that goal. Give yourself opportunities to practice presentations with smaller audiences and deliverables. BAs need to be able to clearly articulate challenges and opportunities that will drive decision makers forward to achieve value from your change efforts.

When you are preparing for a formal presentation, be sure that you understand the reason for the presentation: Are you making a recommendation? Are you notifying management of implementation plans? Are you informing business workers about how their jobs will change with the implementation of the solution? Think about why you are presenting. Be sure to communicate the main points concisely and clearly and allow time for questions and answers. Be positive, even when you have to deliver bad news. Try to predict all of the questions the audience may ask and prepare answers for those questions. If you are nervous about presenting, focus less on being right or *good* and more on ensuring that your information is correct, data is accurate, and that you have the necessary information prepared for decision makers.

Skill: Facilitate and Build Consensus

Every business analysis professional needs to master the skill of facilitation. To facilitate is *to make easy*. This skill is used in almost every interaction, not just in formal requirements workshops. BAs are constantly helping stakeholders to easily express their needs, problems, and preferences. It is common to hear IT people complain that the users do not know what they want. Often, they simply do not know how to articulate their wants and needs. A business analysis professional knows how to ask questions, discuss answers, and provide suggestions to facilitate (make it easy for users to explain) what they want. This is a valuable skill in any pro-

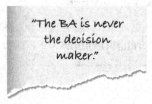

"The BA is never the decision maker."

fession. The ability to listen carefully, interpret unclear statements, ask clarifying questions, and help to bring people to a common understanding is a skill worth developing. Remember, the BA is never the decision maker but they constantly find themselves moving people forward with decision making on change efforts. Facilitation will be both planned and occur ad hoc. Collaborative requirements sessions are best facilitated by an analytical BA.

To improve your ability to facilitate, first concentrate on your active listening skills. Second, improve your verbal presentation skills. Speak precisely and concisely and be direct and honest. One of the difficult aspects of facilitation is enforcing session rules and remaining fact-based and unbiased. Use a non-judgmental tone and stay focused on the goal, not the people. You will know when your skill is improving because co-workers will begin to ask you to help them resolve issues between other people.

A facilitator often helps a group build consensus or agreement so the participants will all support the decisions or ideas generated by the session. During a facilitated session, many ideas are recorded or discussed. It is the group's responsibility to narrow those ideas down and come to an agreement that meets the objective of the session (see the section on facilitated sessions in Chapter 4). While doing this, the group may want to review the list and eliminate some of them. Once the list is narrowed down to real possible solutions, the facilitator helps the group make a decision.

Consensus is a collective opinion arrived at by a group of individuals working together under conditions that permit open and supportive communication, such that everyone in the group feels they have had a fair chance to influence the decision. Participants in consensus agree to decisions even though they may not personally prefer them. A facilitator's goal is to help the group achieve consensus, if possible. The facilitator creates the environment to foster these conditions. Be aware of the potential results of a group decision when consensus cannot be reached. Table 7.2 lists types of group decisions and considerations.

Skill: Conduct Effective Meetings

Business analysis professionals are often responsible for scheduling and leading meetings. This is a core skill that every BA should develop. Many of the activities and behaviors that are used to run an effective meeting are simple and straightforward. The trick is to remember to use them consistently.

There are many reasons why a BA may decide to schedule a meeting. Examples include to consult with a group of stakeholders on the business analysis plan, to develop or confirm the scope of the analysis area, or to brainstorm on solution alternatives. It is important to define your objective for a meeting. Without a strong reason for getting people together, you may waste their time. Think about whether your goal could be accomplished in a different way. If you are simply giving stakeholders the status of your progress, would an e-mail message work just as well as an in-person meeting? If you need help getting started with your requirements document, could you meet with a senior BA to get that help? If you need requirements from one department, is there one key stakeholder who could answer the majority of your questions? Any time that you can accomplish your goal without holding a meeting, you have saved your company valuable

Table 7.2 Types of decision making

	Consensus	Unanimity	Majority vote	Compromise
Definition	100% support	100% agreement	51% wins	Halfway point for all
Pros	All members will support	All members will support	Majority will support	All will support partially
Cons	Time consuming	Unrealistic	Creates win/lose scenario	Creates win/lose scenario
When to use	Support is needed	Clear cut issue	To narrow a list	Need breakthrough
When not to use	Short time frame	Complex issues	To make a final decision	Support is needed

time and money. A good exercise for any BA is to calculate the cost of meetings. Think not only about the hourly amount each individual's wages may be, but also consider that the meeting is taking these individuals away from completing other work. Make sure the outcome of the meeting is worth the cost and effort. And then prepare to ensure that the intended outcome is achieved.

When you have decided that a meeting is the appropriate forum to accomplish your objective, take some time to plan the meeting. Select the appropriate attendees, develop an agenda, conduct the meeting efficiently, and follow up after the meeting is over.

Prepare for the Meeting

The leader or organizer of a meeting should prepare themselves and the participants for the meeting in order to be effective. Clear objectives are necessary to describe specifically what the meeting is to accomplish. The leader should create an agenda and estimate the time required for each topic or activity in the meeting. Based on the objective of the meeting, select participants who will contribute to the objective. Be sure to only include necessary participants. The more people in a meeting, the greater the potential to waste time. Other interested people may be informed about the meeting and sent the meeting minutes.

Determine a time and location for the meeting that best meets the needs of the participants. Since *all* of your participants are necessary to accomplish your goal, aim for 100% attendance. If a key stakeholder is unable to attend, reschedule the meeting. Be mindful that not all meetings have to be in person. This is often not feasible when working with distributed teams. Ensure that your time and location best supports your audience attendance. Practice with various technologies so that you get comfortable conducting effective meetings with virtual attendees. Plan beforehand how you are going to capture the decisions and outcomes of the meeting. Does your organization have templates already? And where will the information be posted or shared and communicated and referenced?

Meeting Agenda

The meeting agenda should be prepared in advance and distributed to participants. This allows everyone to adequately prepare for the objective of the meeting. One of the worst feelings is when someone asks why they are invited. Be clear about this up front. New topics added during the meeting should be noted and scheduled for future discussions unless the group agrees to adjust the agenda. An agenda should include the following items:

- Objective of the meeting (including the expected outcome)
- Date of the meeting along with a start and end time
- Location
- Meeting participants
- Topics, with estimated time for each topic
- Person assigned to lead or present each topic

When the BA spends a few minutes thinking through the meeting agenda, a meeting is more likely to be well run and effective. Although not all meetings will proceed as planned, having a plan sets everyone's expectations and clearly shows when the discussion is getting off topic (Brassard and Ritter 1994).

Conducting the Meeting

The BA or meeting leader should be constantly alert and focused on making the meeting successful. Meetings have become known as time wasters to many people because they are often not well planned or well run. A BA will demonstrate their value to the organization by running effective meetings. As your reputation for being prepared and well organized grows, people will be more willing to attend and participate in your meetings, causing them to arrive at your meetings on time with an optimistic attitude. Your success will breed even more success.

The following list contains some tips for conducting successful meetings:

- Always start on time; invite latecomers to stay after the meeting to hear what they missed.
- Consider scheduling meetings to start 15 minutes after the hour instead of on the hour. This gives participants time to travel from their last meeting to yours.
- Begin with emphasizing what the objective is and ask if anyone has questions before moving forward.
- Introduce participants to each other and explain why each was included in the meeting. This lets everyone know the role they are expected to play and encourages every attendee to participate.
- Restate the meeting objective and review the agenda; ask for suggested changes or any clarifications before getting started.
- Walk through the agenda, one item at a time, making sure that all attendees feel each item is complete before moving on to the next. Post outstanding items and issues on an issues list for follow up.
- Be sure to watch the time and keep the group focused. Stop side conversations if they arise.
- End the meeting on time. If halfway through your meeting, you are concerned about achieving the objective within your time frame, pause the meeting to state this fact and ask the stakeholders to remain on topic or agree to a follow-up meeting before you even finish. This shows respect and value for their time.
- Re-emphasize the objective that was achieved at the end of the meeting. Assign outstanding items to appropriate team members, along with expected completion dates.
- Thank participants for attending and emphasize the value of the work that was accomplished.
- Make participants feel good about how their time was spent.

Follow Up

Meeting minutes can serve a valuable purpose in business analysis work. They provide a written record of decisions and confirm consistent understanding of the agreements made during a meeting. Meeting minutes are *not* meant to capture every word said. Consider them a summary of decisions and outstanding actions that push the team forward—toward completing their change effort. Discussions can be ambiguous and easily misinterpreted, especially with a large number of people. By writing out the meeting results, the BA helps to articulate a single version of the meeting's outcomes that the team can confirm or correct. Consider capturing the outcomes live during the meeting. Do not be afraid to share your screen with the attendees so they see what decisions you are capturing and to whom you are assigning action items. If the BA was misunderstood, a correction can be identified immediately. Then, as soon as your meeting ends, send the resulting meeting minutes to all who were invited and to those who should be aware of the outcome. Try to avoid long time periods between the meeting and sending your key takeaways so that everyone can quickly move forward.

Real World Example: Meeting Artifacts

On a project, part of defining the information management requirements was identifying templates for preserving the minutes of the meeting. It was known there would be a number of meetings conducted by both the PM and the BA. The template was pre-filled with a list of primary stakeholders that were identified as critical to the discussion about the solution. There was also a section for secondary stakeholders that listed all of the people who should be informed, but did not need to be consulted for decision making. This made it easy to schedule meetings because you knew who was involved and who you could simply *cc* on e-mails. This template also had space for a desired outcome, agenda, decision log, and action log.

In prepping for meetings, I only had to fill out the top portion through to the agenda. I would include this with the meeting invites. During the meeting, I would pull up this template and as I walked through it, I would add decisions to the decision log. Any actions identified were then added to the action log. I shared my screen on the projector in the conference room (as many meetings were in person at the request of the sponsor). As I would type, the attendees would correct me, clarifying terminology and acronyms and agreeing on who the assignee of action items should be. This facilitated greater engagement and buy-in from the attendees. At the end of the meeting, I would save and post the template—which was now filled out with only decisions and actions—and notify both the attendees and team members to be informed. This was done during the meeting so I did not have to go back and spend hours trying to "clean up" meeting notes. Following the template also created a standard that the participants stated was easy for them to go back and reference for information because they knew exactly where to look.

Make sure to follow up on any issues that were not resolved during the meeting. If a participant volunteers to get back to you with answers, make sure that they do. This is a great way to build better relationships as you reach out to people to ensure that actions are being completed by offering any assistance necessary. Let the entire group know, though, if issues are resolved outside of the meeting. Following up on loose ends demonstrates thoroughness and a concern for quality.

Skill: Conduct Requirements Reviews

A requirements review session is a formal working session where participants ask questions, make suggestions, and improve the quality of the requirements being reviewed. While many BAs work with requirements often, conducting reviews of any business analysis artifact can and should happen frequently. Analysis practices today should focus more on collaborating *with* your stakeholders rather than doing work in a back office and handing over a solution. Any approach where you get valuable, real-time feedback on solution development is a must for successful business outcomes. For any BA, starting with requirements reviews is a great way to get comfortable eliciting feedback and ideas to work collaboratively with your stakeholders. Requirement deliverables are naturally very complex and difficult to perfect. Rarely would an analyst be able to capture all of the requirements correctly and completely for a project without the help of a review. Keep in mind that reviews are also referred to as walk-throughs, peer reviews, and inspections.

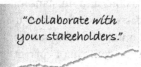

"Collaborate with your stakeholders."

Many studies show that projects often fail because of missing or poorly defined requirements (PMI 2014). Having requirements reviewed before using them to develop a solution is the single best way to mitigate this risk. One missed requirement discovered during a review could save the project team hundreds of hours of work later during testing or after implementation. In addition, having your work reviewed helps you learn and produce improved requirements for the next project.

Analysts must encourage others to review their work as frequently as possible and must be open to suggestions. This requires an analyst who welcomes constructive criticism. Remember that requirements and other BA artifacts are often in support of the business stakeholders. They are not *your* requirements, but rather the product owner's or other decision makers on the team; thus, you must always think about those who need to use the requirements. When you get feedback, remember it is not about you, but about the work. Keep the attitude that you are there to help find the best solution, regardless of who originally created the ideas or who will deliver the end product.

How to Conduct a Review

All of the recommendations for conducting effective meetings also apply to reviews. To make the best use of participants' time and have an effective review, there are specific steps that you should follow:

1. Have a clear objective for doing a review
2. Schedule time with participants
3. Distribute review materials
4. Have participants review materials prior to the session
5. Conduct the review session
6. Record review feedback and changes and update material
7. Share material for awareness and any final confirmations
8. Conduct a second review if absolutely necessary

This review process should be incorporated into every BA plan and should become a regular practice in your organization by being included in the overall project plans. It is also supported by all of the major quality initiatives (i.e., CMMI, ISO) as the best method for *testing* the requirements for quality.

Step 1—Have a Clear Objective for Doing a Review

Any deliverable can undergo a formal review. The more requirements deliverables for which you conduct reviews, the better the quality of your solution.

- Reviews can be used for project initiation documents to confirm understanding of project scope and to gain approval to move forward.
- Reviews conducted for business requirements are opportunities for the business SMEs to carefully verify the results of elicitation sessions and validate that their core business needs are articulated clearly and correctly, as well as to define acceptance criteria.
- Technical requirements and specifications are great candidates for reviews because they lay out the *blueprint* for IT work. Any questions or inconsistencies found in these blueprints help to improve the foundation upon which solution designs are built.
- IT teams often conduct reviews of programs to ensure standards are met and that software will be easy for other developers to understand and maintain.

- Test plans and test cases are also good candidates for reviews. Reviews can compare the tests against the requirements to make sure that all requirements are covered by the testing plans.

These reviews help your stakeholders understand the testing involved. They also help validate the solution by confirming expected behavior.

Also, your planning must include a decision as to what will be the product of the meeting. Gathering lots of input as notes that you take back to your desk to organize and update the reviewed item can be inefficient if your update only generates more questions. A great approach is to bring in an editable version of your artifact and update it *live* as you get input. Remember, people pay more attention in meetings when they can watch you create the item and literally see what is going on. They also will quickly correct you to ensure that the information is accurate.

Step 2—Schedule Time with Participants

Determining who will participate in the review is an important step in making the review successful. First, think about the scope of the content that is being reviewed. Are these high-level business requirements to clarify general goals and objectives? Or are these detailed technical requirements to be used by the developers? Be clear on the scope of the content. Managers may insist on being invited to every review session. However, they may not know the level of detail at which you are expecting to discuss your requirements or other business analysis work. Being clear on the scope and explaining the kinds of materials you plan to review along with what questions you want to ask will help the managers understand the type of information you need. Since a review is intended to be a discussion about a deliverable, a participant's title and position in the organization should not be relevant during the session. The review is not a discussion about the author's productivity or proficiency. It is a discussion about a product. This clarity may lead them to identify an SME who might better help you. You can always send copies of the outcome to those who are interested but could not attend.

Also consider that you might need to break your content up into different sessions in order to best scope the review segments. The bigger the scope the higher the number of participants you will want; although, a large number of participants is harder to manage. You can break up the content in any way that best supports collaborative and productive groups. For instance, you might invite the decision makers and business owners to the first session to validate the goals, objectives, and high-level business requirements first. With those validated, SMEs might be your next group with which to review whether or not the solution requirements align to and support business requirements. Then, with the key functionality defined in your solution requirements, you might conduct another session with the technical teams to talk through the technical requirements and validate design assumptions. Make sure that every review session is always scoped to the goal of that session, including attendees—nothing more and nothing less.

Always think about who is getting value out of the item being reviewed. With requirements reviews, you always want those people who will be consuming the requirements to participate. Then, you should also think about who could provide clarification on the details. For example, the technology team attends because they will be building the technical solution. If they have a question about a business process, who from the business would you want there to clarify? If you do not have SMEs from that business area attend, then the questions will be aimed at you, expecting you to know the answer. You also want any of your decision makers included. If a question comes up and a decision needs to be made, who would be making that decision? It is okay to allow those attending the review session to agree as a group, but you need to make this determination ahead of time.

Another great resource for requirements reviews is quality assurance. A quality assurance analyst will look at each requirement and think about how it could be tested. If a requirement or design element is too vague or ambiguous to be tested, it needs to be further defined or described.

A helpful reviewer, if you can get them, is another BA. A BA peer can look for holes or inconsistencies even if he or she is not involved with the particular project or is not knowledgeable about the business area being analyzed. In fact, this is sometimes better because this forces you and the work products to be as clear as possible.

Steps 3 and 4—Distribute Review Materials and Have Participants Review Materials Prior to the Session

Have participants review any materials prior to the meeting so that they come prepared to engage and collaborate. If all of the participants reviewed the materials prior to the meeting—at their own pace, making notes about their questions—the review typically goes much faster and more effectively. It gives people time to absorb concepts. Point out areas that are critical for each participant to review (when everyone does not need to review the entire document). The BA should deliver the materials to the participants far enough in advance of the session to give them adequate time for a quality review. Participants are responsible for committing to this work and telling the BA when they need more time.

However, be prepared for attendees to come not having read the materials. Many reviews take the approach of a structured walk-through so that the team can literally review each item together. While it is more helpful if attendees understand the general context of what is going on, consider whether or not they need to read *everything* before coming. When you review materials *live* together, you bring the team together to collaborate on topics. This can actually keep your attendees focused and on topic by only addressing the materials you are discussing. And there is often greater collaboration across the team as they talk through concepts.

Step 5—Conduct the Review Session

When participants come prepared, a review session is easy to run. Set the ground rules first, especially when new participants are involved. Reinforce the goal of the session that you plan to achieve. It is a good idea to also reinforce the time allotted for the meeting, setting the expectation that you will start and finish on time. Again, this is a sign of respect—being aware of other people's time—that builds trust with your stakeholders. Lead the discussion through the materials, focusing on one section at a time. Do not assume that everyone understands every word. Do not be afraid to ask if there are questions or confusion on topics, especially if you feel that this may be the first time some people are seeing this material. Comments, suggestions, and criticisms must all be directed at the document, not the person who created it, anyone offering feedback, or yourself as facilitator. Go back to your goal of the session as often as you need in order to direct the attendees back toward producing the outcome versus trying to produce blame. It is best to make changes live in front of all participants so that they can see and confirm that the correct change is being made. Do not be afraid that people are watching you type or draw. The attendees are looking at whether or not the content is correct, not if it is aligned and *pretty*. You can always clean up the materials after the meeting before sending it on to the attendees.

As you move through the session, do not be afraid to do a time check. This is simply pausing for a moment, acknowledging how much time has elapsed or is left of the meeting and articulating how much of the goal has been achieved. It can be as simple as stating, "It's 9:30 a.m. We are halfway through our allotted time for this review and we are only 30% through the documentation. Let's stay focused on completing the validation of these requirements that are presented today so we can complete the review by our scheduled time of 10:30 a.m." Being aware of this time frame will help you complete your review as scheduled. You want to scope enough work to fill the time, but no more.

Rules for a Formal Requirements Review

1. Present a clear objective and outcome of the review session
2. All participants must come prepared
3. Critique the deliverable, not the facilitator
4. All participants carry equal weight during the session (*leave titles outside the room*)
5. Make suggestions and ask questions to improve the quality of the deliverable being discussed
6. Stay on topic
7. End on time

Steps 6 and 7—Record Review Notes, Update Material, and Share with Stakeholders

The formality of your notes should be determined by the project and organizational context in which the deliverable is being reviewed. If you have a highly regulated or risk averse project with a strict change control process on your requirements, then any decisions that are made should be clearly captured during the session. However, if you are working in a less formal setting, making the changes live to the documentation is all that is required. Regardless, try to do as much of the recording and updating during the session as possible. Enlist the help of another analyst if necessary so that you can focus on facilitating. Try to do as little work as possible "back at your desk" after the session. You want to send the outcomes of the review session as close to the end of the actual session as possible when ideas are still fresh. Minimize trying to add more material to share with attendees. Simply send the product of your review, as per your original goal, with a statement of appreciation for their time to move the overall change effort forward. And the *notes* can be as simple as stating that you achieved the goal and the updated contents are in the collaboration workspace.

Step 8—Conduct a Second Review if Absolutely Necessary

Good planning of the session in order to have a very focused and narrow objective with an engaged and collaborative audience should often be enough to prevent having to conduct a second review. If the group decides that significant changes were found, attendees may request a second review. In more traditional and formal environments, the subsequent review is conducted in exactly the same way as the first one. However, if there were new ideas or challenges working through the material, do not be afraid to change some of the approach. The same steps are still required, but the facilitation style may need to change. You might consider brainstorming or a collaborative games approach to elicit feedback on the item being reviewed. Or you might involve new participants to get other opinions on the artifact being reviewed. Unless it is planned from the beginning to iteratively review artifacts as a team, you will want to try to minimize having to schedule additional review sessions. These take significant time, not only of the stakeholders to attend but also from you as the BA to prep for, conduct, and follow up on. Value your time and the time of others to move the change forward as quickly as possible.

To get the most value out of that time, reviews must be supported by operations and project management. Time for reviews should be built into every project plan. Reviews must be held consistently for quality requirements deliverables. In addition, it is critical that reviews are not sacrificed when a project has fallen behind schedule. In the frenzy of a looming deadline, it is easy to start cutting corners and skipping tasks, but skipping quality reviews will almost guarantee project failure. Mistakes in requirements cost anywhere from 10 to 1,000 times more to fix when they are found after development (National Institute of Standards and Technology 2002). Review, review, review—this is a guaranteed method for improving the quality of your requirements.

Informal Reviews

While formal, structured, walk-through reviews are extremely effective at ensuring that all of the details of BA deliverables are verified and validated, do not discount the value of informal reviews. Informal reviews are the ones that may not be planned, scheduled, or even expected. These types of reviews are great for ensuring that the entire scope has been considered, bringing up ideas that have not been discussed, and helping make material presentable to multiple audiences.

Real World Example: Informal Reviews

A manager of mine liked to do *walking touchpoints*. These were essentially 30-minute, one-on-one meetings where we left the building and went for a walk—meaning we did not take our laptops or other work materials with us. However, I had (almost) the undivided attention of leadership for those 30 minutes. While we had general goals of the meeting to update status and discuss any issues we were currently having, agendas were not preset and we allowed ourselves the freedom to explore topics. These meetings were a great way for me to bounce ideas off my manager on my BA work. Once, I needed to present the business case for a major initiative that a specific business area was pushing hard for. I asked him his thoughts on who should be involved in helping create and validate the business case. I shared with him my ideas on presentation format. He gave very open and candid feedback as we walked. He recommended certain individuals in finance and other business areas that I had not yet considered to help review. He discussed the office politics involved in this project and words I needed to use wisely. He essentially was reviewing my BA plan for this business case and giving me the needed feedback for success. All of this was achieved while walking and admiring the great outdoors with no agenda, meeting minutes, or even artifacts—other than the valuable feedback that I promptly put to good use.

Typical Review Session Feedback

When conducting your reviews, while the goal is the updated, verified, and even validated work products, your primary mission is to elicit as much feedback as possible from stakeholders to collaborate on solutions. The feedback is extremely valuable, regardless of whether it "seems" positive or negative. As

"Do not take feedback personally!"

the BA, you need to keep an objective perspective and take all feedback into consideration. The first rule on this feedback is to not take it personally. They are critiquing the artifacts, not the person who created it. Yes, you should always have room to grow, learning to apply the feedback from one session to the next; however, when stakeholders argue or dislike the presented materials, aim to collaborate with them to help make it correct. A stakeholder telling you that you are wrong on everything is more valuable than a stakeholder who says nothing. Anything that you feel you can add to improve future reviews should go into your lessons learned and BA action plans. Do not let negative feedback stop you. It should push you to move forward. Leave your ego outside the session and be open to all suggestions.

While focusing on the materials, be aware the *type* of feedback you are getting. Corrections are common and expected. The stakeholder is validating that the item is required. They are simply giving you the minor adjustments to make it completely accurate and clear. You are trying to get on the same page and articulate the picture that your stakeholders are envisioning. If you need help pulling out the details your stakeholders are trying to communicate, do not be afraid to bring in other techniques during your review session. Prototypes are a great way to visualize solutions that you can constantly edit and rework until the stakeholder is accepting of the design.

What you really want to look for are new ideas or topics that are discussed since these are often a sign of missing components. This is where doing smaller, more frequent reviews can be really helpful. If you chose a small portion of the work to review and then give your stakeholders time to go and think about it, they often will come back with more ideas and questions. They will have considered what else may or has happened in the past and add requirements to the solution. However, be careful that the scope does not go too wide in your discussions, which is why it is important to have a goal of any review, formal or informal. Re-stating why you need the feedback can focus the attendees on the necessary discussions to achieve this goal. Even a BA can be guilty of scope creep as they continue to ask more probing questions during review sessions. Avoid this by focusing on obtaining the goal of the session in as efficient a manner as possible.

Adaptive Project Review Sessions

While much of the discussion on reviews is focused on traditional approaches to solutions and aiming to eliminate risk through verification and validation, these same concepts apply to adaptive and iterative environments. In fact, agile teams do a significant number of review sessions during each iteration on work that has been completed, challenges, deliverables, and the prioritizing of requirements. Most of these are still planned activities with a goal. The often smaller, colocated teams make it easy to collaborate on discussion points and think through ideas. These teams may not have a dedicated facilitator, but there are leadership and decision-making roles that still exist to keep the team focused on the goal of the session. In fact, agile retrospectives take the review session and apply it to the team itself. If you find yourself in any kind of analyst role on an adaptive project, remember to consider the *reviews* that are so essential for the team. Identify the goal of any review, confirm who needs to be included, and lead the discussion to address the topic or deliverable while trying to incorporate the feedback live. The formality, structure, change control, and documentation level may not be the same as with a traditional approach, but the goals of eliciting feedback still exist and are extremely valuable.

SHARPEN YOUR ANALYSIS SKILLS

As a BA, one of the most valuable traits you can possess is to never stop learning. Constantly learn about the organization, learn the environment, learn the technologies, and especially learn from the situations you encounter. Every circumstance, product, and result can provide valuable insight into what helps deliver success—all things that you can apply in your next change effort. Learning will never end for a BA. People are drawn to this career because they love learning new things. This love of learning makes BAs very effective because when you are gathering requirements, you are learning. When you are eliciting and asking questions, you are learning. You are learning how the business makes decisions, how the business gets work done, why the business does its work, and how customers are satisfied by the business. This education continues on every project. There is always more to know even if you have worked in the same industry or in the same business area for your entire career. You will never know everything. Businesses change constantly and BAs must keep up with the current standards, policies, product offerings, and market trends.

Staying up-to-date on trends requires the business analysis professional to not only learn about new techniques and concepts but also to be able to apply those concepts to the existing organization. Understand how pieces fit into the whole. Step outside the boundaries of your current organization's thinking and see how a new concept might work in your business.

Technique: Avoid Analysis Paralysis

As you continue to learn, ensure that you do not fall into the trap of *analysis paralysis*. Many BAs have experienced this at least once in their careers. This phrase describes the situation when you keep thinking about and analyzing a problem, doing more research, documenting it, and then repeat. Think, research, document, think, research, document—it is the BA's equivalent of an infinite loop in programming. You get stuck in this cycle and cannot seem to get out. Why does this happen and what can you do to get out of it?

There are a couple of common reasons for analysis paralysis. One can be when your research gives you a *different* answer then what you thought was true when you started. Therefore, you keep looking for more information that would support your original theory because you want to be right. In addition, if you are wrong, you want to make sure that you are really convinced because you will have to convince others about this new direction.

Another common reason for analysis paralysis is when your answer will not be one that your boss is going to like. In this case, it is a good idea to make sure that you have really done your research and thought through this carefully because you become the bearer of bad news.

Finally, analysis paralysis may be caused by a lack of confidence in your work. New BAs may not be sure that their conclusions or recommendations are correct, so they continue to prove the same point using different techniques or approaches. This is typically solved with experience and is common with new BAs.

Every single thing a BA does should add value. If it is not adding value (or even feels like you are doing *busy work*), then pause and reassess. Ask yourself if the activity you are currently doing is really needed and creating value for the organization. Some questions to consider when evaluating how you are spending your time each day include:

> "A BA's whole existence is to provide value."

- Have you gotten off track?
- Have you wandered down a path that is very interesting to you but is really outside the scope of your task?
- Are you spending time detailing a requirement that will never be automated because it's too complex?
- Are you looking for something that you may never find (i.e., a software package that meets the user's exact need)?
- Are you overanalyzing how the work is currently done when your project will be changing that procedure anyway?
- Are you brainstorming about better ways of operating the business when you should be focused on understanding the core processes?
- Will the additional work you are doing lead to a different result than if you present/share/communicate the work in its current state?
- Am I trying to do everything myself when I should be collaborating with others for their feedback and input?

Whatever you are spending time doing, ask yourself if it is the very best use of your time—if not, stop and change direction. A busy analyst does not have time to get distracted. Spend time asking your stakeholders what they need or are expecting versus guessing. This will save you a significant amount of time while clarifying your role and how you can best support the team.

How do you stop analysis paralysis? First you must learn to be aware that you are doing it. This is often the most difficult part. BAs must *look up* from the details periodically and make sure that the work they are doing is the most important work to be done at that moment. This is a good reason for leaving a task incomplete at the end of the day and giving it a fresh look the next morning. In the light of a new day, the problem may suddenly appear clear or less important. Ideas for getting *unstuck* include:

1. *Ask a fellow BA or coworker (or any friend) to listen to you talk about the problem*: just talking about it out loud sometimes helps you to figure out why you are stuck
2. *Give yourself a time limit*: I am going to work on this for one more hour, and then, wherever it is at that point, it will be done
3. *Sit down with the SME and review the work that you have done so far*: explain that it is a draft and ask for help to find the missing pieces
4. *Sleep on it*
5. *If you have time, put it aside for a few days*: this is the best way to get perspective
6. *Try a different requirement technique to represent the situation*: for example, if you are using a process model with swim lanes, try an entity relationship diagram
7. *Know the 80/20 rule*

An important fact to remember about business analysis work is that the requirements will never be 100% complete and will never be perfect. If you are a perfectionist, be prepared to feel a little frustrated. Hugh Prather, an inspirational speaker and writer, once said: "Perfection is a slow death." When you are stuck in the details of a problem (analysis paralysis), you lose perspective. Change your perspective so that you can see things differently in order to get unstuck.

Skill: Clear Statements of Situations

As your BA career grows, you will find yourself being asked for information by stakeholders. These will range from simple, informal questions to formal presentations of recommendations. Regardless of the request, practice getting good at presenting clear, concise, objective, organizationally focused information. Try a structured format that keeps you focused. A great example is:

- Need
- Background
- Assessment
- Recommendation

This approach takes out the *noise* we often include in our writing. When working with others, always restate the goal or, in this case, the *need*. The background information is the space to talk about what is going on that generated this need. The assessment then is your analysis of what is happening and what could happen. And then, of course, comes your recommendation. And remember, recommendations should include alternatives. The more practice you get at presenting information to stakeholders, the better you get at it. This is a key skill that is required as you advance your career and work with more senior organizational members. When in doubt, try to write your thoughts down and then go back and take out a third of the content before sharing. This will help keep you focused.

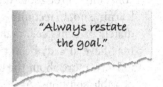

"Always restate the goal."

Skill: Make Recommendations for Solutions

BAs are skilled at understanding problems and developing solutions. They also see approaches for taking advantage of business opportunities. BAs have the skills necessary to evaluate possible solutions, looking at feasibility and cost compared to benefits to determine the best solution, not just for the business area but for the entire organization.

The following three components are essential for making excellent recommendations:

1. Understand the problem
2. Imagine possible solutions
3. Evaluate solution options to select the one that best addresses the need

New or junior-level BAs need to be careful not to make recommendations before they truly understand business requirements and technical options. This is a value that an experienced BA can provide to a business. New BAs should learn to float ideas by showing their analysis skills using the same type of format as in the previous list. An example might be:

> *"With our goal of increasing ease of use and given that the design changes may require a lot of time and money, could we possibly consider modifying the options in the menu versus changing the whole menu?"*

This type of question is a great way to show off your analysis skills while still learning by getting valuable feedback. You have clearly stated the goal, emphasized constraints, and then presented an option. Even if the stakeholders do not go with your choice, you have done a good job of getting stakeholders to at least consider an alternative as part of their own analysis.

Understand the Problem

Understanding the business problem is the main job of every BA. If a business only wanted the quickest, easiest solution, it would not have invested in a BA. A technology person can always come up with a quick idea for how software and/or hardware can improve the business without investigating the cause of the problem. An experienced analyst will thoroughly analyze the problem and consider possible solutions before jumping to any solution.

Imagine Possible Solutions

The second step is to brainstorm possible solutions. Experienced BAs will be imagining possible solutions constantly throughout the requirements elicitation process. One of the challenges of being a BA, though, is learning not to recommend a solution too early in a change effort. Although an obvious solution may immediately present itself, many times the most obvious solution is not the best. Also, the most obvious solution may have already been tried. If the answer was that easy, a BA would not really be needed. As you begin to learn more about the business, its people, its processes, and its deliverables, you will see more and more possible solutions. As you learn more, some of your earliest ideas may prove to be inadequate, or you will find yourself refining your ideas, working to find the perfect solution. This is a natural activity for most BAs.

Experienced BAs have learned to build ideas with others. The more they collaborate and shape ideas with stakeholders, the more ownership the stakeholders take of the ideas. One of the best things a BA can do is to share an idea in an informal manner that stakeholders then take, mold, modify, and present as their own. Practice asking *what-if* questions during brainstorming sessions with stakeholders. Help nurture ideas that resonate with your decision makers by providing analysis and asking good questions. The ideas to present are not meant to always be solutions. Present ideas around what else could happen. To help pull in different perspectives on the ideas, ask questions such as: "What if no one used the solution?" "What if a million people used it?" "What if it was free?" "What if it was really expensive?" or "What if our competitor saw this idea?" Experienced BAs will not let themselves get tied to any particular solution too early in requirements elicitation and analysis. They will recognize that a solution idea may change (and most often do) or may even be eliminated at any time as more information becomes available.

Evaluate Solutions to Select the Best

After extensive information gathering, observation, and analysis, there may be more than one possible solution. How do you decide which one to recommend? This is when a different flavor of analysis is required. Cost/benefit analysis, feasibility analysis, and business case development are all names given to the activity performed by the BA to evaluate possible solutions. These are great for formal recommendations where business owners are looking for ideas. BAs use data for analysis to make recommendations, but the stakeholders—primarily the sponsors—make the final decision. Present each option along with its strengths and limitations to give the sponsor the information needed to make a good decision.

As you collaborate more directly with stakeholders on ideas, three key areas that are important for considering solutions are the feasibility, viability, and desirability of the idea. You want to look for a solution that will satisfy all three areas (see Figure 7.5). *Your* BA skills are valuable in helping understand the feasibility and viability of solution ideas. However, you need input from stakeholders and what they are willing to support and take ownership of (i.e., what is desirable to them). Work *with* stakeholders to think through the options presented along with any analysis work you have done. Useful techniques and approaches are

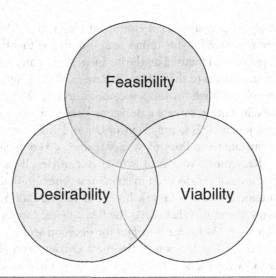

Figure 7.5   Idea considerations

collaborative team-building activities found in design-thinking approaches (see Additional Reading and References on design thinking at the end of this chapter).

Skill: Provide Objective Analysis

Clarity is important because the role of the BA requires the individual to remain objective. The BA's role is to support those making business decisions in such a way that helps drive continuous value for the organization. However, sometimes those decision makers may make a decision with which you do not agree. As the analyst, your role is to provide as much information as possible so that any decisions are the result of being well informed and knowledgeable about what is going on in the enterprise.

Occasionally a BA will see that a proposed solution is not appropriate for the business need. If a solution was proposed before the root cause of the problem was identified, the solution may be less than optimal. If the BA determines that the proposed solution is not the best, he or she must clearly articulate the analysis results that led him or her to a different conclusion. This requires three components: (1) get your facts together, (2) present the facts without emotion or bias, and (3) be willing to accept the decision and move forward. One additional component that is very useful is having an alternate plan. These components allow the business analysis professional to communicate the difference of opinion objectively and offer the highest likelihood that the mistake will be corrected.

Get your facts together, either formally or informally. Use your business case skills to help show management why a proposed solution may not provide a good return on investment or may cost more money than it saves. Be prepared to answer detailed questions about why your argument is correct. Be aware of how much time and money have already been spent on this solution. The more an organization has invested, the more difficult it may be to get the group to change direction. The money already spent is a *sunk cost* according to accounting principles and should not be factored into any decision going forward, but it is human nature to want to complete the original project and not waste the time and money already spent.

Present facts without emotion. Oftentimes, an emotional plea will not be supported or accepted. Be careful with your choice of words. Avoid saying things like, "I don't feel that this is a good idea." Don't personalize the issue. Keep it objective and focused on the business impact and what each option means to the organization. Provide factual statements to show that you have carefully considered the issues. Be prepared to face emotion from the people with whom you are communicating. Members of management may be vested in the idea or may be reluctant to reverse a decision. They may not want to address the issue with their management. Making major changes to project priorities and direction can shake up an organization, and most managers will be reluctant to do this unless they really see a compelling reason.

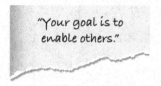

"Your goal is to enable others."

Remember, your goal is to enable others. It can be hard to remember that you are not the decision maker. Sometimes, no matter how much data and persuasion you use with stakeholders, they may still make a decision that you feel is not the most valuable. As the BA, you need to focus on your ability to remain objective. No matter how *bad* the decision seems to you, your role as the BA is to deliver the decision in the most efficient and effective way possible. If you feel the business is foolishly throwing money at a crazy idea, then your job is to help them efficiently and effectively spend its money and help deliver the "crazy" idea. Your work does not end at implementation, but rather continues to post-implementation assessment. Go and get the analysis and objective information on how well the solution is performing once implemented. Avoid saying, "I told you so" and let your analysis results speak for themselves.

Skill: Be Able to Accept Feedback

Being able to accept feedback, especially when it feels negative, is one of the most difficult things for human beings to do. Hearing that you have made a mistake or missed an important requirement is never

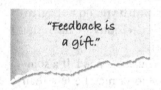

"Feedback is a gift."

enjoyable. However, consider that feedback as a gift. This means that someone actually took the time to consider your deliverables and make them better. Do not take negative feedback personally. Focus on the artifact, the approach, or the work that is getting critiqued. Even if you feel that they are calling you out directly, focus on the deliverables and project goals. Use feedback as a learning experience so it brings value to future projects and initiatives.

One of the best ways to practice accepting feedback is to also give it. Having opportunities to review and provide feedback on others' work helps you put the feedback you receive in a more objective light. Look for opportunities to review other BAs' work. Practice giving them feedback that is focused on solution success, not the BA's competency. You will not only gain confidence and possibly learn something, but you will also be helping to mentor the other BA at the same time.

START ADDING VALUE

As mentioned throughout, business analysis planning should be done before jumping into any kind of analysis activity. Spending a small amount of time to understand the change, context, stakeholders, scope, and even your own skill set can save you valuable time and resources, which in turn increases your value to the organization. Planning the analysis work involves identifying the people with whom you will be working and understanding their communication needs. It requires the BA to decide which requirements analysis techniques to use and which requirements deliverables need to be created. It also involves estimating analysis time. Laying out your BA task list helps focus your attention on having an immediate positive impact.

Technique: Creating a BA Task List

Arranging your BA work in a structured task list is a great communication tool for articulating where your time is being spent and how soon the organization will receive value from your efforts. It can be a formal document that is generated from a template or a simple task list found in one of your productivity tools. Regardless of your method of capturing information, write down the activities so that you and your team are clear as to what you plan to do and when you plan to deliver. Dates drive results!

Identify the Type of Work

While project-based work is the most common for BAs (eliciting requirements, testing, validating solutions, etc.), it is not the only place where BAs add value. Many junior BAs will often support operations and help with troubleshooting issues. This type of work often requires understanding of processes, information and data flows, and root cause analysis work. BAs in lines of business often do a lot of solution evaluation and process improvement work. Here, you are looking to help the organization get more value out of their already invested solutions. This work requires understanding of how users interact with solutions—eliciting their processes, expectations, and even ideas. This will require collaboration with stakeholders and results in brainstorming ideas, prototypes and testing, and managing changes. Senior BAs often spend a lot of time working with stakeholders and doing strategic planning. This requires market research and competitive analysis and delivers business cases based on financial analysis and measurements. Table 7.3 shows an example of a BA task list to help plan and then estimate business analysis work.

Determine the Scope of the Change Work

One of the reasons for thoroughly analyzing scope is to have the facts necessary to build a realistic plan. Project and business analysis planning are complex activities even when change objectives are well

Table 7.3 Example BA task list

Activity	Deliverable	Task	Due Date
Elicit Requirements	Requirements Package	• Review documentation • Schedule requirements workshops • Conduct requirements workshops • Obtain approval	10/1
Build Test Plans	Test Plan	• Create test cases • Schedule test plan review session	11/2
Validate Test Plans	Validated Test Plan Results	• Review and analyze test plan results • Troubleshoot issues	11/15
Build Operational Support Model	Operational Support Model	• Schedule process review session with support staff • Create RACI matrix and support models • Review and validate support models	12/15

understood. The better the understanding of change expectations, the faster you will be able to develop an accurate plan.

Use your analysis techniques to learn as much about the change effort as possible before deciding what business analysis activities you plan to do. You will want to determine the status of the change. Is this an idea that is just now being discussed or has this been a long-standing problem in the department? If the changes have already begun and are being looked at by others, you can save time on your analysis activities by leveraging the work that has already been done. Once you know the current status of the effort, you can begin to plan your business analysis work. Without clearly defined objectives and scope, successful analysis will be difficult.

Technique: Assess Business Impact

Business impact is a measure of the criticality of a change effort to the business stakeholders and their work. Business impact describes the ramifications or effect of a change on the business environment. Being aware of a change effort's importance to the organization allows the BA to stay focused on the most important requirements and stakeholder issues.

Business impact is an important characteristic of a change that must be understood as early as possible. Although all of the factors may not be completely known at the beginning of a project, the BA should consider all that is known and assess the potential business impact. Factors that help in understanding this impact (and, therefore, scope of the change) include:

- Number of users of the solution being implemented or affected
- Number of stakeholders working on the change
- Type(s) of stakeholders
- Geographic location of stakeholders
- Business complexity
- Business risk

Often, the greater the number of people involved—whether end users, support staff, or change agents—the larger the change scope is. Even if the impact of influence is relatively low, that is still one more individual or role to consider in your analysis work. When discussing the type of stakeholders, their role in the organization can greatly affect the scope and type of business analysis work that you need to perform. Senior executives will want status updates in short, formal presentations and will need information to quickly make key decisions. Junior staff are often focused on tasks and due dates and will want detailed information specific to their area of change. These micro-detailed team members may not understand how each effort helps the overall goal and will often look to the BA to validate that the work being done is aligned with the change effort's goals. Geography is going to come into play the more you work with distributed teams. Time zones and coordination of work gets more complex the more distributed you are.

The complexity of the business itself will increase the complexity of the business analysis work. Complex business areas typically have many business rules (i.e., insurance, government regulatory agencies) and/or involve processes that require high levels of knowledge and experience on the part of stakeholders (e.g., financial securities trading, legal systems, chemical/pharmaceuticals). Coupled with that is the business risk. Business risk is defined as the potential for significant business success or failure as a result of a project. While the PM will track project risks, being aware of the business risk is important in understanding the decision-making approach that the business takes and what information these same decision makers will be looking for over the course of the change effort. All of these factors will often have you not only tailoring your approach to your business analysis work, but will also require you to consider what additional activities you will need to add to your BA task list. The more detailed and defined your task list, the more accurate your estimates and communication, and ultimately, the more value you will add.

SUMMARY OF KEY POINTS

Great BAs live their profession in their heart and soul. They are intelligent, well educated, and have significant experience. But even intelligence, training, and background are not enough. To be truly excellent, you have to love what you are doing. And loving business analysis means enjoying problem solving, working patiently with people, and being an advocate for the business. BAs enjoy learning new things and have a natural curiosity. In addition, they have a rare combination of the ability to see the big picture (conceptual thinking) while being detail oriented. This combination of traits results in a successful business analysis professional who is in great demand. The following list will help you to understand the unique combination of traits that are required for successful business analysis and create an appreciation for the complexity of the role, which helps to explain why it is difficult to master:

- Before performing analysis work, understanding the nature and scope of the change effort is key to adding value and more accurately defining business analysis work and deliverables.
- BAs need to consider how the organization approaches the change effort; how stakeholders are organized and participate in those efforts; what structure is in place that guides business analysis activities and the deliverables, changes, and approvals; and how the organization is structured to reuse and leverage business analysis work.
- BAs should critique their own performance with the same rigor and analysis as they would project/ change efforts in order to identify competencies and necessary skill sets and then build structured, measurable plans to improve them.
- As the demand for analysis work continues to increase, BAs need to ensure that they prioritize their time and devote their energy to only the activities that produce the most value for the organization.
- To be successful, BAs need to listen and collaborate with their stakeholders throughout all of their activities and stay focused on achieving defined goals.
- Communication must remain clear and concise to support faster decision making by the organization.
- Laying out the BA work in discrete tasks helps you not only stay organized and focused, but also helps you define the scope of business analysis work that is required to help changes add value to the organization.

BIBLIOGRAPHY

The Agile Alliance. (2018). *Glossary*. https://www.agilealliance.org/glossary/.

Brassard, M. and D. Ritter. (1994). *The Memory Jogger II*. First Edition. GOAL/QPC.

CMMI Institute. (2018). *The Capability Maturity Model Integration (CMMI)®*. https://cmmiinstitute.com/capability-maturity-model-integration.

International Institute of Business Analysis (IIBA). (2015). *Business Analysis Body of Knowledge® (BABOK® Guide)*. IIBA: Toronto, Ontario, Canada.

IIBA. (2017). *Agile Extension to the BABOK® Guide*. IIBA: Toronto, Ontario, Canada.

ISO. (2018). *International Organization for Standardization*. https://www.iso.org/home.html.

National Institute of Standards and Technology. (2002, May). "The Economic Impacts of Inadequate Infrastructure for Software Testing."

Project Management Institute (PMI). (2014). *PMI's Pulse of the Profession®: Requirements management—A core competency for project and program success*. PMI: Newtown Square, PA.

ADDITIONAL READING AND REFERENCES

Brian Tracy International. (2018). *Achieve All of Your Goals Faster Than You Ever Thought Possible*. https://www.briantracy.com/.

Covey, S. (2008). *The SPEED of Trust: The One Thing That Changes Everything*. Free Press Publishers: New York, NY.

Derby, E. and D. Larsen. (2006). *Agile Retrospectives: Making Good Teams Great*. Pragmatic Bookshelf: Raleigh, NC.

Hasso Plattner Institute of Design. (2017). *Design Thinking Bootleg*. https://dschool.stanford.edu/resources/design-thinking-bootleg.

Hasso Plattner Institute of Design. (2017). *A Virtual Crash Course in Design Thinking*. https://dschool.stanford.edu/resources-collections/a-virtual-crash-course-in-design-thinking.

IDEO. (2018). *Design Thinking*. https://www.ideou.com/pages/design-thinking.

International Institute of Business Analysis (IIBA). (2015, November). "Evolution of the BA Role." *BA Lens*. IIBA. http://www.iiba.org/News-Events/ba-lens/issue1.aspx.

IIBA. (2017). *Business Analysis Competency Model® v4*. IIBA: Toronto, Ontario, Canada.

IIBA. (2017, November 6). "The Digital Transformation Is Here, Relevant and Your Opportunity for Success." *BA Lens*. IIBA. http://balens.iiba.org/?q=content/digital-transformation-here-relevant-and-your-opportunity-success.

IIBA and KPMG. (2016). *Business Analysis—Positioning for Success*. Impact study by IIBA and KPMG. http://www.iiba.org/Learning-Development/L-D/research-and-study-impact2016.aspx.

Lencioni, P. (2002). *The Five Dysfunctions of a Team: A Leadership Fable*. Jossey-Bass: Hoboken, NJ.

Leverage Networks, Inc. (2018). "The Systems Thinker." https://thesystemsthinker.com/.

Project Management Institute (PMI). (2017). *Project Manager Competency Development Framework, 3rd ed.* PMI: Newtown Square, PA.

Whittenberger, A. (2017). "How Business Analysis Services Add Business Value." IIBA. https://www .iiba.org/ba-connect/2014/august/how-business-analysis-services-add-business-value.aspx.

INDEX

Note: Page numbers followed by "f" indicate figures; and those followed by "t" indicate tables.